REVISE KEY STAGE 2 SATs
English

REVISION GUIDE

Above Expected Standard

Series Consultant: Janice Pimm

Author: Helen Thomson

This revision guide is written for students who aim to perform above the expected national standard in English in their Year 6 SATs.

For students who hope to perform at the expected standard, check out:

Revise Key Stage 2 SATs English Revision Guide:
Expected Standard   9781292146010

Revise Key Stage 2 SATs English Revision Workbook:
Expected Standard   9781292146003

For the full range of Pearson revision titles visit:
www.pearsonschools.co.uk/revise

ALWAYS LEARNING

PEARSON

Contents

Grammar

Punctuation

Spelling

Writing

Reading

A small bit of small print

The Standards and Testing Agency publishes Sample Test Materials on its website. This is the official content and this book should be used in conjunction with it. The questions in *Now try this* have been written to help you practise every topic in the book. Remember: the real test questions may not look like this.

Introduction

About your tests

At the end of Year 6, you will take tests to find out about your English skills. This book will help you revise all of the important skills you need for your tests.

- There will be one **spelling** test. Your teacher will read 20 words out loud. You need to write down the correct spellings. This test will take about 15 minutes.

- There will be one **grammar** test. This test will ask you questions about spelling, punctuation and grammar. You will have 45 minutes to do this test.

- There will be one **reading** test. You will have to read three texts and answer questions about them. You will have 1 hour to do this test.

Your teacher will look at some of your pieces of **writing** but there won't be a writing test.

Using this book

Each page of this book is about a different skill. Use the checkboxes at the top of the page to track your progress:

Had a look ☐ Tick this box when you've read the page.

Nearly there ☐ Tick this box when you understand the page quite well.

Nailed it! ☐ Tick this box when you understand the page really well.

Pronouns

Pronouns are words that take the place of nouns, such as **the woman**, **the football**, or a name such as **Sarah**.

Examples of pronouns are: **I**, **she**, **it**, **you** and **him**.

Using pronouns

Use pronouns in place of nouns so that you don't repeat the same nouns.

> She took the bracelet to the jewellers because <u>the bracelet</u> was broken.

> She took the bracelet to the jewellers because <u>it</u> was broken.

pronoun 'it' replaces bracelet

Example

Rewrite the text below, replacing the nouns with pronouns.

Aurek and Flo usually walk to school but sometimes Aurek and Flo catch the bus. When Aurek and Flo catch the bus Aurek and Flo get off the bus at the third stop. Aurek and Flo prefer to walk than to catch the bus.

The nouns 'Aurek and Flo' and 'bus' have been replaced with the pronouns 'they' and 'it'.

Aurek and Flo usually walk to school but sometimes they catch the bus. When they catch the bus they get off it at the third stop. They prefer to walk than to catch the bus.

Now try this

1. Rewrite the text, replacing nouns with pronouns where appropriate. Which words did you change?

   The elephants are kept in an enclosure near the edge of the zoo. The elephants are fed by the keeper at four o'clock every day. The elephants stretch their long trucks towards the keeper and the keeper hands the food to the elephants.

Noun phrases

A **noun phrase** is made up of a **noun** and all the words that describe it.

Simple noun phrases

The noun is the main word in a noun phrase. A simple noun phrase is made up of a noun and a determiner. There are three simple noun phrases in this sentence.

simple noun phrases →

The girl won some vouchers in a competition.

A noun phrase can always be replaced by a **pronoun.**

Expanded noun phrases

See page 4 for more information about deteminers.

Expanding noun phrases can make your writing more interesting and more detailed. There are three expanded noun phrases in this sentence.

expanded noun phrases ↙

The clever, red-headed girl won some holiday vouchers in a national mathematics competition.

Adding adjectives is an easy way to expand a noun phrase.

Example

If you can replace the whole phrase with a pronoun, it is a noun phrase: **He** is the conductor.

Expand the underlined noun phrase in the sentence below.
That man is the conductor.

That smiling, moustached man at the front is the conductor.

Now try this

1. Expand the noun phrases in the sentences below.
   a) The footballer is my brother.
   b) That man owns the shop.
2. Rewrite the sentences below, using noun phrases in place of the pronouns.
   a) They can't come until next week.
   b) She went to Spain last summer.

Possessive pronouns

You use a **possessive pronoun** to show who or what **owns** something.
A possessive pronoun replaces a noun and a possessive apostrophe.

used with nouns	replacing nouns
my	mine
your	yours
his/her/its	his/hers/its
our	ours
their	theirs

its = belongs to it
it's = it is

With nouns

A possessive pronoun can act as a determiner with a noun or noun phrase.

possessive
pronoun

> Suzie's violin case was damaged.
> Her violin case was damaged.

Replacing nouns

As with other pronouns, a possessive pronoun can **replace** a noun or noun phrase.

Never put an apostrophe in a possessive pronoun.

> The damaged violin case was Suzie's.
> The damaged violin case was hers.

possessive
pronoun

Example

Rewrite the sentence below, replacing the noun and possessive apostrophe with a possessive pronoun.
Sam's teacher was not at school today.

His teacher was not at school today.

Now try this

1. Rewrite the sentences below, replacing the noun and possessive apostrophe with a possessive pronoun.
   a) Ahmed's cousin lives close to the sea.
   b) The spaniel's obedience won it the first prize.
   c) Catherine of Aragon was King Henry VIII's first wife.

Determiners

A **determiner** is a word that comes before a noun. In an expanded noun phrase, the determiner always comes first.

What do determiners do?

Examples of determiners: *a, an, the, this, his* and *her*

Determiners can make the noun more specific.

These determiners tell you which cup is dirty and which is clean. ➡ <u>This</u> cup is dirty and <u>that</u> cup is clean.

Determiners can also make the noun more general.

<u>A</u> giraffe eats more than 45 kg of leaves and twigs every day. ⬅ This means all giraffes in general.

Possessive pronouns are also determiners. They show the ownership of the noun.

determiner and possessive pronoun ➡ <u>Their</u> house is on a hill.   See page 3 for more about possessive pronouns.

Numbers can also be determiners.

determiner ⬅

Jade bought <u>five</u> pens.

Example

Underline all of the determiners in the sentence below.

<u>The</u> <u>three</u> brothers took <u>that</u> box and carried it into <u>their</u> house.

Now try this

1. Find all of the determiners in the sentences below.
   a) The six enormous, black cats ate their dinner and then ran to their baskets.
   b) That amount of confidence is unusual in young singers.
   c) Even four people couldn't lift his weight.
2. Rewrite the sentence below with determiners.
   We put shopping in car, took it back to house then gave it to neighbour.
3. Write a sentence including the following determiners: *an, four* and *their*.

Adjectives and adjectival phrases

An **adjective** adds detail to a noun.

Adjectives

Adjectives can come before or after a noun.

| The colourful balloons looked pretty. |

adjective ➘

| The balloons were colourful. |

Using more than one adjective to describe a noun makes your writing more interesting.

Example

When you list adjectives, you must separate them with commas.

Add three adjectives to this sentence.

The wild, golden, majestic lion prowled across the plain.

Adjectival phrases

An **adjectival phrase** is a group of words that gives more information about a noun or pronoun.

↙ adjectival phrases ➘

| The cars queued down the brightly lit street. | | She is taller than I am. |

Example

Underline the adjectival phrase in the sentence below.

The roller coaster was going faster and faster.

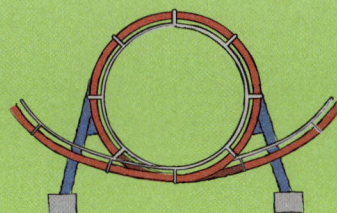

Now try this

1. Write a description of a fairground ride. Use adjectives to make your description more interesting.

2. Write out and complete the sentences below with adjectival phrases.

    a) The holiday was …   **b)** The horse …

Verbs

Verbs describe what someone or something does, or something that happens.

Verbs

Verbs describe actions, events, situations and changes.

> My mum <u>watches</u> TV while she <u>is ironing</u> clothes but my dad often <u>changes</u> the channel.

All these words are different forms of verbs.

A sentence must have a verb to make sense.

'Being' verbs

Verbs can also describe what something is, or is **being**.

> The children <u>are</u> very hot. Sandra <u>feels</u> sad.

being verbs

Verbs are often called 'doing' words, but they can also describe what something is 'being'.

Example

Underline all the verbs in the sentence below.

The farmer <u>has</u> ten acres of fields and cattle <u>are grazing</u> in most of them.

Now try this

1. Identify the verbs in the sentence below.
   Matthew found the bicycle wheel lying in the gutter.
2. Write a sentence containing a verb describing people spending the day at a swimming pool.

Present and past tense

Verbs describe an action. This action might be taking place now (present) or in the past or future.

Calendar

Sun	Mon	Tue	Wed	Thu	Fri	Sat
	1	✗	3	4	5	6
7	8	9	10	11	12	13
14	15	16	17	18	19	20
21	22	23	24	25	26	27
28	29	30	31			

Monday 1st   Tuesday 2nd   Wednesday 3rd

Yesterday it was rainy.   Today is cloudy.   Tomorrow will be sunny.

Past   Present   Future

Present tense

The **present tense** describes an action that is happening now, a habit or a repeated action.

My brother usually <u>cycles</u> to work but today he <u>is catching</u> the bus.

present tense

Past tense

Use the **past tense** to describe actions that have happened in the past.

Last week we <u>went</u> to the cinema and <u>watched</u> a film that <u>had been made</u> in America.

past tense

There are many different forms that the past tense can take. Simple rule: if the action is in the past then it should be in the past tense.

Now try this

1. Rewrite the sentences below, changing the verbs into the present tense.
   a) Jude watched a movie.   b) Patrick studied for his test.
2. Rewrite the sentences below, changing the verbs into the past tense.
   a) Fatma sails the boat around the bay, which has lovely calm water.
   b) The American astronauts arrive at the space station and discover a new form of life.

Future tense

There are different ways to describe actions which take place in the future.

Future tense

Here are three different ways of writing a sentence in the **future tense**.

You can use **will** to show something will happen in the future.

> The aeroplane <u>will arrive</u> at nine o'clock.

You can use **going to** to show something will happen in the future.

> We <u>are going to have</u> pizza for dinner.

You can use the present tense to show something will happen in the future.

> He <u>is playing tennis</u> tomorrow.

By using the word **tomorrow** we know that this action is set in the future.

Example

Underline all of the future tense verbs from the text below.

We <u>will take</u> the six o'clock bus because Ali is <u>cooking dinner</u> for everyone tonight so <u>we are going to help</u> him.

Now try this

1. Rewrite this sentence in the future tense.

   Kate was babysitting her younger sister yesterday as her parents went to meet their friends and left the house at seven o'clock.

2. Rewrite the sentences below, putting the verb in brackets in the correct form.

   a) It is thought that by the year 2040 human kind _____ (colonise) other planets and there _____ (be) cures for all diseases.

   b) My uncle and I _____ (go fossil-hunting) next weekend and _____ (collect) as many as we can.

Modal verbs

Use **modal verbs** to talk about how likely it is that something will or won't happen.

Modal verbs show possibility

Modal verbs always come in front of another verb.

If it is sunny at the weekend, dad <u>might</u> take Henry to the beach.

modal verb

verb

> It is not certain that dad will take Henry to the beach so it is only a possibility.

The sun <u>will</u> rise at six o'clock tomorrow morning.

modal verb

> It is definite that the sun will rise so we use 'will'.

We <u>must</u> finish our homework before we go out.

modal verb

> The writer knows this definitely has to happen before he can go out.

> Some common modal verbs are: **would, can, could, should, shall, must** and **will.**

Example

Underline the modal verb in each sentence and decide whether it shows certainty or possibility.

We <u>may</u> have time to have lunch before the coach leaves. **shows possibility**
The lesson <u>will</u> finish before four o'clock. **shows certainty**

Now try this

1. Copy out the table and underline the modal verb in each sentence.
2. Tick one box in each row to show whether the modal verb indicates certainty or possibility.

sentence	certainty	possibility
There will be a general election next year.		
She's studied hard and should pass the exam.		
I shall bring my didgeridoo.		
There might be a storm tonight.		

Present and past perfect tense

You use the perfect tense when you want to show the order in which events happen.

Present perfect tense

It is formed with either **has**, **have** or **had**.

You use the **present perfect** tense to show an event happened in the past but has an effect on the present.

present perfect

John fell off his bike yesterday and <u>has broken</u> his arm.

The effects of John breaking his arm are still being felt by John because his arm is in plaster.

Past perfect tense

You use the **past perfect** tense when you want to talk about a moment in the past and say that something was completed before it.

When the writer arrived at the bakery (in the past), the bread had been sold already (even further in the past).

The bakers opened early so by the time we arrived they <u>had sold</u> all the bread.

past perfect tense

Example

Complete the sentence below, using either the present or past perfect.

By the time we arrived at the campsite, Alex <u>had put up</u> the tent.

Now try this

Make your sentences as imaginative as you can!

1. Complete the sentences below, using either the present or past perfect.
   a) The explorer Robert Falcon Scott arrived at the South Pole and discovered that his competitor Amundsen _____ (conquer) it the previous day.
   b) Mark dropped the jug and _____ (spill) the milk.
   c) The ambulance _____ (arrive) before the police got there.
2. Write a sentence of your own in the present perfect tense.
3. Write a sentence of your own in the past perfect tense.

Future perfect tense

Use the **future perfect** tense when you want to show the order in which events happen

When do you use it?

Use the future perfect to show that by the time something happens in the future, something else will already have happened.

See page 10 for more about the perfect tense.

The shops closing will happen before the children arrive in town.

Hurry up! By the time we get to town, the shops <u>will have closed</u>.

future perfect

Sorry, we're
CLOSED

Example

Tick the sentence that contains the future perfect tense.

They are going to build a new housing estate on those fields.
If he eats 50 pies in a row he will have achieved a new world record. ✔
We are eating out in a restaurant this evening.

Now try this

1. Which sentence contains the future perfect tense?

    They are opening a new cinema in the shopping arcade.

    There has been considerably more rain this October than in the previous month.

    The plumber will have installed a new bathroom before we get home from our holidays.

2. Using the words in brackets, rewrite the sentences below in the future perfect tense.

    a) I _____ (be) in the hockey team for two years next month.

    b) You _____ (read) the books on the list before the start of the new term.

    c) _____ (you/do) all your homework before youth club?

11

Adverbs

An **adverb** is a describing word that adds detail to a verb, an adjective, another adverb or a whole clause.

Describing verbs

> Most adverbs end in the suffix –ly but some don't, such as **down**.

Adverbs can describe **when**, **how** or **where** a verb is done.

describes the verb <u>started</u> (when)   describes the verb <u>squawking</u> (how)

> The seagull <u>suddenly</u> started squawking <u>noisily</u> as it swooped <u>down</u>.

describes the verb 'swooped' (where)

Describing other words

Adverbs can also describe adjectives, other adverbs or even whole clauses.

> For more on suffixes, see page 39.

describes the adjective <u>black</u>   describes the adverb <u>loudly</u>

> The sky over the city was <u>completely</u> black. The clouds rumbled <u>really</u> loudly as lightning struck the earth. Hours passed and it felt as though the storm would never pass. <u>Eventually</u>, the clouds began to part and the sun shone through.

describes the clause <u>the clouds began to part</u>

Example

Circle all of the adverbs in this passage.

Nervously, she looked down into the frighteningly dark cave. She clenched her fists tightly and strode into the darkness.

Now try this

1. Write a sentence to describe:
   a) How Julie plays tennis – she is a good tennis player.
   b) How Daniel listens – he is a patient listener.

2. Write a match report for your favourite sport. Include at least one adverb to describe:
   - a verb
   - an adverb
   - an adjective
   - a clause.

Adverbial phrases

An **adverbial phrase** is a word, a phrase or a clause that acts as an **adverb**.

Recognising adverbial phrases

Adverbial phrases can describe **where**, **when**, **how** or **why** something happens.

All of the underlined words and phrases are adverbial phrases.

Where did you meet Salma?	We met <u>outside the playground</u>.
When was that?	It was <u>at three-thirty last Wednesday</u>.
Why did you decide to meet there?	We met there <u>so that we could play football</u>.

Example

Underline the adverbial phrase in the sentence below.

We arrived at the station, <u>just in time to catch the train</u>.

Fronted adverbials

Although adverbial phrases usually come at the end of a sentence, they can also come at the beginning to describe the action that follows. These are called **fronted adverbials**.

> You usually need to add a comma after a fronted adverbial.

Example

Underline the fronted adverbial in the sentence below.

<u>Laughing loudly</u>, the children ran into the playing field.

Now try this

1. Identify adverbial phrases in the sentences below.
   a) We will go down to the beach after sunset.
   b) During the match, someone ran onto the pitch.
2. Write a sentence with an adverbial phrase.
3. Write a sentence with a fronted adverbial.

> If you pick a theme for your sentences, you could build them into a short story with lots more adverbials.

Conjunctions

A **conjunction** is a word that you use to link words together inside a sentence.

Co-ordinating conjunctions

This type of conjunction joins together two main clauses or compound sentences.

co-ordinating conjunction

Sabrina likes dancing <u>and</u> Justin likes singing.

Examples of conjunctions: **and, but, because, since** and **or**

See page 23 for more information about compound sentences.

Subordinating conjunctions

This form of conjunction joins together complex sentences. These are sentences that have a main clause and a subordinate clause.

subordinating conjunction

The orchestra played <u>while</u> the *Titanic* sank.

Examples of subordinating conjunctions: **while, before, unless** and **if**

See page 23 for more information about complex sentences.

Example

Rewrite these clauses and join them with a conjunction.
I stayed up until midnight last night / I still got up early for school.

I stayed up until midnight last night, but I still got up early for school.

Now try this

1. Identify the conjunction in each of the sentences below and say what type of conjunction it is.
   a) There was an expectant hush from the audience while they waited for the concert to begin.
   b) You should always fasten your seat belt before setting off in a car.
2. Rewrite each pair of clauses and join them with a conjunction.
   a) There was no food / we were ravenous.
   b) The weather is cold / the weather is sunny.
   c) She won the audition / she was extremely happy.

Prepositions

You use **prepositions** to show time, place or direction.

How to use prepositions

A preposition comes before a noun or pronoun.

- Some common prepositions of **time** include words such as **on**, **before** and **during**.
- Some common prepositions of **place** include words such as **over**, **next to**, **besides** and **in front of**.
- Some common prepositions of **direction** include words such as **towards**, **along** and **into**.

preposition of place

preposition of time

On Saturdays my friends and I meet under the clock tower and walk along the high street.

preposition of direction

Some prepositions such as **on** are used in more than one category.

Example

Underline the preposition in each sentence. Then, decide whether each sentence contains a preposition of time, place or direction.

We drank juice <u>while</u> we waited for the train.　　preposition of time

The cat was hiding <u>under</u> the table.　　preposition of place

The satellite is hiding <u>towards</u> Mars.　　preposition of direction

Now try this

1. Identify the preposition in each sentence and write it down.
   a) He dropped his laptop behind the sofa.
   b) Everyone feels better after a good night's sleep.
   c) The police stormed into the bank.
2. Decide whether each sentence contains a preposition of time, place or direction.

Prepositional phrases

A **prepositional phrase** is a group of words containing a preposition and usually a noun or pronoun.

How do you use a prepositional phrase?

A prepositional phrase isn't a complete sentence and doesn't contain a subject or an object.

prepositional phrase

We camped <u>beside a fast-flowing river</u>.

The preposition in the phrase is the word **beside**.

Examples of prepositional phrases: **up a steep hill** and **with extra marshmallow topping**

Example

Underline the prepositional phrase in each sentence and decide whether each shows time, place or direction.

The children ran <u>around the playing field</u>.   **shows direction**

They ate lunch <u>in the centre of the mall</u>.   **shows place**

<u>On the count of ten</u> the racers set off.   **shows time**

Now try this

1. Identify the prepositional phrase in each sentence and decide whether each shows time, place or direction.

   a) The squirrel scampered down the tree.   b) At the weekends we go hiking.

   c) The birds nested under the eaves.   d) The train hurtled through the tunnel.

2. Write three sentences containing prepositional phrases of:

   a) time   b) place   c) direction

   Write three related phrases and join them together to make a short story or a poem.

16

Subjunctive

You use the **subjunctive** form in two situations: to show **importance** and to show **possibility**.

Importance

You will use the subjunctive form mainly in formal language.

Use the subjunctive to emphasise importance or urgency.

subjunctive form

It is recommended <u>that passengers check in</u> at least two hours prior to departure.

If this was written in a less formal way it would say 'Passengers should check in two hours before departure.'

Possibility

Use the subjunctive to discuss something that is uncertain or has not yet happened.

subjunctive

I insist <u>that you repair</u> the damage to my window.

It's not certain whether the boy will repair the window or not.

Example

Rewrite the sentence below using the subjunctive form.

Competitors should train for three hours a day.

It is recommended that competitors train for three hours a day.

Now try this

1. Which is the subjunctive form in each of the sentences below?
    a) The teacher advises that pupils wear appropriate clothing for the walk.
    b) I propose that we delay giving an answer until we know the facts.
2. Rewrite the sentences below, using the subjunctive form.
    a) He will complete his homework on time.
    b) Please look after your health or you will become ill.

Questions

A **question** is a type of sentence that always end in a question mark.

Writing questions

You can form a question in three ways.

1. You can use a question word such as **who**, **what**, **where**, **when** and **how**.

question word ➡ What are you doing?

2. You can use an inversion such as **have they**, **will you** or **do they**.

inversion ➡ Have they been to school?

3. You can use a question tag such as **isn't it?**, **haven't you?** or **don't they?**

You've forgotten my birthday, haven't you?

question tag

Use question tags to check or confirm something.

Example

Punctuate these sentences.

Will he be able to cut the grass**?**
How many of them will there be**?**
The food was very nutritious**.**
The pudding takes two hours to cook, doesn't it**?**

Now try this

1. Write three questions using each of the question words **who**, **what** and **when**.
2. Write **three** questions using inversions.
3. Change these statements into questions using question tags.
   a) It's very expensive.   **b)** They are very kind.   **c)** We haven't been here before.

Commands and exclamations

Sentences or phrases that have an exclamation mark are usually commands or are expressing surprise.

The imperative

Exclamation marks often punctuate commands.
Commands usually take the imperative verb form.

> Take off your shoes!

An **exclamation mark** shows something that is expressed loudly or with a lot of emotion.

Not all imperative form sentences need an exclamation mark.

> Mix the flour and butter together and then add the sugar.

Exclamations

An exclamation can show that you are surprised, angry or in a hurry. It starts with **what** or **how** and contains a verb.

> What huge teeth you have!

Example

Remember to use an exclamation mark instead of a full stop to form an exclamation.

Underline the imperative sentences.

What lovely stationery you have!
Get on the bus now!
Place the cake in the oven and bake for thirty minutes.
What a surprise this is!

Now try this

1. Decide whether each sentence is an imperative, an exclamation or neither.
   a) What fantastic work you've done! b) How did the spider get into the box?
   c) Quick – hide behind that box! d) The Ancient Egyptians worshipped cats.

Subject and object

In a sentence, or phrase, the **subject** is the person doing something and the **object** is the person having something done to them.

subject ➡ Janice rang Michael. ⬅ object

The subject and object aren't always people, they can be things.

subject   object

⬇   ⬇

The tree dropped all its leaves.

A complete sentence must have a subject and a verb but it doesn't have to have an object.

Phillippa sings.

Example

Underline the subjects and circle the objects in the sentences below.

Dennis cooked (dinner). Julia really enjoyed (it).

Now try this

1. Find the subject and the object in each of the sentences below.
   a) The mechanic repaired the car.
   b) Flowers covered the garden path.
   c) Martina played the piano.
2. Write a sentence containing a subject, a verb and an object. Label the subject, the object and the verb.

Phrases and clauses

The terms **phrase** and **clause** both refer to a group of words.

Phrases

A phrase is a collection of words that may have nouns but does **not** have a subject or a verb.

…up the hill again!

phrase

A phrase is **not** a complete sentence.

Clauses

A clause **has** a subject that is actively doing something.

Although wolves howled in the moonlight, the travellers walked on.

subordinate clause

See page 22 for more about main and subordinate clauses.

Example

Decide whether each of the sentence parts below is a phrase or a clause.

After the initial shock,	phrase
Although he cycled very fast,	clause
Between a rock and a hard place,	phrase
As the horse galloped through the waves	clause

Now try this

1. Decide whether each of the sentence parts below is a phrase or a clause.
   a) The fiddler played
   b) A many-splendoured thing
   c) Actions speak louder than words
   d) A rose by any other name

Main and subordinate clauses

Main clauses and subordinate clauses are used to form sentences.

Main clauses

A main clause can be a complete sentence. It is sometimes called an **independent** clause because it can stand alone.

main clause

We had a fantastic day, even though the weather was horrible.

*If you changed the comma to a full stop, **We had a fantastic day** would be a complete sentence.*

Subordinate clauses

A subordinate clause only makes sense when you use it alongside a main clause.

subordinate clause

Although there was barely any food in the cupboard, Dad made a delicious meal.

You can swap main and subordinate clauses around and the sentence still makes sense.

Example

Decide whether the underlined part of each sentence is a main clause or a subordinate clause.

Greg doesn't eat steak because he's a vegetarian.   main clause
Shamsa, who lives next door, loves horse riding.   subordinate clause
That tractor is old but it still works.   subordinate clause

Now try this

1. Decide whether the underlined part of each sentence is a main clause or a subordinate clause.

   a) Daniel is still fascinated by the tides even though he's afraid of water.

   b) We frequently visit my uncle because he doesn't live far away.

Compound and complex sentences

Both **compound** and **complex** sentences have at least two clauses.

Compound sentences

A compound sentence is made up of two main clauses connected by a **coordinating conjunction**.

co-ordinating conjunction

I love netball <u>but</u> I hate hockey.

See page 14 for more about conjunctions.

Complex sentences

A complex sentence is formed by one main clause and one or more subordinate clauses.

main clause   <u>The shed roof leaks</u> <u>whenever it rains</u>.   subordinate clause

Example

Remember that a main clause could be a sentence on its own.

Decide whether each sentence is a compound sentence or a complex sentence.

Henri devours the chicken but he leaves all the peas.   **compound**

Wherever we went the little dog, which had attached itself to us, followed faithfully.   **complex**

Trudy is a great friend but she is very spoilt.   **compound**

Now try this

1. Decide whether each sentence is a compound sentence or a complex sentence.
   a) Although he kept being interrupted, the comedian continued and made everyone laugh.
   b) Carrie is interested in astronomy and she is fascinated by biology.
2. Write out and complete these sentences with an appropriate conjunction.
   a) _____ she was very sea-sick, she continued on the voyage.
   b) Thomas read a magazine _____ he was waiting for Flora to get ready.

23

Relative clauses

A **relative clause** adds **details** to a noun. It begins after the noun and starts with a **relative pronoun**.

What is a relative clause?

> My uncle, <u>who has lived in Spain for ten years,</u> returned to Britain last week.

← relative clause

Relative pronouns

Relative pronouns are words such as **who**, **which**, **that**, **whose** and **when**.

relative pronoun →

> I have a friend <u>whose</u> mother works in London.

Example

The relative pronoun is part of the relative clause.

Underline the relative clause and circle the relative pronoun.

Buckingham Palace, (which) is in London, is a popular tourist attraction.

Now try this

1. Which part of the sentence is a relative clause?
   My cousin Patricia, who is a talented pianist, also loves football.
2. Write out the sentence below, adding an appropriate relative pronoun.
   a) The dictionary, _____ we needed, was on the third shelf.
   b) This is the route _____ is the quickest.
   c) Winston Churchill, _____ was the Prime Minister at the time, declared war.
   d) There was a time _____ mobile phones had not been invented.
3. Write two sentences containing relative clauses.
   Use a different relative pronoun in each.

Active and passive voice

The **active** and **passive** voice are two different ways of giving the same information. The active or passive voice can change the **tone** of your writing.

The active voice

In the active voice, the subject of the sentence *does* the verb.

subject ➡ Matthew drove the car.

See page 20 for more about subjects and objects.

The passive voice

In the passive voice, the subject has the verb *done* to it.

The car was driven by Matthew.

Passive sentences often have the word **by** in them.

subject

Use the passive voice when you want to sound more formal or to avoid blaming or accusing someone of something.

The vase has been broken.

You don't know who broke it so it's better to use the passive.

Example

Decide whether each sentence is in the active voice or the passive voice.

The jewels were stolen from the bank vault.   passive
The vandals damaged the door.   active

Now try this

1. Rewrite the sentences below in the passive voice.

   a) The children built the snowman.   b) Johann made a sandcastle.

2. Rewrite the sentences below in the active voice.

   a) A car was designed by Tom.   b) The house was hit by a tree.

Standard English verbs

Use **Standard English** when you need to sound more formal, such as when you write a report or an official letter.

Spoken English is often *not* Standard English because it can include slang and dialect.

"Shove all that stuff in the bin."

The words **shove** and **stuff** are slang words and are **not** Standard English.

You might not use the correct subject to verb agreement in spoken language, but it's important when you are writing.

We <u>was</u> really happy because the sun came out.

incorrect verb agreement

In Standard English, you should say: We **were** really happy because the sun came out.

Example

Rewrite the sentences below, using the correct subject to verb agreement.

a) He ain't my cousin, he's my uncle.

He isn't my cousin, he's my uncle.

b) She were working last night.

She was working last night.

Now try this

1. Rewrite the sentences below, using the Standard English subject to verb agreement.

   a) They wasn't in trouble, was they?

   b) She ain't ready yet.

   c) I were so pleased to go horse riding.

   d) We was impressed by the level of service.

2. In which of these situations should you use Standard English?
   Explain your answer.

   a) Writing an email to your cousin

   b) Writing a letter to your head teacher asking permission to take time off

   c) Writing a postcard to a friend

   d) Writing to a restaurant to complain about poor service

Standard English tense and voice

Use Standard English to sound more formal, particularly when you write reports or essays.

The past tense

When you use Standard English, use the correct past tense.

> "I **done** my homework last night."

> The correct past tense in Standard English is **did**.

> See pages 7 and 10 for more about past tenses.

The passive voice

Standard English often uses the passive voice in the past tense.

> The renovation **had** been completed to a high standard.

> See page 25 for more about the passive voice.

Example

Decide whether each sentence is Standard English or non-Standard English.

The facts was clear: the man was guilty.	non-Standard English
They were travelling to Scotland.	Standard English
The carpet were really expensive.	non-Standard English
She done well.	non-Standard English

Now try this

1. Decide whether each sentence is Standard English or non-Standard English. Change any non-Standard English sentences to Standard English.

   a) The balloons was blown up by the clowns.

   b) She has been to France twice this year.

   c) Firemen was working hard to put out the fire.

   d) It was the dog what done it.

Standard English grammar

In Standard English, avoid slang or dialect.

A **dialect** is a way of speaking that is only used in a particular area or region.

Be grammatically correct

In speech, you may use the words **these**, **those** and **them** in a non-standard way.

non-Standard English

> Can we have **them** pies for supper?

Standard English

> Can we have **those** pies for supper?

In Standard English, you should use correct grammar.

non-Standard English

> **Me and my dad** are going swimming this weekend.

Standard English

> **My dad and I** are going swimming this weekend.

Example

Rewrite these sentences in Standard English.

a) Do you have marker pens?

   Have you got any marker pens?

b) She's your neighbour, isn't she?

   Is she not your neighbour?

c) Them shoes are perfect.

   Those shoes are perfect.

d) The concert was called off for now.

   The concert was postponed.

Now try this

1. Rewrite these sentences in Standard English.

   a) Give me them bags.

   b) They claimed that the rides were closed because of bad weather.

   c) He's your friend, isn't he?

   d) It's something like ten miles away.

2. Write a sentence in Standard English explaining that you and a friend are going to the circus tomorrow.

Commas for clarity

A **comma** is used to separate parts of a sentence or items in a list.

Commas in lists

Commas make the meaning of text clear.

> She bought caramel cabbages strawberry sorbet burgers and beef.

Without them, text can be very confusing!

> She bought caramel cabbages strawberry sorbet burgers and beef.

> Let's eat, everyone!

This means everyone should eat!

> Let's eat everyone!

This means we should eat everyone!

Commas in clauses

Commas are often used to separate main, subordinate and relative clauses.

> As she tugged on the door handle, which was ice-cold, she heard a blood-curdling scream.

See pages 22 and 24 for more about different types of clause.

Example

Use commas to mark out the clause in this sentence.

The children, who were on holiday, played in the park.

Now try this

1. Add commas to this sentence to clarify its meaning.
   In my desk you will find a rubber biscuits felt pens paper and an exercise book.
2. Which sentence has the correct punctuation?
   Gradually climbing higher the girl, reached the summit.
   Gradually climbing higher, the girl reached the summit.
   Gradually, climbing higher the girl reached the summit.

29

Parenthesis

Parenthesis is additional information inserted within a complete sentence.

Brackets, dashes and commas

Parenthesis can be indicated by brackets, dashes or commas.

> The sandwich (egg and cress) came with a free bottle of water.
>
> Everyone – except the teachers – got a free go on all the rides!
>
> John, who had already been for lunch, decided to go to the café anyway.

Parentheses and clauses

You use commas to show clauses within or at the beginning of sentences.

> The new girl at school, <u>who has red hair</u>, is really good at netball.

parenthesis

Example

Add brackets to this sentence to indicate parenthesis.

The curry (which was made with coconut milk) was delicious.

Now try this

1. Rewrite these sentences with dashes to indicate parenthesis.

   a) August when we have the school holidays is usually the hottest month.

   b) Carol who will turn 15 next week is a good friend.

   c) The ring which we found on the road is very valuable.

2. Rewrite these sentences and add parenthesis.

   a) Christopher (_____) speaks three languages.

   b) York – _____ – has the River Ouse running through it.

   c) The sunset, _____, was incredibly beautiful.

30

Colons

Use a **colon** to introduce a list or a quotation.

Colons for lists

You can use a colon to introduce a list.

> There is a wide selection of sports to choose from: tennis, badminton, basketball and table tennis.

The items in the list still needs to be separated by commas.

Example

Punctuate this sentence with a colon and commas.

For Charlie's birthday, he would like: a pair of trainers, a mobile phone, a book and a football.

Colons for quotations

Colons are sometimes used to introduce something someone has said.

> The ring master called out: "Ladies and gentleman, take your seats for the most spectacular show on earth."

*Colons are often used to introduce **longer** quotes rather than short ones.*

Example

You will still need to use speech marks and other punctuation.

Punctuate this sentence correctly.

She shouted: "Let me have my books back now or I'll tell Dad."

Now try this

1. Rewrite the sentences below, punctuating them correctly.

   a) The instructor advised us to bring hiking boots a rucksack a change of socks and a sleeping bag.

   b) The policeman addressed the crowd Everyone stand well back and quietly form a queue

2. Write a sentence including a colon to introduce a list.

Semi-colons

Colons and **semi-colons** may look similar but they have different uses.

Semi-colons for clauses

Semi-colons can be used to separate two main clauses in a sentence.

> You should stop eating so much junk food; you are getting very plump.

The two clauses must give information about the **same** topic.

Semi-colons for lists

See pages 22 and 24 for more about clauses.

Semi-colons are used to separate items in a list if the sentence already has commas or is particularly long.

> The subjects are split into four bands: ICT, art and design; English, history and other humanities; physics, chemistry and biology and maths.

Example

Punctuate the sentence below with a semi-colon.

We kept trudging ahead; we were confident that we were almost there.

Now try this

1. Rewrite the sentence below, adding semi-colons and any other punctuation you need.

   To get fit you need to eat a balanced diet swim and walk several times a week not eat fast foods and get plenty of sleep.

2. Explain why semi-colons have been used in this sentence.

   Before you go on holiday abroad you need to: check that your passport is valid, arrange for someone to look after your pets and check your house; buy sun cream; buy travel insurance; wash and pack your clothes and book a taxi to the airport.

Possessive apostrophes

Possessive apostrophes are used to show that something **belongs** to someone or something.

> This car belongs to Tom. It is Tom's car.

Apostrophes for plural nouns

For plural nouns you need to put the apostrophe after the 's'.

> It is at the <u>boys'</u> school.

If a noun has an unusual plural, you add a possessive apostrophe in the same way as you do for a singular noun.

> The <u>children's</u> playground.

Example

Add possessive apostrophes to the sentence below.

Judith's bag was covered in stripes and the bag's handles were sparkly.

Now try this

1. Rewrite the sentences below, adding possessive apostrophes where they are missing.
   a) Minas shirt was a lovely shade of blue.
   b) The mens toilets are on the first floor.
2. Rewrite the sentences below to use possessive apostrophes.
   a) The lorry belonging to Chloes dad transports fruit.
   b) The paintings belonging to grandma are very old.

Apostrophes for contractions

A **contraction** is when two words are put together and letters are removed to make one word. An apostrophe is used to show where letters are missing.

Contractions and speech

Contractions are words that have been shortened to reflect the way we usually speak.

We will becomes We'll

> Don't confuse contractions and possessive apostrophes; they look the same!

> We'll catch the bus at six. When we get home, it'll be time for tea.

> Contractions aren't usually used in formal language.

it will becomes it'll

Now try this

1. Rewrite the sentences, below using contractions.
   a) It is a quite a curiosity.
   b) He will guarantee that the work is completed on time.
2. Rewrite the sentences below in the full form.
   a) I don't want to go.
   b) He hasn't interfered in the past.

Direct speech

Direct speech is how you report what someone has said, using the words spoken.

Inverted commas

You use inverted commas to show what someone said.

Full sentences in direct speech should always begin with a capital letter and include closing punctuation such as a full stop, question or exclamation mark.

> Inverted commas are usually double (") but can be single (').

> Bethany exclaimed, "What huge fish!"

closing punctuation

> Remember that punctuation at the end of what is said comes **inside** the inverted commas.

Interruptions

If the speech is interrupted by words such as **he said** or **she replied** then you use a comma at the end instead of a full stop.

> "I hope we can pet the animals," she said.

comma

Example

Rewrite the sentence below as direct speech. Remember to punctuate your answer correctly.

what amazing news shouted Tim

"What amazing news!" shouted Tim.

Now try this

1. Rewrite the sentences below as direct speech. Remember to punctuate your answers correctly.

   a) it would be so embarrassing if we dropped the plates he said

   b) what a terrible mess exclaimed mum

2. Two people are planning a trip to the cinema.

   Write a paragraph recording their conversation using direct speech.

Bullet points

Bullet points organise information into a **list**. Each bullet point starts on a new line.

Structure

A lead-in clause or phrase or sentence is usually used to introduce a bullet list.

The equipment you need to make a model aeroplane is:

- strong adhesive
- scissors
- strips of wood
- paint
- paint brushes.

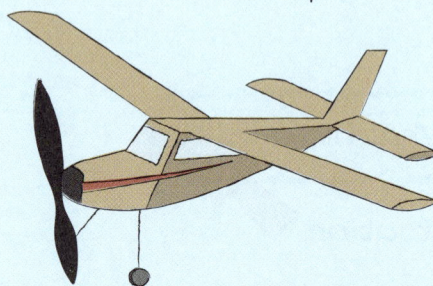

The lead-in phrase/sentence usually ends in a colon.

The last item should have a full stop if the list reads as a sentence.

Example

Rewrite the sentence below, using bullet points and the correct punctuation. To prepare for a camping trip you need to check that your tent is clean make sure your sleeping bag is in a good state of repair pack tins of food fill a container with fresh water

To prepare for a camping trip you need to:
- check that your tent is clean
- make sure your sleeping bag is in a good state of repair
- pack tins of food
- fill a container with fresh water.

Now try this

1. Rewrite the sentence below, using bullet points and the correct punctuation.

   The job requires the successful candidate to be honest reliable trustworthy hard-working

2. Write a list of bullet points, including a lead-in clause or phrase or sentence, to describe the qualities you look for in a friend. Include at least four bullet points.

Hyphens and ellipses

Use **hyphens** to link text and **ellipses** to shorten text.

Hyphens

You use hyphens to make compound words such as **man-eating**, to attach prefixes to other words such as **re-elect** and to show where a word breaks over two lines.

> Hyphens are often confused with dashes but hyphens are shorter and have different uses.

Ellipsis

An ellipsis is a set of dots (…) used to show that you have left out a word, a phrase or some extra text on purpose.

> The prizes were awarded to 10 children from primary schools all over the UK who had travelled to London for the ceremony.

> Ellipses can also be used to create suspense and let the reader **infer** what might happen next. **The door creaked open and then…**

> The prizes were awarded to 10 children … who had travelled to London for the ceremony.

Example

Put a hyphen in the correct place in this sentence.

We could hardly see through the rain-splattered windows.

Now try this

1. Rewrite the sentence below, putting hyphens in the correct places.
   The four year olds were playing in the sand pit.
2. Shorten the sentence below by replacing some words with an ellipsis.
   After school, I went to play basketball at the sports centre in town and then came home.

Prefixes

A **prefix** is a letter or a group of letters that you add to the beginning of a root word to change the meaning.

Prefixes to change adjectives

> Some common prefixes are: **un-**, **re-**, **in-** and **im-**.

Many prefixes are used to give an adjective the opposite meaning.

> He isn't **able** to complete the work. He is **un**able to do it.

         root word   prefix

Prefixes to change nouns

Some prefixes are added to nouns.

subway   ⬅   'sub' means 'below'

autopilot   ⬅   'auto' means 'self'

monorail   ⬅   mono' means 'one'

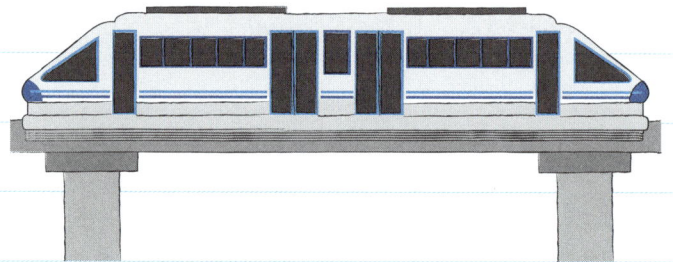

Example

Complete the sentences, using the correct prefixes.

She didn't get any marks because all her answers were <u>in</u>correct.

The band is famous internationally. They are <u>super</u>stars.

Now try this

1. Copy out and complete the sentences, using the correct prefixes.

     1. He is very ___mature for his age.

     2. Keeping wild animals in captivity is cruel and ___humane.

     3. Leaving broken glass in the park is highly ___responsible.

Suffixes

A **suffix** is a letter, or a group of letters, that you add to the end of a **root word** to change its meaning.

Changing word class

Some common suffixes are: **ed**, **ly**, **able**, **ous**, **ness**, **ful** and **tion**.

Notice how the suffixes in **green** change the class of the word.

> It was with great sad**ness** that our teacher gent**ly** broke the news of Mr Green's dread**ful** accident. He had been driving on a danger**ous** bend when a care**less** driver had collid**ed** with him. However, she was hope**ful** that he would make a full recover**y** soon. He is feeling comfort**able** in hospital and his arm is not too pain**ful**.

Changes to the root word

Sometimes you have to change the root word.

> happ**y** → happ**ily**   ta**p** → ta**pp**ing

Example

Rewrite the sentence, adding a suffix to the root word in brackets so that the sentence makes sense.

The police need to collect as much (inform) as they can.

The police need to collect as much information as they can.

Now try this

1. Rewrite the sentence, adding a suffix to the root word in brackets so that the sentence makes sense.

   a) Don't eat those berries they are (poison).

   b) They (dance) on the stage last week.

   c) I feel like (sleep) for a week!

   d) The woman in the painting was very (beauty).

   e) The children wanted to raise (aware) of road safety.

Synonyms and antonyms

Synonyms

Synonyms are words that have the same or similar meanings.

All these adjectives are **synonyms** for the word **big**.

> enormous   huge   gigantic   massive   immense   colossal

Antonyms

Antonyms are words that have opposite meanings.

> tall → short   agree → disagree   detest → adore

Example

Rewrite the sentence below, using a synonym to replace the underlined word.

The patient was <u>brave</u>.

The patient was courageous.

Now try this

1. Replace each of the underlined words with a synonym.
   a) Shamsa was <u>very tired</u> by the time she got home.
   b) Grandma was <u>really pleased</u> to see us.
   c) Mohammed is a <u>clever</u> boy.
2. Match each word in the top row with its antonym in the bottom row.

exhausted   war   cheerful   create
destroy   energised   miserable   peace

Tricky spellings: silent letters

In English, there are a lot of words that don't follow the common spelling rules.

Silent letters

Many words contain letters that you don't say aloud: these are **silent letters**.
The silent letters in the passage below are in **purple**.

When he arrived, which was last Tuesday, the plumber said it was doubtful if he could fix the sink as it had been fitted in the wrong place. He said he would try but couldn't guarantee it. His name was Christopher and he had very gnarled knuckles on his thumbs. He looked like a gnome.

One way to remember the spelling of words that have silent letters is to sound them out saying the silent letter.

Example

Circle the silent letters in the sentences below.

The plumber fixed the tap.

Autumn is my favourite time of year.

Now try this

1. Copy out the sentences below and circle all the silent letters.
   a) It's so cold my feet are numb.   b) You should listen in class.
   c) My grandma has lots of wrinkles.   d) Kneading bread is hard work!
2. Read each sentence aloud, pronouncing the silent letters. Then cover them up and see how many of the silent-letter words you can remember how to spell.

Tricky spellings: pronunciation

Sometimes, sounds in English are spelled in different ways. Other times, the same spelling can be pronounced in different ways.

The ee sound

The most common ways to spell the **ee** sound are **ee**, **ea**, and **y**.

Two other common spellings are **ei** and **ie**.

> These are words such as **green**, **peach** and **key**. What other examples can you think of?

> He bel**ie**ved he hadn't ach**ie**ved good marks so when he passed the test he was very rel**ie**ved. He rec**ei**ved a book called *The Origin of the Species* as a prize.

The letters ough

The letters **ough** are pronounced in many different ways.

> Read this aloud: you can hear that **ough** can be pronounced in several different ways.

> Th**ough** it was cold, and there was a dr**ough**t as it hadn't rained, we b**ough**t ice-cream to put on the d**ough**nuts. I couldn't eat all of mine because I had a c**ough**.

Example

Write a list of as many other **ie** and **ei** words as you can.

| deceive | retrieve | seize | relief | ceiling | mischief |
| receipt | piece | protein | brief | forfeit | priest |

Now try this

1. Study the list of words in the example. Cover it up and rewrite the words with the correct spellings. Check and correct any errors.

2. Write a list of as many **ough** words as you can that have the same sound as **fort**, **huff** or **cow**. Copy the table below and add your word list to it.

fort	huff	cow
thought	rough	plough

Homophones and homonyms

Homophones and homonyms are pairs of words that sound the same but have **different** meanings.

Homophones

Homophones sound the same but have different meanings and are spelled differently.

> The boy **blew** a big **blue** bubble.

Homonyms

Homonyms are pairs of words that sound the same and are spelled the same, but have different meanings.

> Someone had **left** cans and burnt **matches** on the football **pitch**. We had to pick them up before the football **matches** started. Even though we **left** early, it was **pitch** black by the time we got home. We took a wrong turn and went **left** instead of right.

> There are lots of homonym pairs including: flat, long, book, chip, duck and park. How many others can you think of?

Example

Choose the correct homophone to complete the sentence.

Ted cut a huge <u>piece</u> of chocolate cake. (peace / piece)

Now try this

1. Choose the correct homophone to complete the sentence.
   a) They couldn't decide _____ to go or not. (weather / whether)
   b) The ambulance arrived on the _____ as soon as it was called. (seen / scene)
   c) After putting the potato on top, _____ the cheese over it. (grate /great)
   d) The traffic was _____. (stationary / stationery)
2. Write three sentences including the different meanings of homonym pairs **flat**, **book** and **park**.

Audience and purpose

Before you start writing a piece of text, ask yourself: who is my **audience** and what is the **purpose** of the text?

Audience

The people who will read your text are the **audience**. If it's a fiction story about a lost puppy, your audience is probably young children.

> It's important to think about your audience carefully before you start writing so that you can choose the most effective language.

> Sammy was scared. Where was his owner? Now he was all alone. "I want some food," he thought.

> You won't have to do a writing test as part of your Year 6 SATs. Your teacher will look at some of your pieces of writing instead. Use the skills in this section to improve your writing.

Purpose

The **purpose** is the reason for writing a text.

The **audience** is the teacher.

> Dear <u>Mr Brown</u>,
>
> I would be grateful <u>if you could excuse Rachel from PE</u> because the dog has eaten her PE kit.
>
> Yours sincerely,
> Mrs Roberts

The **purpose** is to ask him to excuse Rachel from PE.

Now try this

1. Write down the purpose and an appropriate audience for each text.

   a) a manual on installing a new printer **b)** the biography of a politician

   c) a description of a hotel **d)** a magazine interview with a boyband

   e) a story about teddy bears **f)** a letter to the council about local crime

Planning and organising

Before you start writing, it's important to **plan** your text. Planning your work produces structured, better quality writing.

Planning

When you plan your writing you need to think about:

- what you want to say
- how you are going to say it
- how you are going to set it out.

Organising: beginning, middle and end

Most texts will have: an **introductory** paragraph (beginning), a **main** section (middle) and a **conclusion** (end). You usually need a title too.

Hiking in the mountains

A hiking trip can be great fun, but only if you are well prepared and take all the correct equipment with you.

Before you set off, check that you have a sturdy but light-weight rucksack packed with all the items you will need. Make sure you take plenty of healthy, energising snacks and drinks. Also, check that your hiking boots are comfortable and 'broken in' before you go.

Although there's a lot of effort required to organise a hiking expedition it's well worth the satisfaction you'll gain when you get to the top of the mountain—and don't forget to take your camera to capture the amazing view!

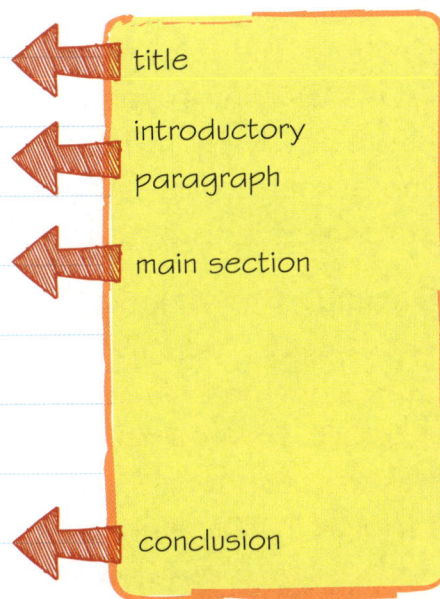

⬅ title

⬅ introductory paragraph

⬅ main section

⬅ conclusion

Being organised will help make sure your paragraphs are correctly formed and in the right order.

Now try this

1. Plan a short piece of text to describe planning a trip such as a holiday or a visit to the cinema. Make sure you have a title, a beginning, a middle and an end.

Drafting and improving

Once you've made a plan, you will be ready to write the first draft.

Drafts

Even experienced writers rarely get it right first time. That's why their first attempt is usually called a **draft**.

This is like an artist doing a quick sketch before they complete the painting.

Improving

Reread your writing carefully. How could you **improve** it? If you're writing a story you could make it more entertaining by selecting interesting **adjectives** and **adverbs**. If it's a set of instructions perhaps there is a way you could make it clearer.

Example

Below is the first draft of a story. Rewrite the first draft to make it more interesting.

In the second draft, use literary devices such as **adjectives, alliteration, similes** and **imagery** to improve the text and make it more interesting.

Draft 1: The long snake slithered across the grass without anyone seeing it. There was a small boy lying in the grass. He was asleep in the sunshine. The snake stopped in front of him and licked his face. The boy screamed in fright and ran away as fast as he could.

Draft 2: The venomous, six-foot snake slithered through the grass unnoticed. The tiny boy was dozing in the August sunshine, his rosy cheek buried in the tall grass like a fallen, ripe peach. The snake stopped, his scarlet, fork-tipped tongue stabbed the air. The snake's tongue flicked against the boy's soft skin. The boy's eyelids snapped open. A blood-curdling scream wrenched from his throat and he fled across the grass like a bullet from a gun.

Now try this

Rewrite the draft below to make the story more interesting. Add your own ending. Remember to organise your paragraphs and use correct punctuation.

It was a wet day and raindrops were falling against the window. Jayden was bored. He hadn't been able to go out and play all week. He had been stuck inside with his annoying sister. He longed to go to the park and play football. Suddenly he had a plan …

Proof-reading

You've finished drafting and writing. Now you need to check for any errors. It's really important to check, as there will always be improvements you can make.

Proof-reading

> It's easy to lose marks through simple mistakes.

Re-read your writing carefully and check for errors, such as spelling and punctuation mistakes, subject to verb agreement and use of correct tense.

Example

> See pages 7, 8, 10 and 11 for more about tenses.

Read the text below and improve it by correcting the errors.

<u>Me and my friend</u> <u>was walking</u> <u>thrugh</u> the long dark tunnel when we saw a huge shape ahead <u>and</u> we <u>run</u> the other way as fast as we <u>can</u>. What was <u>that"</u> said my friend Jack.

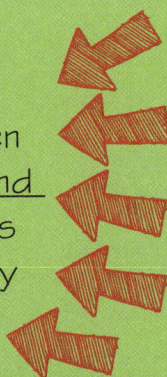

poor grammar and incorrect subject to verb agreement

incorrect spelling

sentence too long

incorrect tense twice

question mark missing

My friend and I were walking through the long dark tunnel when we saw a huge shape ahead. We ran the other way as fast as we could. What was that? said my friend Jack.

Now try this

1. Read the text below and improve it. Make sure that you correct all the errors.

> **The Football Match**
> Me and my sister Holly both love football so when we heard 'The Tamquest Stars' were comeing to play we was really excited.
> The match started at two o clock and me and my sister had wanted to go for yonks. As we walk to the stadium we can hear the supporters in there stands chanting loud. It was them same supporters who were at the last match they were wearing the same colours.
> Lets run," said Holly or we will miss the match.

Writing stories

When you are writing stories (fiction) your purpose is to entertain your audience and make them want to read more.

Creating interesting text

Good writers use a number of methods to attract their audience and keep them interested.

The Duckling Dancer

She had never expected, not in any one single minute of her ten years, that she would one day become a famous ballerina. Not once, in all the years of overhearing her mother's friends saying, "I'm sure she'll grow into those duckling feet of hers one day!" Her mother would sigh and force a smile as she watched her trip up, as her mammoth, flipper-feet somehow managed to catch each other and send her flying like a goose that's forgotten it's got wings.

But now here she was, standing in the middle of the ballet studio ready for the opening performance of 'Swan Lake'. She was surrounded by glistening, coral-coloured satin pumps, dresses with silken bodices and ruffle after ruffle of sparkling layers, and soon it would be her turn to pirouette onto the stage …

- interesting title
- intriguing first line
- metaphor
- inference about a character
- simile
- effective adjectives

See pages 74 and 75 for more about metaphors and similes

Example

Read the opening extract from the short story and identify the ways in which the writer makes the story interesting.

The writer uses an organised structure, an interesting title and intriguing first line. They use figurative language (similes and metaphors) to create imagery and a range of effective adjectives and adverbs to describe and imply meaning.

Now try this

1. Write the opening two paragraphs of a short story, using the devices identified. Remember to interest your audience and make them want to read more.

Persuasive writing

The purpose of persuasive text is to **persuade** someone to do something. Persuasive language is used intentionally to grab the audience's attention, making them want to know more.

> An advertisement **persuades** people to buy a product.

Making your case

Persuasive text often contains a catchy title, an opening sentence to **hook** the reader, facts to support the point of view and a well-formed argument, using **connectives**. It can also use **emotive language** that appeals to the reader's emotions and sympathies.

A Grey Future Without a Green Future

Can you image a world without trees or meadows? Would you want your family to set out their picnic basket on tarmac without a blade of grass in sight? This is the future we face <u>unless</u> we realise some hard, concrete facts.

In the last three years:

- 247,000 acres of coniferous forest have been cut down
- 7,400 acres of mixed forest have been destroyed
- 35,000 acres of agricultural land have been concreted over.

Unless this ruthless, rampaging destruction is halted the future is grey.

- catchy title
- the 'hook'
- emotive language
- connectives

> **Connectives** link ideas in sentences and paragraphs

Now try this

1. Write a piece of persuasive text to encourage people to stop dropping litter.

Instructions and reports

When you write instructions and reports your purpose is to provide **factual information** in an ordered structure.

> Always use formal language in this type of writing.

Instructions

The purpose of instructional text is to explain **how** to do something. You need to set this out in clear, step-by-step instructions. Always begin with a title.

> We often use the **imperative** and **bullet points** in this type of writing.

Flapjack recipe

Ingredients: 200 g oats, 200 g butter, 100 g brown sugar.

Method: Preheat the oven to 200°C.

1. Melt the butter and stir in the oats and sugar.
2. Pour into a well-greased tin.
3. Bake for 20 minutes.

title

list

instruction

step-by-step

> See pages 19 and 36 for more about the imperative and bullet points.

Reports

The purpose is to inform the audience about what has happened. The events don't need to be presented chronologically but you must include details such as time and place and set out facts clearly.

who?   what?

Dolphin Sighting

Beach-goers were amazed to see two dolphins jumping through the waves close to the beach at Sandy Cove yesterday. The bottle-nosed dolphins are a rare sight in these waters. According to local marine expert, Ronnie Holland, the dolphins had probably become separated from the rest of their pod.

where?

when?

Now try this

1. Write a recipe for making beans on toast.
2. Write a report on a school sports day.

50

Formal letters

If you write a letter to someone you haven't met before, it will usually need to be a **formal** letter. These types of letter have to be set out in a certain format.

Language and structure

Formal letters will be written in formal, or standard English, and often include the **passive voice** and the **subjunctive**.

See page 17 for more about the subjunctive and page 25 for more about the passive voice.

title of the person you are writing to

your address

6 Meadow Close
Newstown
NR6 2EH

date

19th September

Mr John Andrews
Manager
Toys Are Great
New Street
Newstown
NR8 3TH

their address

If you don't know the name of the person you are writing to, use Dear Sir/Madam.

reference title

introductory paragraph

Dear Mr Andrews,

Request for visit to your factory

I am writing on behalf of myself and my classmates in Year 6 to ask if it would be possible to visit your factory.

We are learning about the different methods used to make toys as part of a project involving art and design, ICT and science. It would therefore be particularly valuable if we were able to observe the process and stages involved in toy manufacturing at first hand.

I look forward to hearing from you in the hope that my request will be favourably received.

If you have addressed your letter Dear Sir/Madam, you should close with 'Yours faithfully'.

Yours sincerely,

closing statement

Joanna Greenwood

Joanna Greenwood

signature and name

Now try this

1. Write a formal letter to Ms Alexander, the manager of a local zoo, asking if one of the employees could visit your school and give a talk about what it is like to work there.

Informal letters

Letters written to family and friends are usually **informal.** You can use friendly, conversational language. There are still rules about how to set out the text, however.

Language and structure

> You should still make sure that you use correct spelling and punctuation.

your address → 21 Marston Row
Preston
PR9 6NH

date → 5th January

introductory paragraph ↓

Dear Aunt Agnes,

Thank you so much for the amazing roller blades you sent me for Christmas. It was such a great surprise when I opened the parcel on Christmas morning! I've been practising nearly every day and can even skate backwards now!

← informal language

How are you all up in Scotland? Have you still got lots of snow? It's been very wet here. Dad says that if it keeps raining the river might burst its banks. If that happens my friend Janice will have to come and stay with us as they live near the river. So I don't mind if it keeps raining!

Give my love to Uncle Angus. Please come and see us soon as we haven't seen you for ages.

← informal closing statement

Best wishes,

Catriona x ← handwritten name

Now try this

1. Write an informal letter to a friend or relative who lives in a different part of the country, inviting them to come and stay with you.

Reading skills: close meaning

Sometimes you need to look in detail at certain words or phrases and their meaning. You will need to **scan** the text to find certain things.

Skill 1: find information

You will need to find key details in fiction and non-fiction texts. This may mean finding a single word or a phrase.

Skill 2: explain the meaning

See page 57 for more about finding information.

Some questions ask you to explain what a word means or choose words or phrases with a similar meaning. Think about the **context** (what comes before and after the word) to help you work out what the word means.

The judge threw the <u>case</u> out of court.

Here **case** means a legal investigation, not the judge's suitcase!

Skill 3: explain word choice

See page 63 for more about authors' language.

You will be asked to explain how the words used add to the meaning of the writing. You might need to find words the author uses to create a certain effect.

Skill 4: make inferences

You make inferences when you use clues in the text to figure out things the author hasn't told you directly. You need to provide evidence from the text to support your inferences.

See page 61 for more about inferences.

The words **sheepish, muddy footprints** and **flowerbeds** are strong clues.

Example

What inference could you make from this sentence?

David scowled at his dog's sheepish expression; there were muddy footprints on the floor and the flowerbeds outside were in a mess.

You could infer that David's dog has been in the garden when he wasn't allowed to and has dug it up.

Reading skills: the whole text

Some questions focus on 'the big picture'. You will have to think about the whole text. It is a good idea to **skim read** the text first before you read it through carefully.

Skill 5: summarise

A summary states the main points in a text. You may need to identify the main message in more than one paragraph or put some events in the right order.

Skill 6: make predictions

> See page 62 for more about predicting.

Some questions will ask you to make a prediction about what happens next. Think about what has already happened and how the characters might behave.

Example

> We know David is annoyed and his dog feels sheepish. This means the dog probably feels bad about his actions.

Use clues from this sentence to continue the story.
David scowled at his dog's sheepish expression; there were muddy footprints on the floor and the flowerbeds outside were in a mess.

David shouted and told his dog off for digging up the garden. His dog lay down with his tail between his legs.

Skill 7: explain how things are related

You may need to explain the theme of a story or explain how different pieces of information in a non-fiction text create the overall meaning of the whole text.

> See page 68 for more about themes.

Skill 8: make comparisons

Some questions will ask you to compare information, characters or events from different parts of the text. For example, you may be asked to explain how a character's mood changes.

> See page 67 for more about character.

Now try this

1. Create a poster explaining these skills in your own words. Use examples to show what you mean.

Fiction text

This is an extract from *The Railway Children* by Edith Nesbit. It was first published in 1906. The story is about a family that has moved from London to Yorkshire and who now live near the railway. Read the extract as preparation for completing activities later in the revision guide.

The Railway Children

So they went along the fence towards the little swing gate that is at the top of these steps. And they were almost at the gate when Bobbie said:

"Hush. Stop! What's that?"

"That" was a very odd noise indeed — a soft noise, but quite plainly to be heard through the sound of the wind in tree branches, and the hum and whir of the telegraph wires. It was a sort of rustling, whispering sound. As they listened it stopped, and then it began again.

And this time it did not stop, but it grew louder and more rustling and rumbling.

"Look" — cried Peter, suddenly — "the tree over there!"

The tree he pointed at was one of those that have rough grey leaves and white flowers. The berries, when they come, are bright scarlet, but if you pick them, they disappoint you by turning black before you get them home. And, as Peter pointed, the tree was moving — not just the way trees ought to move when the wind blows through them, but all in one piece, as though it were a live creature and were walking down the side of the cutting.

"It's moving!" cried Bobbie. "Oh, look! and so are the others. It's like the woods in Macbeth."

"It's magic," said Phyllis, breathlessly. "I always knew this railway was enchanted."

It really did seem a little like magic. For all the trees for about twenty yards of the opposite bank seemed to be slowly walking down towards the railway line, the tree with the grey leaves bringing up the rear like some old shepherd driving a flock of green sheep.

"What is it? Oh, what is it?" said Phyllis; "it's much too magic for me. I don't like it. Let's go home."

But Bobbie and Peter clung fast to the rail and watched breathlessly. And Phyllis made no movement towards going home by herself.

The trees moved on and on. Some stones and loose earth fell down and rattled on the railway metals far below.

"It's *all* coming down," Peter tried to say, but he found there was hardly any voice to say it with. And, indeed, just as he spoke, the great rock, on the top of which the walking trees were, leaned slowly forward. The trees, ceasing to walk, stood still and shivered.

The Railway Children

So they went along the fence towards the little swing gate that is at the top of these steps. And they were almost at the gate when Bobbie said:

"Hush. Stop! What's that?"

"That" was a very odd noise indeed — a soft noise, but quite plainly to be heard through the sound of the wind in tree branches, and the hum and whir of the telegraph wires. It was a sort of rustling, whispering sound. As they listened it stopped, and then it began again.

And this time it did not stop, but it grew louder and more rustling and rumbling.

"Look" — cried Peter, suddenly — "the tree over there!"

The tree he pointed at was one of those that have rough grey leaves and white flowers. The berries, when they come, are bright scarlet, but if you pick them, they disappoint you by turning black before you get them home. And, as Peter pointed, the tree was moving — not just the way trees ought to move when the wind blows through them, but all in one piece, as though it were a live creature and were walking down the side of the cutting.

"It's moving!" cried Bobbie. "Oh, look! and so are the others. It's like the woods in Macbeth."

"It's magic," said Phyllis, breathlessly. "I always knew this railway was enchanted."

It really did seem a little like magic. For all the trees for about twenty yards of the opposite bank seemed to be slowly walking down towards the railway line, the tree with the grey leaves bringing up the rear like some old shepherd driving a flock of green sheep.

"What is it? Oh, what is it?" said Phyllis; "it's much too magic for me. I don't like it. Let's go home."

But Bobbie and Peter clung fast to the rail and watched breathlessly. And Phyllis made no movement towards going home by herself.

The trees moved on and on. Some stones and loose earth fell down and rattled on the railway metals far below.

"It's *all* coming down," Peter tried to say, but he found there was hardly any voice to say it with. And, indeed, just as he spoke, the great rock, on the top of which the walking trees were, leaned slowly forward. The trees, ceasing to walk, stood still and shivered. Leaning with the rock, they seemed to hesitate a moment, and then rock and trees and grass and bushes, with a rushing sound, slipped right away from the face of the cutting

Retrieving information

Many of your reading test questions will ask you to **retrieve** (find) information from a text. You will need to identify exactly which part of the text the question is about.

Selecting the correct answer

Think carefully about what information you need to find.

For example:

Read all of the text in the question to make sure you give the correct answer.

- If you are asked **where** something happened, give a place.
- If you are asked **when** something happened, give a point in time.
- If you are asked **who** did something, give a character.
- If you are asked **why** something happened, give a reason.

Example

There is quite a lot of information in this text that you need to read through to pick out the correct answer.

Read the text below, taken from *The Railway Children*. Where were the children when they first heard the noise?

So they went along the fence towards the little swing gate that is at the top of the steps. And they were almost at the gate when Bobbie said – 'Hush. Stop! What's that?'

'That' was a very odd noise indeed – a soft noise, but quite plainly to be heard through the sound of wind in the tree branches, and the hum and whir of telegraph wires. It was a sort of rustling, whispering sound. As they listened it stopped, and then it began again.

And this time it did not stop, but grew louder and more rustling and rumbling.'

'Look – 'cried Peter, suddenly – 'that tree over there!'

They were at the top of the steps.

Now try this

Read the text above again to find the answers to these questions.

1. Who heard the noise first?

2. What other noises did the children hear?

Recording information: selecting an answer

Your test questions will ask you to provide answers in different types of format.

Selecting the correct answer

Many of the questions will ask you to select an answer from a list of options.

These often ask you to circle or tick the correct answer.

Look at this extract from the text and how the questions are formatted.

> The tree he pointed at was one of those that have rough grey leaves and white flowers. The berries, when they come, are bright scarlet, but if you pick them, they disappoint you by turning black before you get them home.'

Be careful with these questions as it's easy to make a mistake and circle or tick the wrong box!

The berries on the tree were:

Circle **one** answer.

black   (red)   grey   white

If you didn't read the paragraph or the question carefully you might circle *black* which would be the wrong answer because the question asks you about the berries when they are on the tree.

How does the boy feel when the berries turn black?

Tick **one**.

delighted ☐
let down ☑
angry ☐
miserable ☐

The question clearly instructs you to 'Tick **one**'. If you tick more than one you will not get any marks – even if one is the correct answer.

Now try this

1. Using information from the text above, decide whether each statement is true or false.

The tree had white berries.

The tree had smooth leaves.

The berries turn black.

Recording information: free answers

Some of your test questions will ask you to write your answer **on lines** or inside a **box**.

Free answers

Here you might be asked to describe or explain something, select and write words from the text or use evidence from the text to support your answer.

Question: Describe how Peter spoke.

Evidence:

> The trees moved on and on. Some stones and loose earth fell down and rattled on the railway metals far below.
>
> "It's all coming down,' Peter tried to say, but he found there was hardly any voice to say it with. And, indeed, just as he spoke the great rock, on the top of which the walking trees were, leaned slowly forward. The trees, ceasing to walk, stood still and shivered.'

The number of lines and the size of the space provided suggests how long your answer should be.

Answer: He spoke in a quiet voice
which you could only just hear.

Now try this

1. Read the paragraph above. What do you think might happen to the great rock?

2. According to the text, what fell onto the railway metals? Give two examples.

Using evidence

Some questions in your test will ask you to find and provide **evidence** within the text to support your answers. Use the Point, Evidence, Explain (PEE) method.

Explaining your answer

When a question asks you to explain your answer, use all the **relevant** evidence from the text you are given.

Example

> To answer this type of question you need to locate the exact words and phrases that give you the information.

Explain how the description of the trees and rocks falling onto the railway line supports the idea that this was a serious event.
Use evidence from the text to support your answer.

Leaning with the rock, they seemed to hesitate a moment, and then <u>rock and trees and grass and bushes</u>, with a rushing sound, slipped right away from the face of the cutting and fell on the line <u>with a blundering crash</u> that could have been heard half a mile off. <u>A cloud of dust rose up</u>. ⬅ relevant phrases

The writer stresses the amount of things that fall on the line by dividing the list up with and to emphasise that absolutely everything fell on the line: rocks and trees and grass and bushes.

We know that it caused a lot of damage because the writer says that a cloud of dust rose up.

We know that it caused a lot of noise because the writer tells us that there was a blundering crash that could have been heard half a mile off.

Now try this

1. Read the text below. What sort of person do you think Jed is?

   Use evidence from the text to support your answer.

   I like my mate Jed, I really do. I know that he'd do anything for me, but sometimes I get so fed up with him turning up late, or even forgetting completely, that we were supposed to be going out.

Inference

Text, particularly stories and poems, is more interesting when the writer doesn't give the reader all the information directly. Instead they let the reader **infer** (work out) meaning for themselves through **hints** and **clues**.

Looking for clues in the text

When you are reading a text look out for clues and hints about what else might be happening, or is about to happen.

> The writer doesn't use the word **worried** or state it explicitly, but the reader can work this out (infer) from the clues in the text.

clue

Emily's <u>brow creased</u> as she stared out of the window and saw the bank of purple, storm clouds rolling in.

Only an hour ago the sky had been clear azure but now they were approaching like an army of furious warriors. They were advancing towards the village from the sea, within a couple of hours they would be over the moors. Then they would strike, unleashing their fury on the wind-swept moorland.

Her brother's extra bag lay next to the door – the one containing his water-proof jacket and sleeping bag.

<u>Emily dialled his mobile again</u>, but there was still no answer. <u>She sighed as she hung up.</u>

clue   clue

Example

> The writer has used descriptions of facial expressions, actions and sounds to hint to the reader.

How can you tell that Emily is worried?

Her brow is creased, she keeps trying to call her brother but he is not answering his phone and she sighs when she fails to reach him again.

Now try this

> Look for clues in the text that might explain why Emily is worried.

1. Explain why you think Emily is feeling worried.

Prediction

Predicting

Some questions in your test will be about **predicting** what might happen in texts.

> The fire alarm went off. Mr Adams ordered everyone to "Leave all your bags and make a line at the door!"
>
> As we filed down the corridor Form 2R were coming the other way. Amber and Dawn were giggling in that irritating way of theirs, although at least their mate Gemma wasn't shouting her mouth off as usual.
>
> "Hey Dawn, where's Gem?" shouted Ben.
>
> "Quiet!" called Mr Adams.
>
> Dawn shrugged her shoulders.
>
> Outside the classes lined up. The screech of sirens grew as fire engines raced towards the school. Everyone was quiet, as their teacher called the register.
>
> "Amber Johnson."
>
> "Yes, miss."
>
> "Dawn Matthews."
>
> "Yes, miss."
>
> "Gemma Green."
>
> There was complete silence.
>
> "Gemma Green... where's Gemma?" shouted the teacher.
>
> Everyone looked at each other, no one spoke...

The text doesn't directly tell us that Gemma has been left inside the school but we can infer it from these phrases.

Example

Based on what you have read, what might happen next? Use evidence from the text.

I think the teacher will discover that Gemma has been left inside the school, she doesn't answer when the register is called: '"Gemma Green." There was complete silence.' Additionally, her friends don't know where she is: '"Gemma Green... where's Gemma?" shouted the teacher.'

Now try this

1. Continue the story in the example using your own words. Add hints so a reader can predict what might happen later.

Authors' language

To create **interesting text** writers choose their words carefully to enhance the meaning and mood.

Creating themes

Some questions in the test will ask you to comment on how the writer has used particular words to convey the mood and theme.

> 'And, as Peter pointed, the tree was moving — not just the way trees ought to move when the wind blows through them, but all in one piece, as though it were a living creature and were walking down the side of the cutting.
>
> "It's moving!" cried Bobbie. "Oh, look! And so are the others. It's like the woods in Macbeth."
>
> "It's magic," said Phyllis, breathlessly. "I always knew this railway was enchanted."'
>
> It really did seem a little like magic. For all the trees for about twenty yards of the opposite bank seemed to be slowly walking down towards the railway line, the tree with the grey leaves bringing up the rear like some old shepherd driving a flock of green sheep.

Macbeth is a play by William Shakespeare which is full of references to enchantment. By mentioning Macbeth the writer adds to the magic of the situation.

Example

Find and copy two words from the text above that suggest something particularly strange and unknown is happening.

1. magic   2. enchanting

Now try this

Reread the text above.

1. What does the word 'breathlessly' tell you about how Phyllis was feeling?

Non-fiction text:
Endurance

The vast frozen land of Antarctica lies at the southernmost end of the world. The coldest, windiest continent on Earth, it is ringed by the planet's stormiest seas.

It is no wonder that, for centuries, people could only guess that any land might be there, and marked it on maps as *Terra Australis Incognita,* or *Unknown Southern Land.*

Antarctica

The first people to discover Antarctica were whale- and seal-hunters. An American sealer, John Davis, may have made the first known landing in 1821. Two years later a ship, captained by British sealer James Weddell, sailed into the sea that now carries his name.

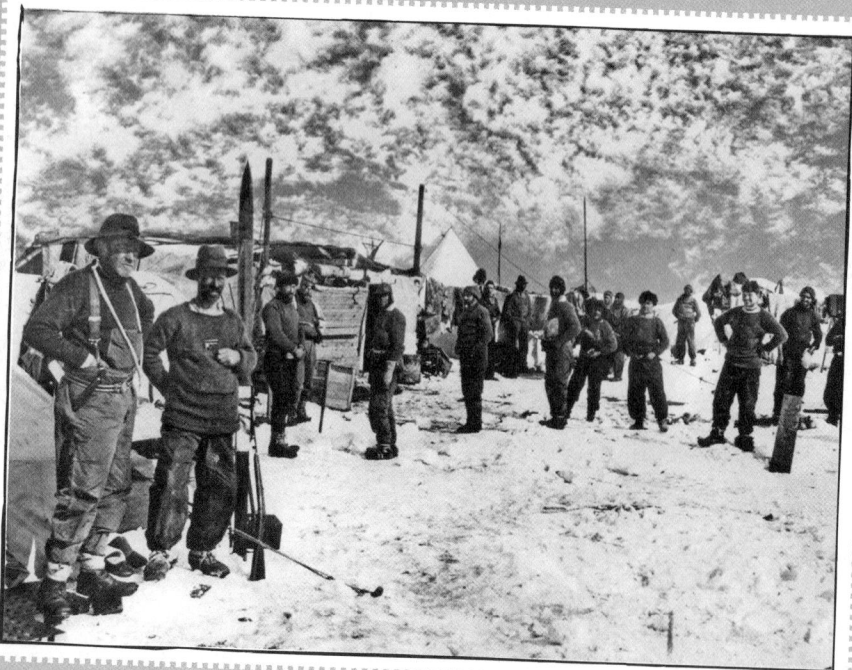

Expeditions

At the end of the 19th century and beginning of the 20th century expeditions were launched from several different countries, including Belgium, Britain, Germany and Sweden. The aim of these expeditions was to learn more about the science and geography of Antarctica, but the race was also on to become the first to reach the South Pole, whatever the cost.

Shackleton

Key among the explorers willing to risk their lives on the ice was Ernest Shackleton. Born in Ireland on 15th February 1874, Shackleton was the son of a doctor. He did not want to follow in his father's footsteps but, instead, joined the merchant navy as an apprentice and went away to sea at the age of 16. By the time he was just 24 years old, he had qualified as a master mariner, able to command a British ship anywhere in the world.

Ernest Shackleton

Antarctica statistics

Area: 14,200,000 square kilometres
Average thickness of ice: 1.9 kilometres
Lowest recorded temperature: −89.2°C
Highest point: Vinson Massif −4,897 metres
Biggest ice shelf: Ross Ice Shelf −965 kilometres

Word meanings

You will find questions in your test that will ask you to explain the **meaning of words** from a text. The next sections in the revision guide relate to the text *Endurance* on pages 64 and 65.

Words in context

When you answer these questions you must think carefully about what the words mean within the **context of the text**. This means thinking about the words used in relation to the **subject** of the text.

> The vast frozen land of Antarctica lies at the southernmost end of the world. The coldest, windiest continent on Earth, it is ringed by the planet's stormiest seas. It is no wonder that, for centuries, people could only guess that any land might be there, and marked it on maps as *Terra Australis Incognita*, or *Unknown Southern Land*.

Example

Find the two words below in the text and explain what they mean.
a) vast   **huge or enormous**
b) ringed   **surrounded by**

See page 40 for information about synonyms and antonyms.

Now try this

1. Find and copy words in the text that mean the same as the words below.
   a) hundreds of years
   b) wrote the name as
   c) speculate.

2. Reread the extract of *Endurance* on pages 64 and 65 and find words that mean the same as:
   a) goal
   b) lead
   c) journeys into unknown lands.

Inference about characters

Writers use **inference** as a way of creating interesting characters. By picking up **hints** and **clues** about how characters think and behave, the reader feels as if they are getting to know the character for themselves.

Looking for clues

Some of the questions in your test will be about inferring information about characters.

> **Inference** helps to bring stories and characters to life.

> Key among the explorers willing to risk their lives on the ice was Ernest Shackleton. Born in Ireland on 15th February 1874, Shackleton was the son of a doctor. He did not want to follow in his father's footsteps but, instead, joined the merchant navy as an apprentice and went away to sea at the age of 16. By the time he was just 24 years old, he had qualified as a master mariner, able to command a British ship anywhere in the world.

> Even though the words **adventurous**, **courageous** and **determined** aren't used by the writer the reader is able to infer this information from other information given about Shackleton.

Example

Circle **three** words which best describe Shackleton's character.

timid   ⟨adventurous⟩   boring   ⟨courageous⟩   conventional   ⟨determined⟩

Now try this

1. Using information from the text above, decide whether each statement is true or false. Give evidence from the text to support your answers for each statement.

   Shackleton was a strong, independent character.

   Shackleton didn't have the right aptitude or natural skills as a mariner.

   Shackleton had the opportunity to become a doctor.

Summarising themes

Some of your test questions will ask you to **summarise** information from different paragraphs in a text.

Linking information

When you answer questions like this you often have to link information from different paragraphs in the text.

Example

Reread the extract from *Endurance* on pages 64 and 65.
Using information from the text, tick one box in each row to show whether each statement is true or false.

	True	False
By the beginning of the 20th century an expedition to Antarctica was a safe journey to undertake.		✓
Sealers and whale hunters were the first people to visit the area which was known as *Unknown Southern Land*.	✓	
The whalers were willing to risk their lives because they wanted to discover more about the science of the area surrounded by the stormiest seas on Earth.		✓

Now try this

> To be able to answer these questions you need to read and understand the text as a whole – you can't just pick out the answers from separate sections.

1. Reread the extract from *Endurance* on pages 64 and 65.

   Using information from the text, decide whether each statement below is true or false.

   Ernest Shackleton didn't want to explore *Terra Australis Incognita*.

   The lowest temperature recorded in the *Unknown Southern Land* is -89.2°C.

   John Davis was a scientist.

2. How can you tell that an expedition to Antarctica is dangerous?
   Give **two** examples from the text.

Making comparisons

Some of your test questions will ask you to **compare** information in different parts of the text to see how the information fits together.

Comparing information

You may be asked to compare moods, how the story progresses or how events unfold.

In the example below, you are asked to look at how people's knowledge develops over time. To do this, you need to make sure you are clear on what happened when. A helpful way to do this would be to sketch a timeline or underline all of the dates in the extract.

Example

Reread the extract from *Endurance* on pages 64 and 65.
Describe how people's knowledge of Antarctica developed and changed from pre 1821 to the beginning of the 20th century.

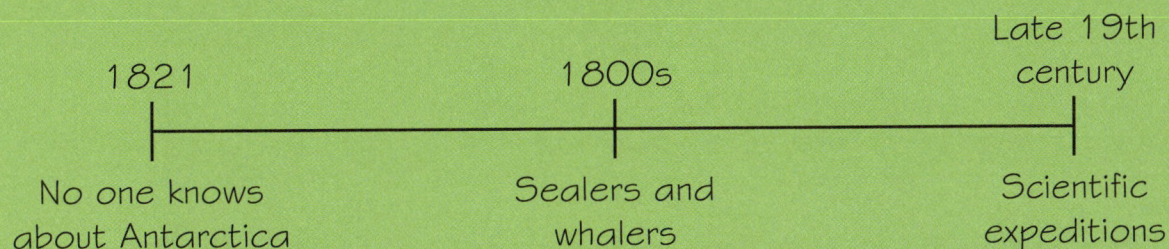

1821	1800s	Late 19th century
No one knows about Antarctica	Sealers and whalers	Scientific expeditions

Prior to 1821 nothing was known about Antarctica because no one had been there. For hundreds of years people only guessed about what might be there. Sealers and whalers first started venturing there in the 1800s. Scientific expeditions from several different countries started in the late 19th century and beginning of the 20th century. This started a race to be the first explorer to reach the South Pole. One of the explorers who set their sights on journeying there was Ernest Shackleton.

Now try this

1. Reread the extract from *The Railway Children* on pages 55 and 56.

   Explain how the children's feelings change from the beginning of the extract to the end.

   Use evidence from the text to support your answer.

Poems

The Jealous Ones

Don't look over your shoulder. We're coming soon
with hungry hands that reach and snap like jaws,
fingers like sharp teeth. We want what's yours

and will not stop until we've pulled it down,
until it's stung by sticks or stones, until it's useless
as a juicy toffee apple stamped into the dirt.

And all because we can. Because your happiness itches
under our skins. And when we have it, tethered, leashed,
we'll roll over ourselves, each of us wanting to be the one

to burst your bright red bubble. But for now we'll wait
in shadows, watching. You'll feel our eyes on your back.
And when we come for you, you'll hear us,

baying at your pride and joy — the way it floats
beyond us — we'll howl across the distance
as if it were a fat, red, candied moon.

Jacob Sam-La Rose

Fossils

At midnight in the museum hall,
The fossils gathered for a ball,
There were no drums or saxophones,
But just the clatter of their bones,
Rolling, rattling carefree circus,
Of mammoth polkas and mazurkas,
Pterodactyls and brontosauruses
Sang ghostly prehistoric choruses,
Amid the mastodonic wassail
I caught the eye of one small fossil,
"Cheer up sad world," he said and winked,
"It's kind of fun to be extinct."

Ogden Nash

Tree

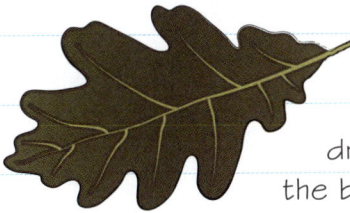

A tree
is not like you and
me – it waits around quite
patiently – catching kites and
dropping leaves – reaching out to touch
the breeze...A tree all day will stand and stare
clothed in summer, winter : bare – it has no shame
or modesty...Perhaps its generosity is the greatest in
the world – it gives a home to every bird, every squirrel,
feeds them too – to every dog it is a loo...And after dark
what does it do? Catch a falling star or two? Shimmy
in the old moonlight? Or maybe have a conker fight?
A tree can give an awful lot : the wood to make a
baby's cot – pencils, paper, tables, chairs – lolly
sticks as well as stairs ...Without a tree we
could not live – a tree, it seems just
loves to give –
but us :
we
chop
we
take
we
burn
that's
what we
do in return

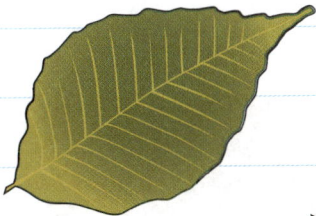

James Carter

71

Reading poetry

There are many different types of poem, but they all express feelings and ideas. Read a poem a few times and consider how the poet is using **form** and **imaginative language** to create meaning.

Form

The form of a poem means its rhythm, rhyme, repetitions, where lines start and end, and its shape. The form helps to give a poem its meaning.

Look back at the poem *Tree* on page 71. The poem is shaped like a tree. As you read down the trunk, the lines get shorter. This reflects how our actions are slowly destroying trees.

The poem *Fossils* on page 71 has pairs of rhyming lines.

> At midnight in the museum <u>hall</u>,
> The fossils gathered for a <u>ball</u>,

This makes you read the poem in a rhythm.

Imaginative language

Poets also make feelings or ideas in poems more intense by using interesting vocabulary or figurative language.

These similes emphasise how scary and dangerous the creature is.

> with hungry hands that reach and <u>snap like jaws</u>, <u>fingers like sharp teeth</u>. We want what's yours

For more on similes, see page 74.

Now try this

1. The poem *Fossils* on page 71 was written to accompany a piece of music called *Carnival of the Animals*. How does the form of the poem give it a musical feeling?

Alliteration

Poems are much shorter pieces of text than stories or non-fiction articles so poets must select their words carefully to create the effect they want.

What is alliteration?

Alliteration is when a writer links a sequence of words that start with the same letters, or repeat the sound within the word. Usually these are words that follow on from each other (consecutive words).

> Tongue twisters are an example of alliteration: Peter Piper picked a peck of pickled peppers.

Writers use alliteration to create a number of effects:

- direct attention to particular words
- create rhythm
- make associations between words

> The writer uses alliteration to make the poem more powerful.

> Don't look over your shoulder. We're coming soon, with <u>h</u>ungry <u>h</u>ands that reach and snap like jaws, fingers like sharp teeth. <u>W</u>e <u>w</u>ant <u>w</u>hat's yours.

← alliteration

> For the whole poem *The Jealous Ones*, see page 70.

Example

How does the writer use alliteration to create mood?

The use of alliteration emphasises the mood of grasping and taking by stressing those words.

Now try this

1. Read *The Jealous Ones* on page 70.
   a) Find an example of alliteration.
   b) Explain how this makes the poem more powerful.

Personification

Writers use **personification** as a way of adding interest and understanding to their writing. Personification is a handy tool to help the reader build a picture from your writing.

What is personification?

> You often find personification in poetry.

Personification is when a writer gives human qualities or characteristics to an object or animal.

> The book was extremely popular, it was flying off the shelves.

personification

> The book wasn't actually flying. So many people were buying the book that the books were being taken off the shelves as quickly as they could be put on there.

Example

> In this text, the tree is described as if it has human emotions.

Read the poem *Tree* on page 71. How does the poet use personification to make the reader feel a greater appreciation of trees?

A tree all day will stand and stare clothed in summer, winter bare – it has no shame or modesty … Perhaps its generosity is the greatest in the world – it gives a home to every bird, every squirrel, feeds them too – to every dog it is a loo.

The poet makes the reader think of the tree as a kindly human being.

Now try this

1. Give two examples of human characteristics that the poet attributes to the tree.
2. Write two sentences of your own, using personification to describe a tree.

Onomatopoeia

Poets have to make every word matter, as they can sometimes have only a few lines in which to put their message across.

What is onomatopoeia?

Onomatopoeia is when the sound of a word mimics (repeats) the sound of the thing being described. Writers use it to make the reader imagine the sounds associated with the poem.

> In the poem a raven is tapping with its beak at the door. The poet uses **onomatopoeia** to bring this image to life.

> Once upon a midnight dreary, while I pondered, weak and weary,
>
> Over many a quaint and curious volume of forgotten lore—
>
> While I nodded, nearly napping, suddenly there came a <u>tapping</u>,
>
> As of someone gently <u>rapping</u>, <u>rapping</u> at my chamber door.
>
> "'Tis some visitor," I muttered, "<u>tapping</u> at my chamber door—
>
> Only this and nothing more."
>
> Extract from *The Raven* by Edgar Allan Poe

cuckoo cuckoo

onomatopoeia

meow

Cuckoo, meow, boom, crash are all examples of onomatopoeia.

Example

Read the sentence below and underline the onomatopoeic word.

The song of the <u>howling</u> wolves echoed through the forest.

Now try this

1. Read *Fossils* on page 71.

   a) Give two examples of onomatopoeia used in the poem.

   b) How does the use of these words make the poem more effective?

Similes

Similes are phrases that directly **compare** one thing to something else.

> Similes often contain the words **as** and **like**.

How do similes add interest?

Similes are used frequently by writers and poets to bring the text to life and to make a description more vivid. Using similes stretches your imagination and makes your writing more detailed for the reader.

> We're coming soon, with hungry hands that reach and **snap like jaws, fingers like sharp teeth**. We want what's yours.

simile

Example

> The small boy's cry is compared to an angry lion's roar.

Complete the sentence below with a simile.

The small boy's face crumpled, his mouth widened and he let out a gigantic roar like an angry lion.

Now try this

1. Read the first verse of *The Jealous Ones* on page 70 and identify a simile.
2. Explain why this simile is effective.
3. Use similes to complete the sentences below.
   a) The baby's skin was as soft _____.
   b) The girl ran _____.
   c) The cola exploded out of the can _____.

Metaphor

Writers and poets use **metaphor** to compare two completely different things, to make descriptions of objects, people and actions more powerful and keep the reader interested.

What is metaphor?

A **metaphor** says that one thing is something else without using the words **like** or **as**.

> Don't get confused! 'She is as fierce as a lioness' is a **simile**. Whereas, 'She is a fierce lioness' is a **metaphor**.

Using metaphor makes descriptions of objects, people and actions more powerful and keeps the reader interested and wanting to know more.

> The clouds were cotton wool balls in the sky.

> The exam was the doorway to her future.

EXAM ROOM

FUTURE

> Mya's voice is liquid velvet.

Example

Read the line below from *The Jealous Ones* and identify a metaphor.

And when we have it, tethered, leashed, we'll roll over ourselves, each one of us wanting to be the one to burst your bright red bubble.

your bright red bubble

Why is this metaphor effective?

It compares the person's happiness to a bubble. This shows that the jealous ones believe it is vulnerable, and can be popped and destroyed.

Now try this

1. Identify two examples of metaphor in the text below.

   My mother told me that Mr Davidson was a complete peacock of a man. He was always strutting along the road with his nose in the air wearing his iridescent plumage of velvet, crimson jacket and purple hobnailed boots.

2. Write down, from the list below, two adjectives which most accurately describe Mr Davidson.

   friendly   vain   generous   mean   conceited

Answers

GRAMMAR

1 Pronouns

1. The elephants are kept in an enclosure near the edge of the zoo. They are fed by the keeper at four o'clock every day. They stretch their long trucks towards her and she hands the food to them.
   I exchanged the nouns for pronouns.

2 Noun phrases

1. Answers may vary. Examples:
   a) The footballer in the green jersey running towards the goal is my brother.
   b) That man with the long beard owns the shop.
2. Answers may vary. Examples:
   a) The family who are moving in next door can't come until next week.
   b) The woman I met on the bus went to Spain last summer.

3 Possessive pronouns

1. a) His cousin lives close to the sea.
   b) Its obedience won it first prize.
   c) Catherine of Aragon was his first wife.

4 Determiners

1. a) The six enormous black cats ate their dinner and then ran to their baskets.
   b) That amount of confidence is unusual in young singers.
   c) Even four people couldn't lift his weight.
2. We put the shopping in the car and took it back to the house then gave it to our neighbour.
3. Answers may vary. Example: The four friends had an eventful time on their holiday.

5 Adjectives and adjectival phrases

1. Answers may vary. Example: The brightly coloured horses rose and fell as they paraded around the silver and gold pole.
2. Answers may vary. Examples:
   a) The holiday was an exciting adventure.
   b) The horse raced across the sand, its black mane flying in the air.

6 Verbs

1. Matthew found the bicycle wheel lying in the gutter.
2. Answers may vary. Examples:
   The children were swimming in the deep end.
   The boys dived into the pool.

7 Present and past tense

1. a) Jude is watching a movie.
   b) Patrick is studying for his test.
2. a) Fatma sailed the boat around the bay, which had lovely calm water.
   b) The American astronauts arrived at the space station and discovered a new form of life.

8 Future tense

1. Kate is babysitting her younger sister tomorrow as her parents are going to meet their friends and will leave the house at seven o'clock.
2. a) It is thought that by the year 2040 human kind will colonise other planets and there will be cures for all diseases.
   b) My uncle and I are going fossil-hunting next weekend and are going to collect as many as we can.

9 Modal verbs

1 and 2.

sentence	certainty	possibility
There will be a general election next year.	✓	
She's studied really hard and should pass the exam.		✓
I shall bring my didgeridoo.	✓	
There might be a storm tonight.		✓

10 Present and past perfect tense

1. a) The explorer Robert Falcon Scott arrived at the South Pole and discovered that his competitor Amundsen had conquered it the previous day.
   b) Mark dropped a jug and has spilt the milk.
   c) The ambulance had arrived before the police got there.
2. Answers may vary. Example: The horses have escaped from the meadow.
3. Answers may vary. Example: She had bought all the Christmas shopping by December 1.

11 Future perfect tense

1. The plumber will have installed a new bathroom before we get home from our holidays.
2. a) I will have been in the hockey team for two years next month.
   b) You must have read the book list before the start of the new term.
   c) Will you have done all your homework before youth club?

12 Adverbs

1. Answers may vary. Examples:
   a) Julie plays tennis well.
   b) Daniel listens patiently.
2. Answers may vary.

13 Adverbial phrases

1. a) We will go down to the beach after sunset.
   b) During the match, someone ran onto the pitch.
2. Answers may vary. Example: They caught the bus, with moments to spare.
3. Answers may vary. Example: After the test, I am going to relax.

14 Conjunctions

1. a) There was an expectant hush from the audience <u>while</u> they waited for the concert to begin.
   Subordinating conjunction

   b) You should always fasten your seat belt <u>before</u> setting off in a car.
   Subordinating conjunction

2. Answers may vary. Examples:

   a) There was no food <u>so</u> we were ravenous.

   b) The weather is cold <u>and</u> sunny.

   c) She won the audition <u>so</u> she was extremely happy.

15 Prepositions

1 and 2.

	Time	Place	Direction
He dropped his laptop <u>behind</u> the sofa.		✓	
Everyone feels better <u>after</u> a good night's sleep.	✓		
The police stormed <u>into</u> the bank.			✓

16 Prepositional phrases

1.

	Time	Place	Direction
The squirrel scampered <u>down the tree</u>.			✓
<u>At the weekends</u> we go hiking.	✓		
The birds nested <u>under the eaves</u>.		✓	
The train hurtled <u>through the tunnel</u>.			✓

2. Answers may vary. Examples:

   a) The film is shown <u>on Saturdays.</u>

   b) The garage is <u>beside the house.</u>

   c) The rabbits ran <u>into the woods.</u>

17 Subjunctive

1. a) The teacher advises <u>that pupils wear</u> appropriate clothing for the walk.

   b) I propose <u>that we delay</u> giving an answer until we know the facts.

2. Answers may vary. Examples:

   a) <u>I insist that he complete</u> his homework on time.

   b) <u>I recommend that you look after</u> your health or you will become ill.

18 Questions

1. Answers may vary. Examples:
   Who is on the team?
   What are you doing on Saturday?
   When are you going in holiday?

2. Answers may vary. Examples:
   Do they have a nice teacher?
   Will you be going on holiday?
   Have they been to the fair?

3. a) It's very expensive, <u>isn't it</u>?

   b) They are very kind, <u>aren't they</u>?

   c) We haven't been here before, <u>have we</u>?

19 Commands and exclamations

1. a) exclamation   b) neither

   c) imperative   d) neither

20 Subject and object

1. a) The <u>mechanic</u> (S) repaired the <u>car</u> (O).

   b) <u>Flowers</u> (S) covered the <u>garden path</u> (O).

   c) <u>Martina</u> (S) played the <u>piano</u> (O).

2. a) Answers may vary. Example:
   The child burst the balloon.
   subject   verb   object

21 Phrases and clauses

1. a) clause   b) phrase

   c) clause   d) phrase

22 Main and subordinate clauses

1. a) subordinate   b) main

23 Compound and complex sentences

1. a) complex

   b) compound

2. a) <u>Although</u> she was very sea-sick, she continued on the voyage.

   b) Thomas read a magazine <u>while</u> he was waiting for Flora to get ready.

24 Relative clauses

1. My cousin Patricia, <u>who</u> is a talented pianist, also loves football.

2. a) The dictionary, <u>which</u> we needed, was on the third shelf.

   b) This is the route, <u>that</u> is the quickest.

   c) Winston Churchill, <u>who</u> was the Prime Minister at the time, declared war.

   d) There was a time <u>when</u> mobile phones had not been invented.

3. Answers may vary. Examples:
   My teacher, whose name is Mr Robinson, is very kind.
   The ornament, which was on the shelf, was covered in dust.

25 Active and passive voice

1. a) The snowman was built by the children.

   b) A sandcastle was made by Johann.

2. a) Tom designed a car.

   b) A tree hit the house.

26 Standard English verbs

1. a) They <u>weren't</u> in trouble, <u>were</u> they?

   b) She <u>isn't</u> ready yet.

   c) I <u>was</u> so pleased to go horse riding.

   d) We <u>were</u> impressed by the level of service.

2. Answers may vary. Example: You should use Standard English to write a letter to your head teacher and to complain about poor service in a restaurant. This is because these are formal situations where you don't know the people you are writing to very well.

27 Standard English tense and voice

1. **a)** Non-Standard English: The balloons were blown up by the clowns.
   b) Standard English
   c) Non-Standard English: Firemen were working hard to put out the fire.
   d) Non-Standard English: It was the dog that did it.

28 Standard English grammar

1. **a)** Give me <u>those</u> bags.
   b) They claimed that the rides were closed <u>due to</u> bad weather.
   c) Is he <u>not your</u> friend?
   d) The distance <u>is approximately</u> ten miles.

2. Answers may vary. Example: I will be going to the circus tomorrow with my friend Karla.

PUNCTUATION

29 Commas for clarity

1. In my desk you will find a rubber, biscuits, felt pens, paper and an exercise book.

2. Gradually climbing higher, the girl reached the summit.

30 Parentheses

1. **a)** August <u>– when we have the school holidays –</u> is usually the hottest month.
   b) Carol <u>– who will turn 15 next week –</u> is a good friend.
   c) The ring <u>– which we found on the road –</u> is very valuable.

2. Answers may vary. Examples:
   a) Christopher (<u>who has spent a lot of time abroad</u>) speaks three languages.
   b) York <u>– where we bought some amazing ice-cream –</u> has the river Ouse running through it.
   c) The sunset, <u>which we watched from the beach,</u> was incredibly beautiful.

31 Colons

1. **a)** The instructor advised us to bring: hiking boots, a rucksack, a change of socks and a sleeping bag.
   b) The policeman addressed the crowd: "Everyone stand well back and quietly form a queue."

2. Answers may vary. Examples: I have bought: cheese, crisps, grapes, nuts and cake for the party.

32 Semi-colons

1. To get fit you need to: eat a balanced diet; swim and walk several times a week; not eat fast foods and convenience foods and get plenty of sleep.

2. To separate items in a long list of items.

33 Possessive apostrophes

1. **a)** Mina'<u>s</u> shirt was a lovely shade of blue.
   b) The men'<u>s</u> toilets are on the first floor.

2. **a)** Chloe's dad's lorry transports fruit.
   b) Grandma's paintings are very old.

34 Apostrophes for contractions

1. **a)** <u>It's</u> quite a curiosity.
   b) <u>He'll</u> guarantee that the work is completed on time.

2. **a)** I <u>do not</u> want to go.
   b) He <u>has not</u> interfered in the past.

35 Direct speech

1. **a)** "<u>It</u> would be so embarrassing if we dropped the plates<u>,"</u> he said.
   b) "<u>What</u> a terrible mess<u>!</u>" exclaimed Mum.

2. Answers may vary. Examples:
   "Which film would you like to see?" asked Jeremy.
   "I'd really like to see the new sci-fi film," replied Martin.
   "Okay, that sounds good, which viewing shall we go for?"
   "There's one at 6.30, let's see if we can make that one."

36 Bullet points

1. The job requires the successful candidate to be:
   • honest
   • reliable
   • trustworthy
   • hard-working.

2. Answers may vary. Example:
   The qualities I look for in a friend are:
   • kindness
   • a sense of humour
   • loyalty
   • fairness.

37 Hyphens and ellipses

1. The <u>four-year-olds</u> were playing in the <u>sand-pit</u>.

2. After school I went to play basketball <u>…</u> and then came home.

SPELLING

38 Prefixes

1. He is very <u>im</u>mature for his age.

2. Keeping wild animals in captivity is cruel and <u>in</u>humane.

3. Leaving broken glass in the park is highly <u>ir</u>responsible.

39 Suffixes

1. **a)** Don't eat those berries, they are <u>poisonous</u>.
   b) They <u>danced</u> on the stage last week.
   c) I feel like <u>sleeping</u> for a week!
   d) The woman in the painting was very <u>beautiful</u>.
   e) The children wanted to raise <u>awareness</u> of road safety.

40 Synonyms and antonyms

1. Answers may vary. Examples:
   a) Shamsa was <u>exhausted</u> by the time she got home.
   b) Grandma was <u>delighted</u> to see us.
   c) Mohammed is an <u>intelligent</u> boy.

2. exhausted   energised
   war   peace
   cheerful   miserable
   create   destroy

41 Tricky spellings: silent letters

1. **a)** It's so cold my feet are num(b).
   b) You shou(l)d lis(t)en in class.
   c) My grandma has lots of (w)rinkles.
   d) (K)neading bread is hard work!

2. Answers may vary.

42 Tricky spellings: pronunciation

1. Answers may vary.
2. Answers may vary. Examples:

fort	huff	cow
thought	rough	plough
sought	tough	bough
wrought	enough	
brought		

43 Homophones and homonyms

1. a) They couldn't decide <u>whether</u> to go or not.
   b) The ambulance arrived on the <u>scene</u> as soon as it was called.
   c) After putting the potato on top, <u>grate</u> the cheese over it.
   d) The traffic was <u>stationary</u>.
2. Answers may vary. Examples:
   The pancake fell flat on the floor of my new flat.
   I am going to read my book and then book a table for dinner.
   Can I park my car near the park?

WRITING

44 Audience and purpose

1. a) To instruct someone how to install a printer; a customer who has bought a new printer
   b) To inform someone about the politician's life; someone interested in history or politics
   c) To inform someone about the hotel; someone wanting to book a holiday
   d) To entertain and to give fans more information about the band; fans of the boyband, probably young people
   e) To entertain; a young child
   f) To inform the council about local crime and to persuade them to do something about it; the council

45 Planning and organising

1. Answers may vary. Example:

Title Into the blue
Introductory paragraph (beginning)
This summer I went on holiday to Greece. I went scuba diving for the first time.
Main section (middle)
What scuba diving was like. The things I saw. How much I enjoyed it.
Conclusion (end)
When I can do it again. Where I would like to do it.

47 Proof-reading

1. Answers may vary. Example:
   My sister Holly and I both love football. When we heard that our favourite team, 'The Tamquest Stars', were coming to play we were really excited.
   The match was starting at two o' clock. My sister and I had wanted to go for ages. As we walked to the stadium we could hear the supporters in their stands chanting loudly. It was these same supporters who were at the last match and they were wearing the same colours.
   "Let's run," said Holly, "or we will miss the match."

48 Writing stories

1. Answer to include:
   • interesting title
   • intriguing first line
   • adjectives and adverbs
   • similes and metaphors
   • inference

49 Persuasive writing

1. Answer to include:
   • catchy title
   • hook
   • emotive language
   • connectives

READING

57 Retrieving information

1. Bobbie heard the noise first.
2. The children could hear the wind in the trees and the buzz of the telegraph wires.

58 Recording information: selecting an answer

1. The tree had white berries. <u>False</u>
   The tree had smooth leaves. <u>False</u>
   The berries turn black. <u>True</u>

59 Recording information: free answers

1. The rock might fall onto the railway lines.
2. stones, earth

60 Using evidence

1. Answers may vary. Example: Jed is a nice person and a good friend: "I know that he'd do anything for me." Annoyingly, he is quite unorganised and forgetful: "I get so fed up with him turning up late, or even forgetting."

61 Inference

1. Answers may vary. Example: Emily is feeling worried because she doesn't know where her brother is. He is out on the moors and a storm is coming in and he doesn't have any warm or waterproof clothing with him. Since he is not answering his phone, Emily thinks that he is in trouble.

Answers

63 Authors' language

1. Answers may vary. Example: The word "breathlessly" suggests that Phyllis is excited and nervous. She can't quite believe what she is seeing and she senses danger in the situation.

66 Word meanings

1. a) for centuries

   b) marked it

   c) could only guess

2. a) aim

   b) the first

   c) expeditions

67 Inference about characters

1. Shackleton was a strong, independent character. <u>True</u>. "Key among the explorers willing to risk their lives on the ice was Ernest Shackleton."

   Shackleton didn't have an aptitude or natural skills as a mariner. <u>False</u>. "By the time he was just 24 years old, he had qualified as a master mariner…"

   Shackleton had the opportunity to become a doctor. <u>True</u>. "Shackleton was the son of a doctor. He did not want to follow in his father's footsteps…"

68 Summarising themes

1. Ernest Shackleton didn't want to explore *Terra Australis Incognita*. <u>False</u>

   The lowest temperature recorded in the *Unknown Southern Land* is -89.2C. <u>True</u>

   John Davis was a scientist. <u>False</u>

2. Answers may vary. Example:

   An expedition of Antarctica is dangerous because firstly, explorers might die: "…among the explorers willing to risk their lives on the ice". Secondly, Antarctica is: "The coldest, windiest continent on Earth, it is ringed by the planet's stormiest seas."

69 Making comparisons

1. Answers may vary. Example:

   At the beginning of the extract the children are curious about the commotion, they don't know what it is making the noise: "Hush. Stop! What's that?"

   As the story develops they become excited about what they are seeing and can't quite believe what is happening: "Oh, look! and so are the others. It's like the woods in Macbeth."

   At the end of the extract the curiosity and excitement have given way to shock and fear: "It's *all* coming down," Peter tried to say, but he found there was hardly any voice to say it with."

72 Reading poetry

1. Answers may vary. Example: The poem has pairs of rhyming lines, which makes you read it in a rhythm.

73 Alliteration

1. Answers may vary. Examples:

   a) "hungry hands"

   b) The use of alliteration draws attention to the words and creates rhythm. The alliterative words suggest that the 'hands' want something you have.

74 Personification

1. Answers may vary. Examples:

   The poet attributes clothing to the tree. The tree isn't wearing clothes – it is covered in leaves.

   The poet attributes pride to the tree. In winter, "it has no shame or modesty" as it is left uncovered by the fallen leaves.

2. Answers may vary. Examples:

   The tree screamed in the stormy wind.

   The tree wept its golden leaves.

75 Onomatopoeia

1. Answers may vary. Examples:

   a) "the <u>clatter</u> of their bones"

   "<u>rattling</u> carefree circus"

   b) The use of these words makes the poem more effective as it brings the poem to life. It helps the reader to imagine the sounds the fossils are making and believe that they are moving around.

76 Similes

Answers may vary. Examples:

1. An example of a simile is: "hungry hands that reach and snap like jaws."

2. This simile is effective because it likens hands to snapping jaws. It suggests something that could quickly and painfully snatch something from you.

3. a) The baby's skin was as soft <u>as a peach</u>.

   b) The girl ran <u>like the wind</u>.

   c) The cola exploded out of the can <u>like a volcanic eruption</u>.

77 Metaphor

1. My mother told me that <u>Mr Davidson was a complete peacock of a man</u>. He was always strutting along the road with his nose in the air <u>wearing his iridescent plumage of velvet</u>, crimson jacket and purple hobnailed boots.

2. vain, conceited

Published by Pearson Education Limited, 80 Strand, London, WC2R 0RL.

www.pearsonschools.co.uk

Text © Pearson Education Limited 2016
Edited by Jane Cotter
Typeset by Jouve India Private Limited
Produced by Elektra Media
Original illustrations © Pearson Education Limited 2016
Illustrated by Elektra Media
Cover illustration by Ana Albero

The right of Helen Thomson to be identified as author of this work has been asserted by her in accordance with the Copyright, Designs and Patents Act 1988.

First published 2016

19 18 17 16
10 9 8 7 6 5 4 3 2 1

British Library Cataloguing in Publication Data
A catalogue record for this book is available from the British Library.

ISBN 978 1 292 14599 0

Printed in Slovakia by Neografia

Acknowledgements
We are grateful to the following for permission to reproduce copyright material:

Text
Extract on page 64 from *Endurance, Shackleton's Incredible Antarctic Expedition*, Wayland (Hachette Children's) (A. Garneri 2015); Poetry on page 71 from *Michael Rosen's A to Z, The Best Children's Poetry from Agard to Zephaniah* (J. Carter), Copyright © James Carter from *Time-Travelling Underpants* (Macmillan). Poetry on page 70 from *Michael Rosen's A to Z, The Best Children's Poetry from Agard to Zephaniah*, (J. Sam-La Rose); Poetry on page 71 from *Carnival of the Animals*, Macmillan Children's Books (Saint-Saen, C. 1998). Copyright by Curtis Brown Ltd, Ginger Knowlton, Agent. Copyright © 1949 by Ogden Nash, renewed. Reprinted by permission of Curtis Brown, Ltd. and for USA, Canada.

Picture Credits
The publisher would like to thank the following for their kind permission to reproduce their photographs:

Alamy Images: Archive Pics 64, Pictorial Press Ltd 65

All other images © Pearson Education

OLYMPIC LEGENDS
TEAM GB

WRITTEN BY

KEIR RADNEDGE & AIDAN RADNEDGE

sona
BOOKS

sona
BOOKS

© Danann Media Publishing Limited 2024

First published in the UK by Sona Books, an imprint of Danann Media Publishing Limited 2024

WARNING: For private domestic use only, any unauthorised copying, hiring,
lending or public performance of this book is illegal.

CAT NO: SONO589

Photography courtesy of

Getty images:

Cameron Spencer	Popperfoto	Gary M. Prior	Scott Heavey	Harry How
Bryn Lennon	Chris Graythen	Simon Bruty	Christie Goodwin	Staff
Ian MacNicol	Clive Brunskill	Bettmann	Scott Barbour	Simon Bruty
Professional Sport	Laurence Griffiths	Inpho Photography	John Gichigi	Mirrorpix
Tom Jenkins	Phil Walter	Tony Duffy	Pool	Stu Forster
Bob Martin	John Gichigi	Rolls Press	Sion Touhig	The Asahi Shimbun
Jack Guez	Clive Mason	Harry Benson	Michael Steele	Gilbert lundt; Jean-Yves
Clive Rose	Bob Thomas	Reg Lancaster / Stringer	Dan Mullan	Ruszniewski
Ross Kinnaird	Bettmann	Keystone	Tim Clayton	
Hulton Archive	Ullstein bild Dtl	William Vanderson	Yuki Iwamura	
Tom Dulat	Rich Clarkson	Stuart Franklin	Jamie McDonald	

All other images Wiki Commons

Book cover design Darren Grice at Ctrl-d

Layout design Alex Young at Cre81ve

Copy Editor Martin Corteel

Proofreader Finn O'Neill

Made in EU.

ISBN: 978-1-915343-50-5

CONTENTS

INTRODUCTION

The Olympic Games is the world's greatest sporting extravaganza. Every four years some 10,500 athletes match talent and ambition, fuelled by personal and national pride, in two weeks of daily dramas which transfix the planet.

Each Games sees its Olympic Flame sparked into life in ancient Olympia in Greece, home of the original competition in BC 776. The original Games attracted widespread popularity across the city states of Greece and lasted until 393 AD when they were discontinued by the Romans. Emperor Theodosius considered the Games a pagan festival.

Nearly 1,400 years later a young Frenchman named Baron Pierre de Coubertin travelled to England and the United States. The popularity of competitive sport in schools, colleges and clubs persuaded him that sporting competition would be beneficial not only for his country and its youth in particular but the world in general.

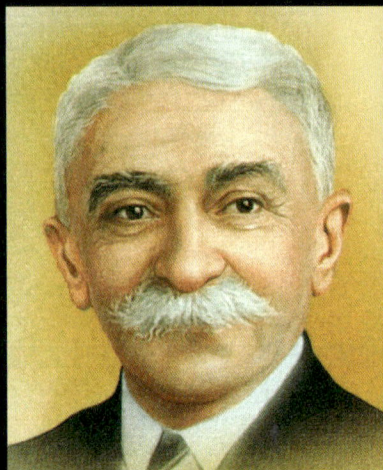

In 1894, still only 31, he summoned a conference at the University of the Sorbonne in Paris which founded the

ABOVE: Pierre de Coubertin

International Olympic Committee. It also decided on a revival of the Olympic Games, appropriately in Athens in 1896.

Modest beginnings saw fewer than 250 athletes compete from a dozen nations. All were men. De Coubertin, who died in 1937, would be amazed to see his legacy. The third Paris Games in 2024, after 1900 and 1924, will see 10,500 athletes representing 206 National Olympic Committees contesting 329 medal events across 28 sports. Half of those athletes will be women.

Just for the record, Great Britain has won 916 summer Games medals, exceeded only by the United States (2,629) and former Soviet Union (1,010). Similarly Team GB stand third in summer gold ranking with 284 champions, trailing only the US (1,061) and USSR (395).

Here are the stories of some of those heroes.

ABOVE LEFT: Poster for the 1904 Summer Olympics in St. Louis, United States

ABOVE RIGHT: The Olympic flame burns brightly from the Thomas Heatherwick designed Olympic Cauldron at the opening of the London 2012 Summer Games

AQUATICS

Diving, swimming, synchronised swimming and water polo make up the Olympics' aquatics programme. Swimming featured at the first modern Games in Athens in 1896, with four men-only freestyle race events. Since 1924 the official Olympic length of a pool became 50m – as it remains today. Only track and field has more medal events than swimming, with 37 at Tokyo 2020 and again at the 2024 Games in Paris. Water polo for men began in 1900, and for women 100 years later, while women-only synchronised swimming was introduced in 1984. Diving was added for men in 1904 and for women eight years later.

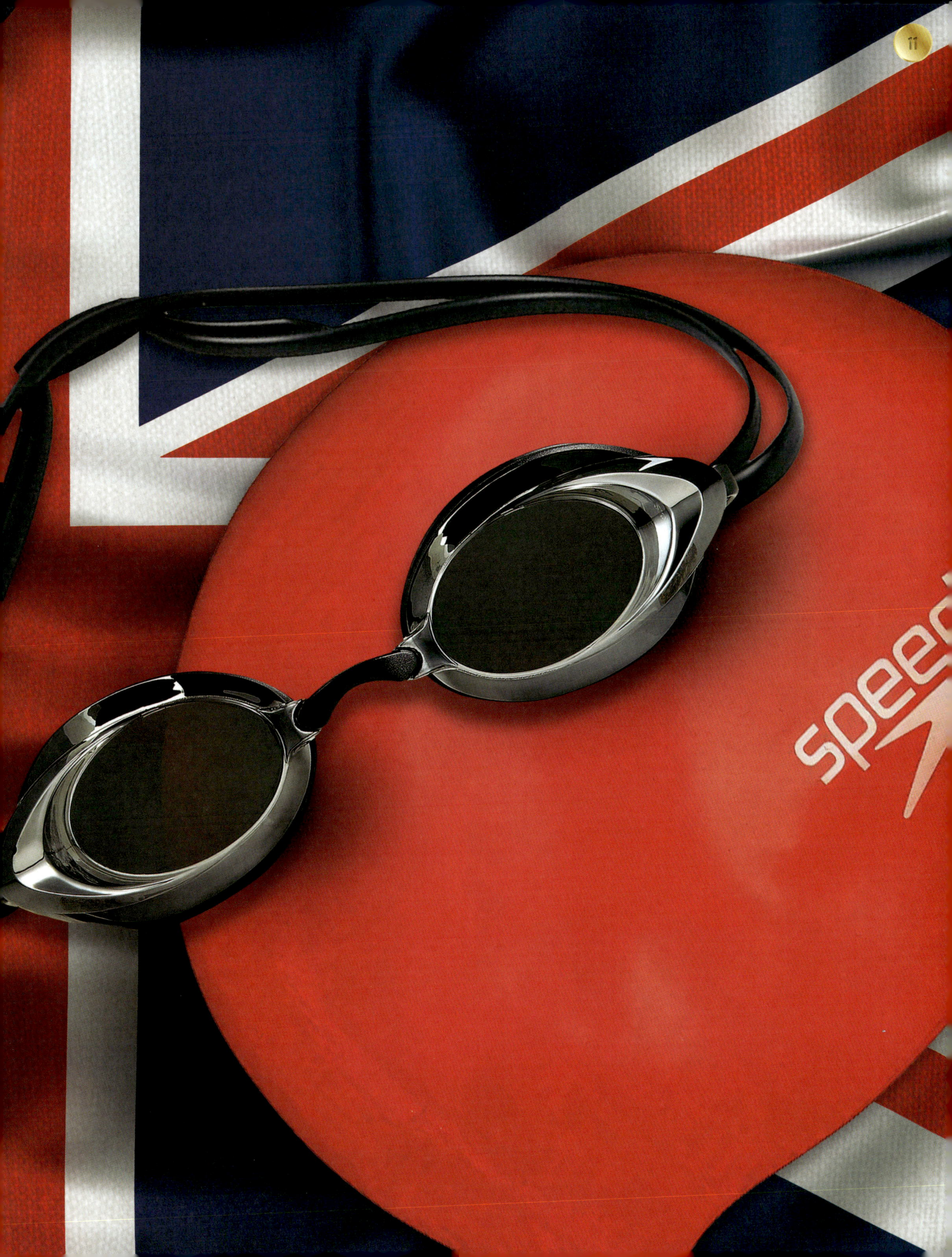

REBECCA ADLINGTON

Rebecca Adlington was seen as a leading contender for 800m freestyle gold at the 2008 Beijing Olympics. But winning the 400m freestyle days earlier came as such a surprise – "an unexpected bonus", as she put it – that her parents had not yet arrived in China to watch. They were there, though, as she won the 800m final while taking two seconds off the world record, finishing in 8:14.10 minutes. Yet just three years earlier then-15-year-old Adlington had suffered a severe health scare, stricken by glandular fever which left her with chronic fatigue syndrome and forcing her to give up on training and hopes of competing at the 2006 Commonwealth Games. Yet she and coaches credit her mental strength with her recovery and subsequent success. Her double triumph at Beijing made her the first British swimmer to win more than one gold at one Games since Henry Taylor's three freestyle triumphs in London in 1908 – and she was the country's first woman to win swimming gold since Anita Lonsbrough in the 200m breaststroke at Rome 1960. Adlington was disappointed not to successfully defend her two Olympic titles at London 2012 but did win bronze in both finals, before retiring the following year.

BORN: February 17, 1989, in Mansfield, Nottinghamshire

EVENT: Swimming - freestyle

GOLD (2): 400m freestyle (Beijing 2008), 800m freestyle (Beijing 2008)

BRONZE (2): 400m freestyle (London 2012), 800m freestyle (London 2012)

TOTAL MEDALS: ⬤⬤⬤⬤

BELOW: Rebecca Adlington competes in the Women's 800m Freestyle heats during Day 6 of the London 2012 Olympics Games

Tom Daley made his Olympics debut in Beijing in 2008 aged just 14, becoming the youngest to reach the final and the youngest Briton at the Games that summer. He had to wait another four years for his first medal, a bronze in the platform event at London 2012 – a year after being the first person to dive into the city's new Olympic Park Aquatics Centre to mark the start of a 12-month countdown to the Games. Daley added further bronzes in the synchronised event at Rio 2016 and again in the platform at Tokyo 2020. His long wait for an Olympic gold finally ended at that pandemic-delayed Tokyo Games in 2021, alongside Matty Lee in the synchronised 10m platform event – beating Cao Yuan and Chen Aisen in a dramatic finale which ended China's winning streak in the event since Sydney 2000. Daley and Lee celebrated wildly after a scoreboard revealed the China pair's final score of 470.58, behind their own 471.81. Daley wept on the medal podium and said afterwards: "I was gone, I was blubbering. To finally have this around my neck – I've been diving over 20 years." A familiar sight throughout Tokyo 2020 was Daley sitting on the sidelines knitting – including an Olympics-themed cardigan – to help calm his nerves.

TOM DALEY

ABOVE: Tom Daley (near) and Matthew Lee perform a dive in the men's 10m Synchro Platform final

BORN: May 21, 1994, in Plymouth, Devon

EVENT: Diving – 10m platform, synchronised 10m platform

GOLD (1): Synchronised 10m platform (Tokyo 2020)

BRONZE (3): 10m platform (London 2012), Synchronised 10m platform (Rio 2016), 10m platform (Tokyo 2020)

TOTAL MEDALS: ●●●●

TOM DEAN

Team GB waited 113 years for a man to win two swimming golds at one Olympics, then three came along at the same Games. Tom Dean was the first of these to do so, at the pandemic-delayed Summer Olympics in Tokyo in 2021. He first triumphed in the 200m freestyle in the 12,000-capacity new Tokyo Aquatics Centre – touching in first in a new British record of 1:44.22 minutes, just ahead of British team-mate Duncan Scott's 1:44.26 to claim silver. That made for the first British one-two on an Olympic swimming medal podium since Henry Taylor and John Arthur Jarvis for the 1500m freestyle in London in 1908. Scott did then win gold in Tokyo, alongside Dean, James Guy and Matt Richards in the 4 x 200m freestyle, setting a European record of 6:58.58. Guy would go on to win a second Olympic gold of his own that summer, as would fellow Team GB swimmer Adam Peaty. Dean's double success was especially notable since his training for the Games was badly hampered by contracting Covid-19 not once but twice – he admitted at times he couldn't even "walk up the stairs without coughing and wheezing". Covid-related spectator restrictions family had to watch the action on TV at home in Maidenhead, Berkshire, where Dean's mother Jacquie Hughes said: "How cheeky is that – to go to your first Olympics and take away two golds."

BELOW: Tom Dean of Great Britain reacts after winning the Men's 200m Freestyle final on day four of the Tokyo 2020 Olympic Games at Tokyo Aquatics Centre on July 27, 2021 in Tokyo, Japan

BORN: May 2, 2000, in London

EVENT: Swimming - freestyle

GOLD (2): 200m freestyle, 4 x 200m freestyle (Tokyo 2020)

TOTAL MEDALS: 🥇🥇

BORN: May 27, 1957, in Marylebone, London

EVENT: Swimming – breaststroke

GOLD (1): 100m breaststroke (Moscow 1980)

BRONZE (1): 4 x 100m medley (Moscow 1980)

TOTAL MEDALS:

DUNCAN GOODHEW

Duncan Goodhew almost missed out on the Olympic race that brought him gold medal glory – he was reading a book to keep his composure before the 100m breaststroke final at the 1980 Games in Moscow and an official had to remind he was being called to the start. Goodhew had set an Olympic record in the 100m heats at the Montreal Olympics four years earlier but later admitted he "froze" in the final, only finishing seventh. In Moscow, however, he won in 1:03.34, just ahead of Soviet silver medallist Arsens Miskarovs in 1:03.82 after overtaking him on the final length. Goodhew added bronze in the 4 x 100m medley, alongside team-mates Gary Abraham, David Lowe and Martin Smith as well as Paul Marshall and Mark Taylor who swam in the heats. Goodhew had insisted on going to the Moscow Games despite a boycott of the Soviet Union by other countries – and also his retired air vice-marshal stepfather Bill Crawford-Compton's opposition and refusal to travel there. He also triumphed despite a shoulder injury preventing him from training properly in the run-up to the Olympics. Goodhew lost all his hair aged just 10, after falling from a tree triggering an autoimmune disease, and was also diagnosed with dyslexia three years later.

JAMES GUY

Team-mate Tom Dean just about beat him to becoming the first male British swimmer to win more than one gold at a single Olympics since Henry Taylor in 1908 – but James Guy came to share the joy when they were on the same side then triumphing in the 4 x 200m freestyle at Tokyo 2020. Guy broke down in tears in response to their victory, Britain's first 4 x 200m freestyle Olympics gold since the 1908 Games in London. The Tokyo 2021 team were just three-hundredths of a second away from the world record. Guy then followed that up with a second gold the first time a both-sexes relay race final was swum at a Games, triumphing in the 4 x 100m mixed medley alongside Adam Peaty, Kathleen Dawson and Anna Hopkin. Guy swam the third leg, his favoured butterfly, as the team won in a new world record time of 3:37.58 ahead of China's 3:38.86 in second. Guy has also won individual gold in the 200m freestyle at the 2015 World Aquatics Championships in Kazan, Russia – beating US six-time Olympic gold medallist Ryan Lochte, who Guy described as "one of my heroes", as he did so.

ABOVE: James Guy of Team competes in the Mixed 4 x 100m Medley Relay Final at Tokyo Aquatics Centre on July 31, 2021 in Tokyo, Japan

BORN: November 26, 1995, in Bury, Greater Manchester

EVENT: Swimming - freestyle, medley

GOLD (2): 4 x 200m freestyle, 4 x 100 mixed medley (Tokyo 2020)

SILVER (3): 4 x 200m freestyle, 4 x 100m medley (Rio 2016), 4 x 100m medley (Tokyo 2020)

TOTAL MEDALS: ⬤ ⬤ ⚪ ⚪ ⚪

Despite the long-time expectations for Tom Daley, Britain's first diving gold at an Olympics came courtesy of Jack Laugher and Chris Mears at the 2016 Games in Rio. They triumphed in the synchronised 3m springboard event with an overall score of 454.32, ahead of Americans Sam Dorman and Michael Hixon on 450.21 and China's Qin Kai and Cao Yuan with 443.70. Laugher, who began diving as a seven-year-old, then became the first British diver to win more than one medal at a single Olympics. He claimed silver in the individual 3m springboard, with Cao Yuan this time taking gold with a score of 547.60 to Laugher's 523.85. Laugher said afterwards: "I always knew I could medal at these Olympic Games – I have been rising each year, but obviously doing it is a completely different story." Five years later he added another medal at the delayed Tokyo 2020 Olympics, completing a full set with bronze in the individual 3m springboard, while he and Dan Goodfellow finished seventh in the synchronised 3m springboard. Laugher also has seven Commonwealth Games golds, a silver and a bronze, as well as five European Aquatics Championships triumphs.

JACK LAUGHER

BORN: January 30, 1995, in Harrogate, North Yorkshire

EVENT: 3m springboard, synchronised 3m springboard

GOLD (1): Synchronised 3m springboard (Rio 2016)

SILVER (1): 3m springboard (Rio 2016)

BRONZE (1): 3m springboard (Tokyo 2020)

TOTAL MEDALS: 🥇🥈🥉

LEFT: Jack Laugher and Chris Mears compete in the Synchronised 3m springboard, Rio 2016

One of Britain's first gold medallists in diving had been told just a few years before he would never dive again after illness. Chris Mears was 15 when he suffered a ruptured spleen in January 2009, was rushed to hospital and on losing two litres of blood was given only a five per cent chance of survival. After being discharged he then suffered a seven-hour seizure and spent three days in a come but even after recovery he was told his diving prospects were over. Yet he persisted and managed to return to competition at the 2010 Commonwealth Games in Delhi. His greatest moment came six years later at the Rio Olympics where he and Jack Laugher won Britain's first ever diving gold, in the synchronised 3m platform. The pair, who first teamed up in 2013, also won gold in the same event at both the Commonwealth Games in Glasgow in 2014 and the Gold Coast in 2018. Mears retired from diving in August 2019 to focus instead on a music career, having started playing guitar while recovering from his illness and using computer technology to produce from his bedroom studio.

CHRIS MEARS

BORN: February 7, 1993, in Reading, Berkshire

EVENT: Diving – 3m springboard, synchronised 3m springboard

GOLD (1): Synchronised 3m springboard (Rio 2016)

TOTAL MEDALS: 🥇

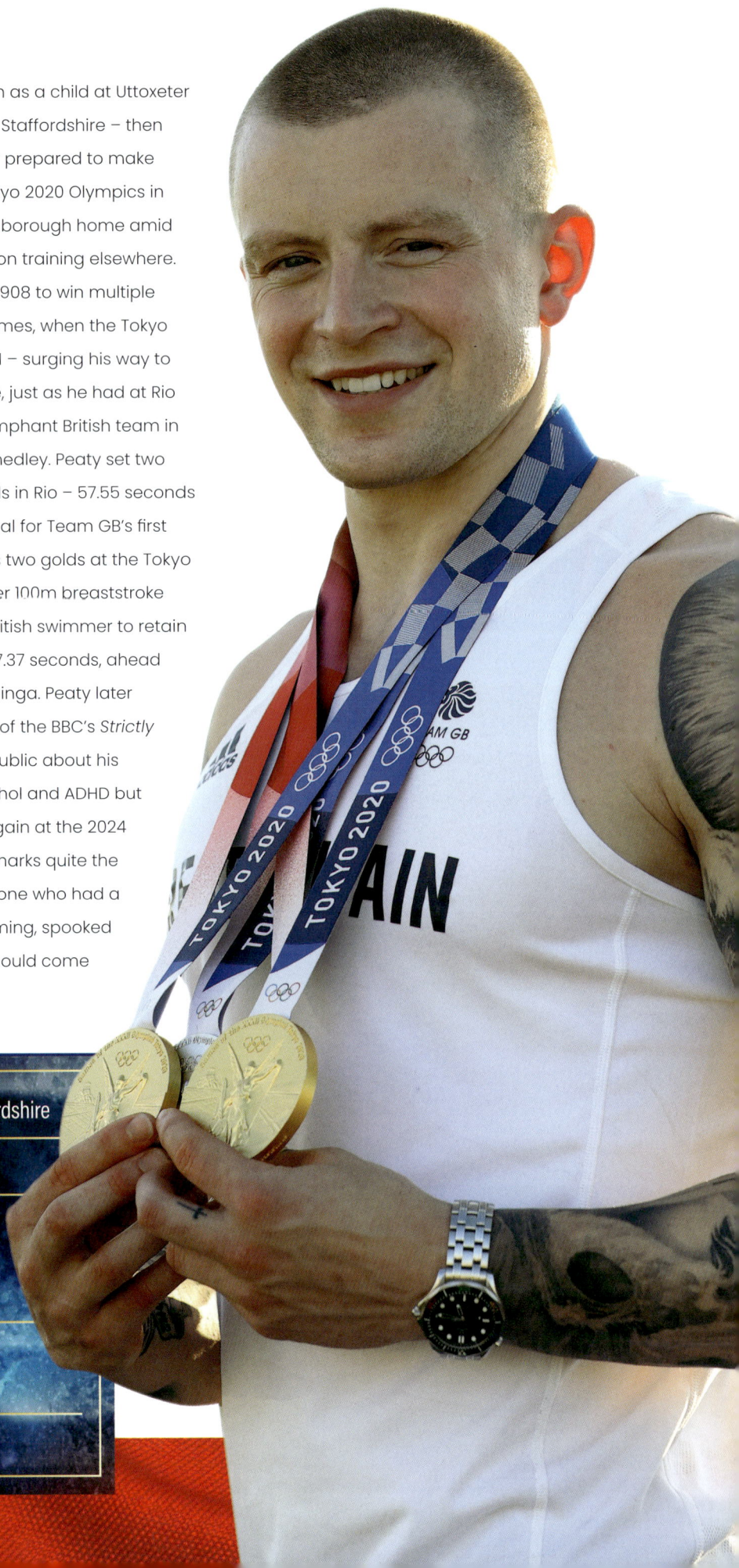

ADAM PEATY

Adam Peaty swam as a child at Uttoxeter Leisure Centre in Staffordshire – then many years later prepared to make history at the Tokyo 2020 Olympics in a flown-in 5m pool at his Loughborough home amid Covid-19 lockdown restrictions on training elsewhere. He became the third Brit since 1908 to win multiple swimming golds at a single Games, when the Tokyo event finally went ahead in 2021 – surging his way to victory in the 100m breaststroke, just as he had at Rio 2016, and being part of the triumphant British team in the inaugural 4 x 100m mixed medley. Peaty set two world 100m breaststroke records in Rio – 57.55 seconds in the heats, then 57.13 in the final for Team GB's first gold of 27 that summer. Peaty's two golds at the Tokyo 2020 Olympics included another 100m breaststroke triumph, making him the first British swimmer to retain an Olympic title – finishing in 57.37 seconds, ahead of the Netherlands' Arno Kamminga. Peaty later finished ninth in the 2021 series of the BBC's *Strictly Come Dancing*, before going public about his struggles with depression, alcohol and ADHD but committing himself to going again at the 2024 Olympics in Paris. His success marks quite the turnaround, however, for someone who had a fear of water as a boy – screaming, spooked by his brothers' claims sharks could come up through the plughole.

BORN: December 28, 1994, in Uttoxeter, Staffordshire

EVENT: Swimming – breaststroke, medley

GOLD (3): 100m breaststroke (Rio 2016), 100m breaststroke, 4 x 100m mixed medley (Tokyo 2020)

SILVER (2): 4 x 100m medley (Rio 2016), 4 x 100m medley (Tokyo 2020)

TOTAL MEDALS: 🥇🥇🥇🥈🥈

Water polo has been played at every Summer Olympic except for 1896 in Athens and 1904 in St Louis – and the first four golds were won by Great Britain, with Paul Radmilovic on the team at London 1908, Stockholm 1912 and Antwerp 1920. He scored twice when beating Belgium 9-2 in the 1908 final and the winner in a 3-2 victory over the same nation 12 years later, in a finale which prompted violent attacks on the winning team by home supporters. Radmilovic had also previously won gold as a swimmer at the 1908 London Games, in the 4 x 200m freestyle relay – drafted in to swim the second leg as a late replacement, in a race which saw Hungary's Zoltán Halmay start losing consciousness while swimming the anchor leg with his team in the lead. Radmilovic also played Olympics water polo for Britain in 1924 in Paris and 1928 in Amsterdam, a five-Games record not bettered for Britain until fencer Bill Hoskyns competed at his sixth in Montreal in 1976. Radmilovic's tally of four Olympic golds was also the nation's finest until rower Steve Redgrave clinched his fifth in Sydney in 2000. Radmilovic, born in Cardiff to parents with Welsh and Croatian ancestry, later ran a hotel in Somerset resort Weston-super-Mare where his family put his medals on display.

BELOW LEFT: Programme from the 1908 London Olympic Games

PAUL RADMILOVIC

THE GREAT
STADIUM
SHEPHERD'S BUSH LONDON

THE OLYMPIC GAMES 1908
PROGRAMME
6d

BORN: March 5, 1886, in Cardiff

DIED: September 29, 1968, aged 82, in Weston-super-Mare, Somerset

EVENT: Swimming – freestyle; water polo

GOLD (4): Water polo (London 1908, Stockholm 1912, Antwerp 1920), 4 x 200m freestyle (London 1908)

TOTAL MEDALS: ●●●●

DUNCAN SCOTT

Swimming team-mate Tom Dean set himself a target of taking the record from him at the 2024 Olympics in Paris, but Duncan Scott came out of Tokyo 2020 with an all-time British best of four medals at a single Games. That tally included silver, just four-hundredths of a second behind Dean in the 200m freestyle final – though they were later on the same side winning gold in the 4 x 200m freestyle. He also won silver that summer in the 4 x 100m medley, alongside fellow 200m relay gold medallists James Guy as well as Luke Greenbank and Adam Peaty instead of Dean and Matt Richards. Scott's gold and three silvers in Tokyo followed another two silvers at the Rio Olympics in 2016, making him Britain's most decorated Olympic swimmer. Scott's finishing time in the Tokyo 2020 200m medley final was 1:55.28 minutes, a British record but just short of China's Wang Shun and his 1:55.00. Britain came third in the swimming medals table at Tokyo 2020, with eight – four golds, three silvers and one bronze, compared to six at Rio 2016 and three at London 2012. Two years before Tokyo, Scott refused to shake hands and pose for pictures with World Aquatics Championships gold medallist Sun Yang who had previously been given bans for doping offences.

BORN: May 6, 1997, in Glasgow

EVENT: Swimming – freestyle, medley

GOLD (1): 4 x 200m freestyle (Tokyo 2020)

SILVER (5): 4 x 200m freestyle, 4 x 100m medley (Rio 2016), 200m freestyle, 200m medley, 4 x 100m medley (Tokyo 2020)

TOTAL MEDALS:

CHARLES SYDNEY SMITH

While Paul Radmilovic was 42 when he competed at his then-record fifth Olympics in 1928, it is his former team-mate Charles Sydney Smith who holds the record as the oldest water polo player at a Games – having been 45 years and 169 days old when bowing out in Paris four years earlier. Sydney Smith played in goal for the British side which won gold at London 1908 with him as captain, Stockholm 1912 – where he was chosen to be the country's flagbearer at the ceremonies – and Antwerp 1920. His final match at an Olympics was the defending champions' 7-6 first round defeat to Hungary at Paris 1924. Sydney Smith's side had conceded just 14 goals in his previous seven Olympics fixtures including a clean sheet in the 1912 final, an 8-0 win for Britain over Austria. Since the last triumph in 1920, Britain has fared less well in Olympic water polo when occasionally entering a team – with a best subsequent finish of fourth in 1928 and no participation since 1956 apart from coming 12th at London 2012. Yet Britain's four golds – the first was in 1900 – keeps them still second in the overall table only behind Hungary's nine titles. Since women's water polo was introduced at the 2000 Sydney Olympics, Britain has only entered one team which came eighth at London 2012.

For all the success of Britain's swimmers in recent years, none has yet matched Henry Taylor's hat-trick of golds at the 1908 Games in London. The Lancashire cotton mill worker – who trained by swimming in Oldham's Hollinwood Canal or else Chadderton Baths on "dirty water days" with cheaper admission fees – won 400m, 1500m and 4 x 200m freestyle relay gold in London. His 1500m finishing time was recorded as an inaugural world record for the distance, 22:48.75 minutes. Taylor followed up those successes with 4 x 200m freestyle bronze at Stockholm 1912 and the same again in Antwerp eight years later. He had also won three golds at the so-called Intermediary Games in Athens in 1906 – in the 400m freestyle, one-mile freestyle and 4 x 200m freestyle – but this event later had its official status removed by the International Olympic Committee. Taylor died in poverty aged 65 in 1951 – but his memory was evoked by British performances at the Beijing Olympics in 2008. Cyclist Chris Hoy became that summer the first Brit to match his tally of three golds at a single Games, while Rebecca Adlington emulated him in winning multiple swimming golds. A blue plaque commemorating Taylor's achievements has been placed at Chadderton Baths.

HENRY TAYLOR

BORN: March 17, 1885, in Oldham, Greater Manchester

DIED: February 28, 1951, aged 65, in Oldham

EVENT: Swimming – freestyle

GOLD (3): 400m freestyle, 1500m freestyle, 4 x 200m freestyle (London 1908)

BRONZE (2): 4 x 200m freestyle (Stockholm 1912), 4 x 200m freestyle (Antwerp 1920)

TOTAL MEDALS: ●●●●●

BORN: January 26, 1876, in Wigan, Lancashire

DIED: April 6, 1951, aged 75, in Southport, Merseyside

EVENT: Water polo

GOLD (3): Water polo (London 1908, Stockholm 1912, Antwerp 1920)

TOTAL MEDALS: ●●●

FAR RIGHT: A poster by artist Olle Hjortzberg for the 1912 Summer Olympics held in Stockholm

OLYMPISKA SPELEN STOCKHOLM 1912
29 JUNI – 22 JULI

ATHLETICS

Athletics delivers the most-watched and keenly anticipated events at any summer Olympics and offers the most medals – with 48 events across track and field, road running and race walking scheduled for the 2024 Games in Paris. Most are held within the host nation's dedicated Olympic stadium, featuring a 400m-length running track and a field in the middle for events such as the high jump, long jump and triple jump and throwing sports discus and javelin.

HAROLD ABRAHAMS

Paris was given the duty and privilege of hosting the 2024 Summer Olympics – taking place exactly a century after the French capital did so for the second time, having previously staged the 1900 event. Among the most celebrated achievements at the 1924 Games was Harold Abrahams' triumph for Great Britain in the 100m final. His story, along with that of fellow British runner Eric Liddell, featured in the 1981 movie Chariots of Fire which won the Academy Award for Best Film and three more Oscars the following year. Abrahams was knocked out in the quarter-finals in both the 100m and 200m at the 1920 Olympics in Antwerp but prepared for Paris under the coaching of Sam Mussabini, who had already overseen Reggie Walker's 100m gold medal triumph at the 1908 Olympics in Athens. Abrahams developed a training tactic of putting pieces of paper along the track marking out the exact distance each stride should be – and aiming to pick up each one with his running shoes spikes. He won the 100m gold in Paris, equalling the Olympic record of 10.6 seconds, before finishing sixth in the 200m final but helping the British team to silver in the 4 x 100m. He later worked as a broadcaster, lawyer and for the British Amateur Athletic Association as chairman.

BORN: December 15, 1899, in Bedford, Bedfordshire

DIED: January 14, 1978, aged 78, in Enfield, London

EVENT: 100m, 200m

GOLD (1): 100m (Paris 1924)

SILVER (1): 4 x 100m (Paris 1924)

TOTAL MEDALS: 🥇 🥈

ROGER BANNISTER

Roger Bannister failed to win a medal at his only Olympics, the 1952 Summer Games in Helsinki – but the experience helped spur him on to what would be his crowning achievement, becoming the first man to run a mile in under four minutes. He set a new British record of 3:46.30 in the 1500m final in Helsinki, but finished out of the medals in fourth. After this relative disappointment he set himself the new target of beating the four-minute target for the mile – something he managed on 6 May 1954 at Iffley Road Track in Oxford, running the final lap in just 59 seconds and finishing with an overall time of three minutes and 59.4 seconds. Commentating on the run for the BBC was Harold Abrahams, 100m gold medal-winner at the 1924 Olympics in Paris. Bannister went on to win British Empire and Commonwealth Games gold in August 1954, beating Australia's John Landy – a bronze statue of the moment Bannister overtook him was unveiled in 1967 in Vancouver, where those 1954 Games took place. Ahead of the 2012 Olympics in London, Sir Roger – who was knighted in 1975 – carried the Olympic flame in the Oxford stadium where he had broken the four-minute barrier for the first time.

Charles Bennett has the honour of being Britain's first Olympics gold medallist in athletics – yet for many years his accomplishments went neglected. Bennett, a train driver, dominated the 1500m final in Paris at the 1900 Games – only the second Olympics of the modern era – and won in a world record time of four minutes and 6.2 seconds, before celebrating with a visit to the Folies Bergère theatre. He also helped a combined British/Australian team to victory in the 4000m steeplechase team race. This saw a team of five French

BORN: December 9, 1871, in Shapwick, Dorset

DIED: December 18, 1948, aged 77, in Bournemouth

EVENT: 1500m, 4000m steeplechase, 5000m

GOLD (2): 1500m, 5000m team race (Paris 1900)

SILVER (1): 4000m steeplechase (Paris 1900)

TOTAL MEDALS: 🥇🥇🥈

runners go up against four British and one Australian in a mixed side, with each athlete completing ten laps and being given points depending on their finishes. Charles Bennett crossed the line fastest, in a time of 15.29.2, and the British/Australian team won by virtue of having fewer points, 26 to France's 29. Finishing second to Bennett that day was UK team-mate John Rimmer, who nevertheless would beat Bennett in the 4000m steeplechase final. Bennett's abandoned and overgrown grave in Kinson in Bournemouth was given a new headstone in 2011 after being found by his grandson Chris Bennett.

ABOVE: Charles Bennett in 1900

LEFT: Harold Abrahams at the 1924 Olympics in Paris

BORN: March 23, 1929, in Harrow, London

DIED: March 3, 2018, aged 88, in Oxford

EVENT: 1500m

TOTAL MEDALS:

CHARLES BENNETT

CHRIS BRASHER

Chris Brasher was one of Roger Bannister's two pacemakers, along with Chris Chataway, when Bannister became the first man to run the mile in under four minutes – in May 1954. Two years later Brasher enjoyed individual glory of his own, winning gold – an achievement which eluded Bannister – at the 1956 Summer Olympics in Melbourne. But it was, so to speak, a close-run thing. After finishing the 3000m steeplechase – a track race involving hurdles and water jumps – in a winning time of eight minutes and 41.2 seconds, Brasher was disqualified for allegedly impeding Norway's Ernst Larsen. But he was reinstated as champion the following day. His appeal was backed by Larsen, who took bronze, as well as Hungary's Sándor Rozsnyói who came second and was given an International Fair Play Award in 2007 for his actions. Brasher later designed the Brasher Boot, a walking boot popular for its comfort, and co-founded the annual London Marathon in 1981 with friend John Disley. His wife was Shirley Bloomer, who won three Grand Slam titles as a tennis player, and their three children included daughter Kate who reached the second round at Wimbledon in 1980.

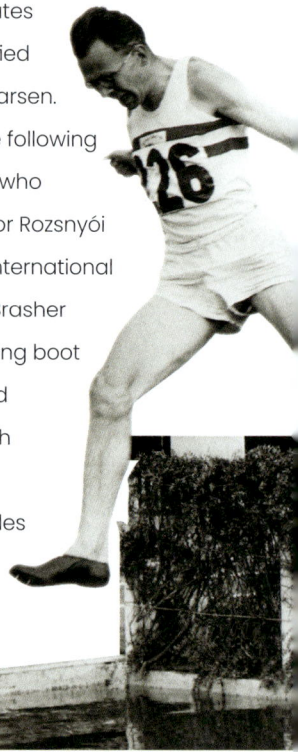

BORN: August 21, 1928, in Georgetown, British Guiana, now Guyana

DIED: February 28, 2003, aged 74, in Chaddleworth, Berkshire

EVENT: 3000m steeplechase

GOLD (1): 3000m steeplechase (Melbourne 1956)

TOTAL MEDALS: 🥇

DAVID CECIL, LORD BURGHLEY

A famous scene in Oscar-winning 1981 film *Chariots of Fire* shows Harold Abrahams achieving the "Great Court Run" feat of sprinting the 367m around the Great Court at the University of Cambridge's Trinity Court in the 43.6 seconds it took the college clock to toll 12 times marking midnight. In fact Abrahams never achieved this but the first person to successfully complete the challenge is believed to have been David Cecil, also known as Lord Burghley after becoming the 6th Marquess of Exeter – though he refused to give film-makers permission to use his name. He followed his 1927 feat by winning Olympic gold in the 400m in Amsterdam the following year, before adding 4 x 400m relay silver in Los Angeles in 1932 when he was Britain's team captain. His training regime involved placing matchboxes on top of hurdles and trying to knock each one off without hitting the hurdles themselves. Burghley had been given special dispensation to compete in the 1932 Games, winning temporary leave from his duties as Conservative MP for Peterborough. He later served on the International Olympic Committee for 48 years and was chairman of the organising committee when London hosted the Olympics in 1948.

BORN: February 9, 1905, Burghley House, near Stamford, Lincolnshire

DIED: October 22, 1981, aged 76, at Burghley House

EVENT: 110m hurdles, 400m hurdles

GOLD (1): 400m hurdles (Amsterdam 1928)

SILVER (1): 4 x 400m relay (Los Angeles 1932)

TOTAL MEDALS: 🥇🥈

Only one British man has won 100m gold at the Olympics, the Commonwealth Games, the World Championships and the European Championships. The greatest of these was Linford Christie's triumph in the 100m final at the 1992 Summer Games in Barcelona, finishing in 9.96 seconds – ahead of Namibia's Frankie Fredericks who ran 10.02 and US athlete Dennis Mitchell's 10.04. Christie, 32 at the time, became the oldest man to win Olympic 100m gold. Four years earlier in Seoul his bronze in the same event was upgraded to silver after Canada's Ben Johnson, who won the race, was disqualified after failing a drugs test. Christie also tested positive that summer, for banned stimulant pseudoephedrine, but he insisted he ingested the small amount accidentally when drinking ginseng tea and the IOC's medical commission voted 11-10 not to punish him. His attempt to successfully defend his Olympic title at the 1996 Olympics in Atlanta ended in disappointment when he was disqualified just before the final for two false starts. He tested positive for banned steroid nandrolone in 1999, despite having retired from representative international athletics two years earlier. He has consistently denied any wrongdoing. Christie was born in Jamaica but moved to England at the age of seven, living with his parents in Acton, west London.

BORN: April 2, 1960, in St Andrew, Jamaica

EVENT: 100m

GOLD (1): 100m (Barcelona 1992)

SILVER (2): 100m, 4 x 100m (Seoul 1988)

TOTAL MEDALS: 🥇🥈🥈

LINFORD CHRISTIE

BELOW: Linford Christie wins the Olympic 100 metres final in a time of 9:96 seconds in the Montjuic stadium in Barcelona, Spain, 1 Aug 1992

SEBASTIAN COE

London-born, Yorkshire-raised Sebastian Coe briefly held four world records in the run-up to the 1980 Olympics in Moscow, having broken three in 41 days the following year – the 800m, 1500m and mile – and then the 1000m, though this was taken from him by long-time rival Steve Ovett within the following hour. Their rivalry was one of the compelling stories of the 1980 Games, which was boycotted by the United States. Coe was thought the favourite in the 800m, Ovett in the 1500m – yet each one the other's supposed specialist event. Coe, whose career was often afflicted by illness, again won 800m silver in Los Angeles four years later before becoming the first and still only man to claim 1500m gold at two Summer Games, this time winning in an Olympic record time of 3:38.40. Coe later went into politics, spending five years as Conservative MP for Falmouth and Cambourne in Cornwall between 1992 and 1997. He was made a life peer in 2000 and then chaired both London's bid for and organisation of the 2012 London Olympics. In 2015 he was elected president of the International Association of Athletics Federations, now World Athletics.

RIGHT: Sebastian Coe victorious after winning the 1500m final at Central Lenin Stadium, Moscow, 1980 Olympics

BORN: September 29, 1956, in Hammersmith, London

EVENT: 800m, 1500m

GOLD (2): 1500m (Moscow 1980), 1500m (Los Angeles 1984)

SILVER (2): 800m (Moscow 1980), 800m (Los Angeles 1984)

TOTAL MEDALS: ⚫⚫⚪⚪

LYNN DAVIES

The physical education teacher known as "Lynn the Leap" saved his best for his fifth and last attempt in the Tokyo 1964 Olympics long jump final – managing 8.07 metres in cold and rainy conditions he later said benefitted him over the favourites Ralph Boston from the United States and the Soviet Union's Igor Ter-Ovanesyan. He could barely watch Boston's final leap which followed his, but the American finished 4cm short. Davies became the first Welshman to claim Olympic gold in an individual event. He went on to win European Championship long jump gold two years later in Budapest and Commonwealth Games titles in 1966 in Kingston and 1970 in Edinburgh. But he had to settle for ninth place in the long jump final at the 1968 Olympics in Mexico City, where he got to watch close-up US athlete Bob Beamon's world record-smashing leap of 8.90m – the admiring Welshman told Beamon afterwards: "You have destroyed this event." Davies carried Britain's flag at the opening ceremony in Mexico City. At London 2012, he was one of seven past Olympians nominating a youngster apiece to carry torches which lit the Olympic Cauldron at that summer's opening ceremony.

RIGHT: Davies jumping at the 1964 Olympics in Tokyo

BELOW: Official 1964 Tokyo Olympic Games poster artwork

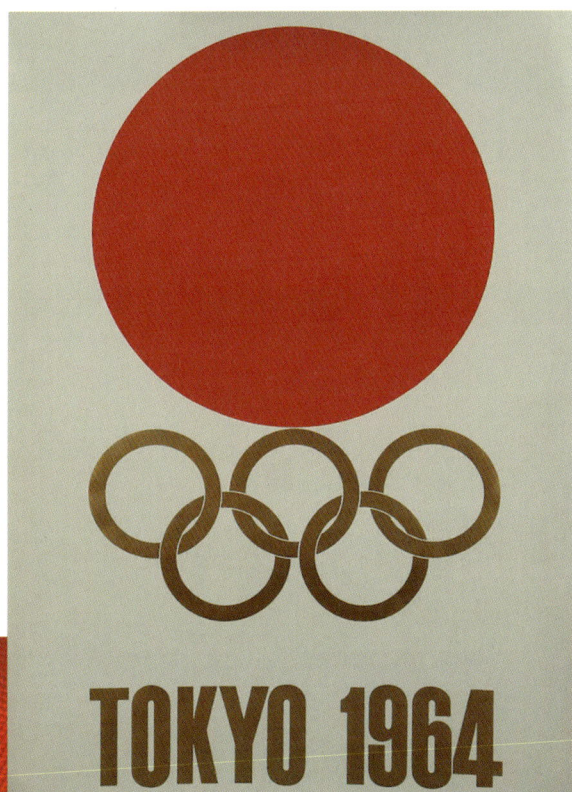

TOKYO 1964

BORN: May 20, 1942, in Nant-y-moel, Wales

EVENT: 100m, long jump

GOLD (1): Long jump (Tokyo 1964)

TOTAL MEDALS: 🥇

JONATHAN EDWARDS

Athletics glory came relatively late to Jonathan Edwards – but what an impact he had when he did begin to dominate his sport, the triple jump. The son of a clergyman had to wait until he was 29 to win his first major international championship title but he went into the 1996 Summer Olympics in Atlanta on a streak of 22 consecutive victories. These included breaking the world record in Salamanca in Spain the previous year, with a jump of 17.98m and then in August 1995 setting a new mark of 18.29m, making him the first man to pass 60ft. He had to settle for silver behind the US's Kenny Harrison in Atlanta – his best effort of 17.88m was the longest ever not to win gold. But he went one better four years later in Sydney, winning the title with a distance of 17.71m. Edwards had previously competed at the 1988 Olympics in Seoul and in Barcelona four years later but finished disappointingly each time. Until a change of mind in 1993 he would not take part in competitions held on Sundays for religious reasons – which included missing out on the 1991 World Championships. After retiring in 2003 he later served on the organising committee for the London 2012 Olympics.

ABOVE: Jonathan Edwards celebrates taking Gold in the Triple Jump at the Sydney Olympics in 2000

BORN: May 10, 1966, in Westminster, London

EVENT: Triple jump

GOLD (1): Triple jump (Sydney 2000)

SILVER (1): Triple jump (Atlanta 1996)

TOTAL MEDALS:

JESSICA ENNIS

Popular Sheffield-born heptathlete Jessica Ennis was one of the most prominent Team GB members going into the London 2012 Olympics but she appeared to wear lightly the pressure of expectations. She confirmed gold as she cruised across the London Olympic Stadium finishing lane ahead of the field in her last heptathlon event, the 800m. This was the first of three track and field gold medals for Britain on an evening which would be dubbed "Super Saturday", when her triumph was followed by victories for compatriots Greg Rutherford in the long jump and Mo Farah in the 10,000m. Ennis ended with a British and Commonwealth record score of 6,955 points – 306 ahead of silver medallist Lilli Schwarzkopf from Germany – and her 12.54-second run in the 100m hurdles was an Olympic record for the heptathlon. Ennis not only won World Championships heptathlon gold in 2009 and 2015 but in 2016 had her 2011 silver upgraded after gold was stripped from Russia's Tatyana Chernova for doping offences. Ennis had to settle for silver when trying to defend her Olympics title at the 2016 Games in Rio, behind Belgium's Nafissatou Thiam who set personal bests in five of the seven events. Since marrying Andy Hill in 2013 she has been known as Jessica Ennis-Hill and is now a Dame, given the honour in 2017 for services to athletics.

BELOW: Jessica Ennis in the Olympic stadium, London 2012, at the end of the 100m hurdles heats of the women's heptathlon

BORN: January 28, 1986, in Sheffield, South Yorkshire

EVENT: Heptathlon

GOLD (1): Heptathlon (London 2012)

SILVER (1): Heptathlon (Rio 2016)

TOTAL MEDALS: 🥇 🥈

MO FARAH

Sebastian Coe has described Mo Farah as "Britain's greatest ever athlete" and no one else in the country's history has matched his four Olympic gold medals on the track. These have been dubbed the "double-double". In Rio in 2016 he became the first man since Finland's Lasse Virén in 1976 to retain Olympic titles from four years earlier in both the 5000m and 10,000m. At London 2012 he was roared around the track in both finals by the home crowd in the 80,000-capacity Olympic Stadium, masterfully timing his runs to emerge ahead of the pack both times. His London 2012 winning times were 27:30.42 in the 10,000m and 13:41.66 in the 5000m seven days later. In Rio he won double gold again, with times of 27:05.17 in the 10,000m – despite falling during the 10th lap – and 13:03.30 in the 5000m. He celebrated each victory with his trademark "Mobot" celebration, using his arms to fashion the letter M on top of his head. He was knighted in 2017. Farah revealed in 2022 that his birth name was actually Hussein Abdi Kahin but he was given another child's identity of Mohamed Farah when he was illegally trafficked to Britain as a nine-year-old from what was then the Somali Democratic Republic.

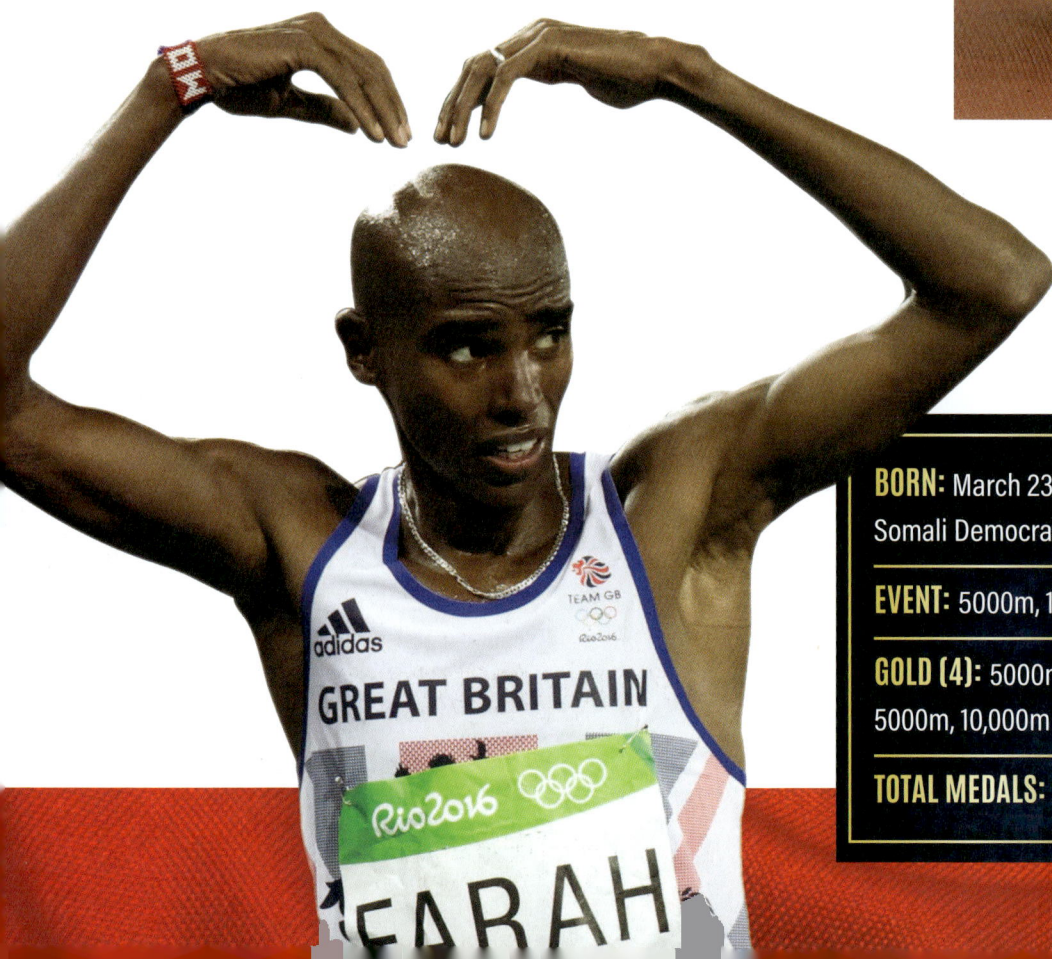

ABOVE: Mo Farah celebrates winning gold in the Men's 5000m Final on Day 15 of the London 2012 Olympic Games

BORN: March 23, 1983, in Gabiley, Somali Democratic Republic, now Somaliland

EVENT: 5000m, 10,000m

GOLD (4): 5000m, 10,000m (London 2012), 5000m, 10,000m (Rio 2016)

TOTAL MEDALS: 🥇🥇🥇🥇

SALLY GUNNELL

The US's Sandra Farmer-Patrick was the favourite but it was a farmer's daughter Sally Gunnell who would triumph in the 400m hurdles final at the 1992 Olympics in Barcelona. Gunnell overtook her rival at the ninth hurdle and stormed across the finishing line 3.5m clear, in a winning time of 53.23 seconds – 0.43 ahead of Farmer-Patrick in second. Gunnell also helped the British team to bronze in the 4 x 400m that summer, taking on the last leg following runs Phyllis Smith, Sandra Douglas and Jennifer Stoute. Gunnell previously finished fifth in the 400m hurdles final at the Seoul Olympics in 1988. She followed up her 1992 Barcelona victory with two more years of dominance, adding World Championships gold in 1993 and European Championships gold the following year. She has also won five Commonwealth Games gold medals, making her the only British athlete to triumph at all four of Olympics, World, European and Commonwealth events. As a youngster she had excelled at long jump, heptathlon and 100m hurdles as well but decided to focus on the 400m hurdles alone – paying off in style in Barcelona.

BELOW: Sally Gunnell after winning the women's 400-meter hurdles at the 1992 Olympics

BORN: July 29, 1966, in Chigwell, Essex

EVENT: 400m hurdles

GOLD (1): 400m hurdles (Barcelona 1992)

BRONZE (1): 4 x 400m hurdles (Barcelona 1992)

TOTAL MEDALS:

DAVID HEMERY

David Hemery's winning margin in thee 400m hurdles at the 1968 Olympics in Mexico City was the largest since the US's F. Morgan Taylor at the Paris Games in 1924. The American won that race in 52.6 seconds, ahead of Erik Vilén of Finland in 53.8. Hemery's new world record of 48.12 was 0.50 seconds ahead of Germany's Gerhard Hennige. Yet it took Hemery some time to realise he had won, needing confirmation from a BBC camera crew. Fellow Briton John Sherwood won bronze, the day after his wife Sheila clinched bronze in the long jump. Hemery added two more medals in Munich four years later, silver in the 4 x 400m relay alongside Martin Reynolds, Alan Pascoe and David Jenkins – beaten to gold by Kenya's team – and bronze in the 400m hurdles. Hemery had spent 10 years of his youth living in the US, due to his father's work as an accountant, and he graduated from Boston University where he later worked as a track coach after retiring from athletics. During the 1970s he enjoyed success in the BBC's Superstars decathlon-style multi-discipline competition, winning the inaugural British edition in 1973 against boxer Joe Bugner, golfer Tony Jacklin, footballer Bobby Moore, Formula One driver Jackie Stewart and tennis player Roger Taylor.

BORN: July 18, 1944, in Cirencester, Gloucestershire

EVENT: 400m hurdles

GOLD (1): 400m hurdles (Mexico City 1968)

TOTAL MEDALS: ⬤

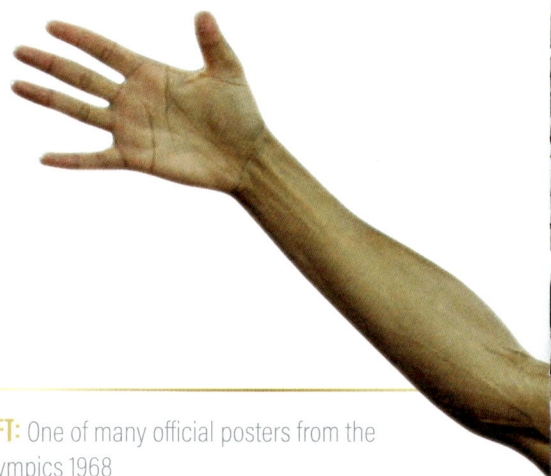

BELOW LEFT: One of many official posters from the Mexico Olympics 1968

BELOW: David Hemery winning the Men's 400 meter hurdles event, at the 1968 Olympics

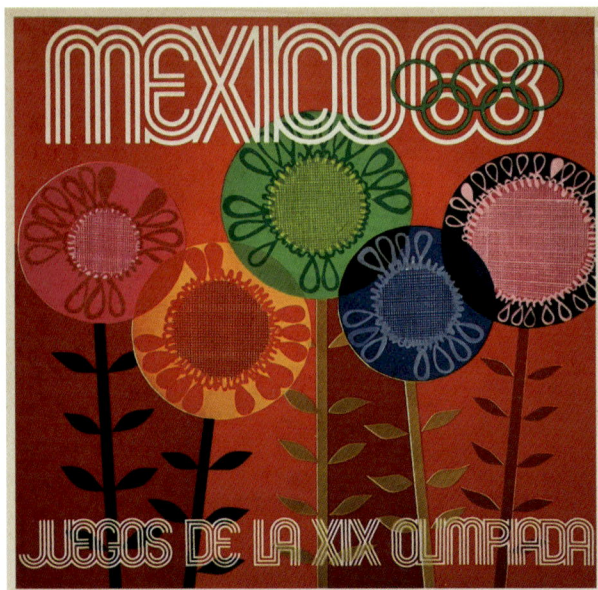

Kelly Holmes timed her running to perfection not once but twice at the 2004 Olympics in Athens, winning both the 800m and then the 1500m five days later by taking the lead with just half a lap to go. At 34 she became the oldest woman to win each of those events and only the second British athlete to win Olympic gold at both 800m and 1500m, after Albert Hill at the 1920 Games in Antwerp. Despite showing promise after taking up running as a 12-year-old, Holmes opted to quit when signing up with the British Army aged 18 and intending to become a physical training instructor – but she reconsidered after watching ex-school rival Lisa York, who Holmes knew she could beat, representing Britain in the 3000m at the 1992 Barcelona Olympics. She won 800m bronze at the 2000 Sydney Olympics, though had been leading before being overtaken by Mozambique's Maria Mutola and Stephanie Graf of Austria in the final 50m. After twice doing better in Athens she was given the honour of carrying the British flag at the closing ceremony, the day after her 1500m run which was in a British record time of three minutes and 57.90 seconds. She was created Dame Kelly Holmes in 2005, the same year she retired from athletics.

BELOW: Kelly Holmes celebrates as she wins the final of the women's 1500m at the Athens 2004 Olympic Games

KELLY HOLMES

BORN: April 19, 1970, in Pembury, Kent

EVENT: 800m, 1500m

GOLD (2): 800m, 1500m (Athens 2004)

BRONZE (1): 800m (Sydney 2000)

TOTAL MEDALS: 🥇🥇🥉

DENISE LEWIS

In Sydney in 2000 Denise Lewis became the first European woman to win the seven-event heptathlon since it replaced the five-event pentathlon in 1984 – and she did so against the odds and in shooting pain. She came into the Olympics with a damaged Achilles tendon and concentrated on intensive physiotherapy instead of training in the three weeks building up to the Games. She was prescribed the highest dose of the painkiller ibuprofen and also competed with both calves and one ankle strapped – yet performed especially strongly in the shot put, with a throw of 15.55m, and the javelin where she threw 50.19m, and finally clinched gold with her finish in the 800m to beat silver medallist Yelena Prokhorova by 53 points. Lewis previously won bronze at the 1996 Olympics in Atlanta, the only medal for a British woman at those Games. She would go on to the 2004 Olympics in Athens but was forced out midway through by injury while British team-mate Kelly Sotherton won bronze. Since retiring she has worked regularly as an athletics pundit on TV, finished runner-up in the 2004 series of the BBC's *Strictly Come Dancing,* and was made a dame in 2023.

RIGHT: Denise Lewis celebrates gold in the Heptathlon at the Sydney 2000 Olympic Games

BORN: August 27, 1972, in West Bromwich, West Midlands

EVENT: Heptathlon

GOLD (1): Heptathlon (Sydney 2000)

BRONZE (1): Heptathlon (Atlanta 1996)

TOTAL MEDALS:

ERIC LIDDELL

Along with that of Harold Abrahams, Eric Liddell's story was dramatised in the 1981 movie *Chariots of Fire*. The film suggests the devout Christian who was born in China to parents who were Scottish missionaries only discovered on the boat to Paris for the 1924 Olympics that the 100m heats would be held on a Sunday. He is shown deciding then to withdraw, because his religious beliefs kept him from competing on Sundays. Yet he had known since the Olympics timetable was drawn up six months earlier and had been concentrating on his 200m and 400m preparations. He spent the Sunday of the 100m heats at a Scottish church in the French capital, giving a sermon before days later winning bronze in the 200m final – with Abrahams sixth – and gold in the 400m. Liddell, known as the "Flying Scot", sprinted into an immediate lead in the 400m from his outside lane and finished in an Olympic record time of 47.6 seconds. Liddell, who also won seven international rugby caps for Scotland, later returned to China where he worked as a missionary before dying of a brain tumour while in a Japanese internment camp.

BORN: January 16, 1902, in Tientsin, now Tianjin, China

DIED: February 21, 1945, aged 43, Weixian Internment Camp, near Weifang, China

EVENT: 100m, 200m, 400m

GOLD (1): 400m (Paris 1924)

BRONZE (1): 200m (Paris 1924)

TOTAL MEDALS: 🥇🥉

CHRISTINE OHURUOGU

Christine Ohuruogu became the first British woman to 400m Olympic gold at the 2008 Games in Beijing – but it had looked for some time as if she would never get to compete at a summer Games. She was given a one-year ban in 2006 for missing three out-of-competition drug tests in ten months. The British Olympics Association barred anyone suspended for a doping offence from representing Britain in the Olympics but she challenged this ban and it was overturned the following year. In the 2008 Olympic final she was trailing in fourth with just 100m to go but pulled clear of Jamaica's Shericka Williams in second, Sanya Richards of the United States in third and Russia's Yulia Guschina just out of the medals. Ohuruogo desperately wanted to retain her title at the London 2012 Olympics, in the Olympic Stadium in Stratford, east London, less than a mile from where she grew up. But she was narrowly beaten to gold by Richards, now competing as Sanya Richards-Ross. Ohuruogu also has two Olympics bronze medals, both in the 4 x 400m – her team finished fifth in Beijing but were awarded bronze after those coming third and fourth were both disqualified and she added another in Rio eight years later.

TOP RIGHT: Christine Ohuruogu at the parade in London to celebrate the British competitors at the 2008 Summer Olympics

BORN: May 17, 1984, in Newham, London

EVENT: 400m

GOLD (1): 400m (Beijing 2008)

SILVER (1): 400m (London 2012)

BRONZE (2): 4 x 400m (Beijing 2008)
4 x 400m (Rio 2016)

TOTAL MEDALS: 🥇🥈🥉🥉

Steve Ovett and Sebastian Coe had only raced each other once before in senior competition ahead of the US-boycotted 1980 Olympics in Moscow and their supposed rivalry captured much of the attention ahead of their 800m and 1500m finals. Coe was said to favour the former, Ovett the latter, but Ovett won the first race – surging past the Soviet Union's Nikolai Kirov in the final 70m to win in 1:45.40 while Coe did just about enough to claim silver. The positions were reversed six days later in the 1500m, when Coe ended Ovett's three-year, 42-race unbeaten streak at 1500m and one mile. Coe finished in 3:38.40, with Germany's Jürgen Straub taking silver 0.19 seconds ahead of Ovett's 3:38.89. Ovett's efforts at the Los Angeles Olympics four years later were ill-fated, as struggled with the effects of bronchitis. He collapsed on the track after his 800m semi-final then finished eighth in the final before spending two days in hospital. He returned for the 1500m final but was unable to complete the race and was taken off on a stretcher. Ovett retired in 1991, a year after Coe had done so, and later moved to Canada and then to Australia.

STEVE OVETT

FAR LEFT: Steve Ovett in the 800 metres quarter-final at the 1984 Summer Olympics

BORN: October 9, 1955, in Brighton, East Sussex

EVENT: 800m, 1500m

GOLD (1): 800m (Moscow 1980)

BRONZE (1): 1500m (Moscow 1980)

TOTAL MEDALS:

ANN PACKER

Ann Packer had run the 800m only six times as she lined up for the final at the Tokyo Olympics in 1964 and one of those had been the semi-final in which she was the second slowest of the qualifiers. Yet she later proclaimed "ignorance proved to be bliss" as she surged through the field on the final lap to win in a world record 2:01.1. She had considered not taking part in the final and going shopping instead but reconsidered after her fiancé Robbie Brightwell was disappointed to finish fourth in his 400m final the previous day. Brightwell,

captain of the British team for that Olympics, did later win 4 x 400m silver. Packer had already won Olympic silver herself that summer in her 400m race, which had become her favoured event in 1963 when she attended an athletics meeting in Reading and there were no 100m or 200m races scheduled. After her Olympic gold, Packer immediately retired from athletics at the age of 22. Two months later she and Brightwell married and would have three sons – two of whom, Ian and David Brightwell, played top-flight football for Manchester City in the 1980s and 1990s.

LEFT: Ann Packer and Maryvonne Dupureur 1964

BORN: March 8, 1942, in Moulsford, Oxfordshire

EVENT: 200m, 400m

GOLD (1): 800m (Tokyo 1964)

SILVER (1): 400m (Tokyo 1964)

TOTAL MEDALS: 🥇 🥈

Mary Peters had her father to thank for encouraging her athletics efforts as a teenager by providing a long jump pit in the family's back garden as a present for her 16th birthday – later laying concrete for a shot put circle. She took part in her first Olympics in Tokyo in 1964, when the five-event pentathlon was included for the first time, and finished fourth – then ninth at the Games in Mexico City four years later. She finally clinched a medal, and the gold one at that, in Munich at the 1972 Olympics. The then-33-year-old, who had been working as a secretary in Northern Ireland, charmed the German crowd despite competing against home favourite Heide Rosendahl. Peters recorded personal bests in two of her three events on the first day, a 1.82m high jump and running the 100m hurdles in 13.29 seconds

and also did well in the shot put with a throw of 16.29m to lead East Germany's Burglinde Pollak by 97 points and Rosendahl by 301. The following day Peters's long jump best was 5.98m, to Rosendahl's 6.83m, but her final 200m run of 24.08 seconds was enough to secure gold despite Rosendahl crossing the line in 22.96 seconds. If Peters had finished one-tenth of a second slower, the gold would be her rivals – but she won with a world record 4,801 points. Peters was one of the seven British Olympians chosen to nominate a young person to help light the London 2012 Olympic cauldron.

MARY PETERS

BELOW: Mary Peters competing in the long jump section of the Women's Pentathlon competition during the 1964 Summer Olympic Games in Tokyo

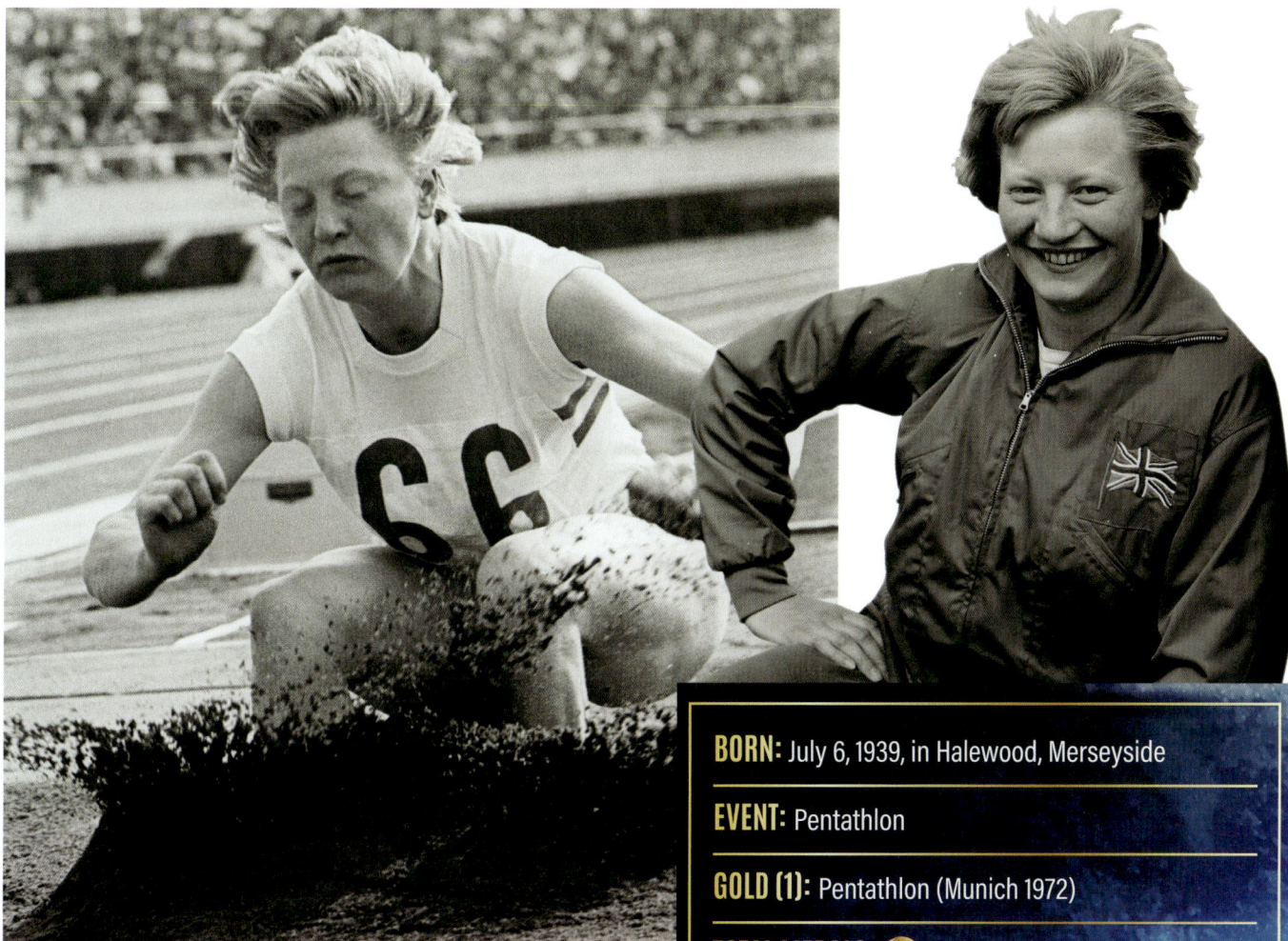

BORN: July 6, 1939, in Halewood, Merseyside

EVENT: Pentathlon

GOLD (1): Pentathlon (Munich 1972)

TOTAL MEDALS:

MARY RAND

No British woman had won an Olympic gold in athletics until Mary Rand's world record-breaking long jump triumph at the 1964 Games in Tokyo – one of three medals she claimed that summer, a tally no other female Brit has matched at a single Summer Olympics. The long jump final in Tokyo first saw her leap a British record of 6.59m first then a new world record distance of 6.76m at her fifth attempt. She went on to add silver in the pentathlon and helped Britain to bronze in the 4 x 100m alongside Janet Simpson, Daphne Arden and Dorothy Hyman – making up for her disappointment four years earlier in Rome where, competing under her maiden name Mary Bignal, she had only finished ninth in the long jump and fourth in the 400m hurdles. The second of her three husbands was US athlete Bill Toomey, who she wed in 1969 the year after he won decathlon gold at the 1968 Olympics in Mexico City. Rand had retired from athletics in September 1968 after failing to make the British team for that Games.

BORN: February 10, 1940, in Wells, Somerset

EVENT: 100m, long jump, pentathlon

GOLD (1): Long jump (Tokyo 1964)

SILVER (1): Pentathlon (Tokyo 1964)

BRONZE (1): 4 x 100m (Tokyo 1964)

TOTAL MEDALS: 🥇🥈🥉

BELOW: July 1964 - Leading British athlete Mary Denise Rand training in a field near her home in Henley-on-Thames. In the same year, she became the first British woman to win an Olympic gold medal

GREG RUTHERFORD

Day eight of the London 2012 Olympics was quickly dubbed "Super Saturday" after six gold medal triumphs for Team GB – including three packed into just 46 minutes in the Olympic Stadium, staging its second day of that summer's athletics programme. There had been sky-high hopes for Jessica Ennis in the heptathlon and Mo Farah in the 10,000m – but between their two triumphs a far less expected champion: Greg Rutherford in the long jump. It only gradually dawned on many of the 80,000 spectators with their eyes trained on the track just what he was achieving in the field and he took gold with a winning jump of 8.31m, 15cm ahead of Australia's Mitchell Watt in second. He had finished tenth in the long jump final at the 2008 Olympics in Beijing but after striking gold in London he went on to add bronze at Rio 2016. Since retiring from athletics in 2018 he has pursued an interest in bobsleigh but was unable to secure a place on Britain's team for the 2022 Winter Olympics in Beijing. His grandfather John Rutherford and great-grandfather Jock Rutherford both played First Division football for Arsenal in the 1920s, with Jock also winning 11 England caps.

LEFT: Greg Rutherford's distance after his gold-medal-winning jump at the 2012 London Olympics

BORN: November 17, 1986, in Milton Keynes, Buckinghamshire

EVENT: Long jump

GOLD (1): Long jump (London 2012)

BRONZE (1): Long jump (Rio 2016)

TOTAL MEDALS: 🥇 🥉

TESSA SANDERSON

Jamaican-born Theresa "Tessa" Sanderson, who grew up in the West Midlands after moving aged six, became the first British woman to win Olympic gold in a throwing event, at the 1984 Olympics in Los Angeles. She had been inspired to pursue an athletics career after seeing Mary Peters win pentathlon gold at the 1972 Games in Munich – and Peters, then team manager, was among the first to congratulate Sanderson after her LA triumph. Her winning throw was 69.56m, putting her 56cm ahead of silver medallist Tiina Lillak from Finland, Another Brit Fatima Whitbread, with whom Sanderson had a long-running rivalry, claimed bronze with her fifth effort covering 67.14m. Sanderson's other Olympics finishes were 10th at Montreal 1976, 19th at Moscow 1980, 21st at Seoul 1988 where Whitbread won silver, fourth at Barcelona 1992 and 14th at Atlanta 1996. That final appearance made her only the second person to compete in athletics in six different Olympics, after Romanian discus thrower Lia Manoliu who competed at Games from 1952 to 1972. Since retiring Sanderson's activities have included being vice-chair of public body Sport England between 1999 and 2005 and joining the Olympic Park Legacy Board charged with developing and managing the space in and venues in Stratford, east London, used for the London 2012 Games.

ABOVE: Posters from the 1976 Montreal and 1984 Los Angeles Olympic Games

BORN: March 14, 1956, in St Elizabeth, Jamaica

EVENT: Javelin

GOLD (1): Javelin (Los Angeles 1984)

TOTAL MEDALS:

Francis "Daley" Thompson was a no-nonsense performer. After finishing 18th in the decathlon at the 1976 Olympics in Montreal, he went into the Moscow Games four years later having sent a postcard to the US's double Olympic decathlon champion Bob Mathias vowing: "I'm going for three!" Thompson would "only" emulate Mathias by winning two in a row, marking his second triumph at Los Angeles 1984 by running his victory lap after the final 1500m event in a top complaining about the host country's US bias in TV coverage. Thompson, the son of British Nigerian father Frank and Scottish mother Lydia, was given his nickname Daley from one of his middle names Ayodélé, meaning "joy come home". He switched to the decathlon as a teenager after failing in three individual athletics events at an amateur championships in 1974. He was helped in the decathlon by the fact it started with his best two events, the 100m and long jump, but few would dispute his status as one of the greatest decathletes of all-time and certainly Great Britain's best. He broke the world record four times – including his 1984 Los Angeles tally of 8,798 points, having won 8,495 in Moscow – before finishing fourth at the 1988 Olympics in Seoul. True to his convention-challenging persona, Thompson collected his 1982 BBC Sports Personality of the Year award not in formal attire but instead in a tracksuit.

RIGHT: Poster for the 1980 Moscow Games

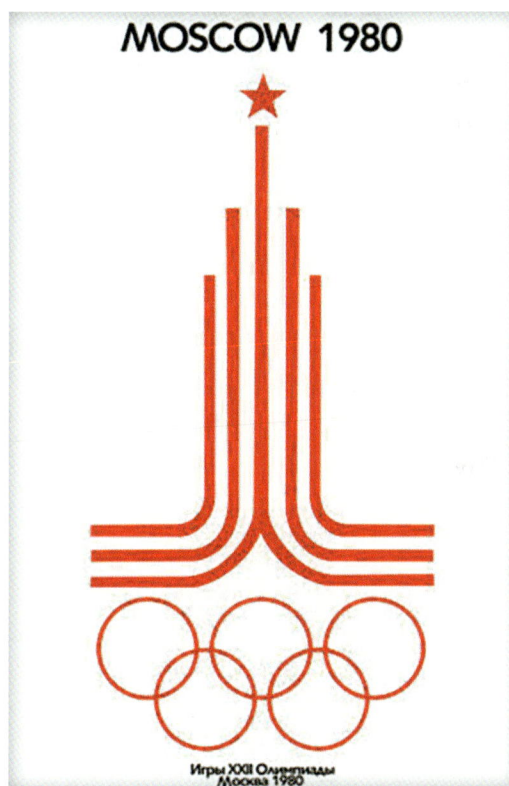

DALEY THOMPSON

MOSCOW 1980

Игры XXII Олимпиады
Москва 1980

BORN: July 30, 1958, in Notting Hill, London in England

EVENT: Decathlon

GOLD (2): Decathlon (Moscow 1980) Decathlon (Los Angeles 1984)

TOTAL MEDALS: 🥇🥇

ALLAN WELLS

It took a photo finish – and a skilful final dip of the head and shoulders – to narrowly clinch Allan Wells his 100m gold at the 1980 Olympics in Moscow – with Cuba's Silvio Leonard given silver despite having the same finishing time of 10.25 seconds. Wells, 28, became the oldest man at that time to win Olympic gold in that event – having only come late to sprinting after first concentrating on the long jump, inspired by 1964 Olympic champion Lynn Davies. There was another agonisingly close finish in the 200m final in Moscow, but this dipping his head at the line was not quite enough for Wells – he won silver, with a time of 20.21 seconds, just behind Italy's Pietro Mennea's 20.19. Wells then helped the British team finish fourth in the 4 x 100m final won by the Soviet host nation's team. Wells was the first British man to win the Olympic 100m since Harold Abrahams at Paris 1924. Amid some cynical suggestions he was helped by the American boycott of the 1980 Games, he responded a fortnight later by winning a 100m race in Cologne, Germany, featuring the best US sprinters of the time.

RIGHT: Allan Wells listens to the national anthem on the podium after winning the Men's 100m final at the 1980 Summer Olympic Games in Moscow

BORN: May 3, 1952, in Edinburgh

EVENT: 100m, 200m

GOLD (1): 100m (Moscow 1980)

SILVER (1): 200m (Moscow 1980)

TOTAL MEDALS: 🥇 🥈

Car mechanic Harold Whitlock remains Britain's oldest athlete to compete internationally, being aged 48 years and 218 days when he finished 11th out of 31 in the 50km walk race at the 1952 Olympics in Helsinki. But his greatest success had come 16 years earlier when winning the same event at the 1936 Games in Berlin, where his prize of an oak tree sapling was presented to him by Nazi dictator Adolf Hitler. Whitlock later gave the sapling to his former school, Hendon School in north London. Whitlock won in Berlin despite suffering from severe sickness at the 38km mark, which continued for 5km, before he recovered and continued on in first place. Whitlock later coached Don Thompson, who won 50km walk gold at the 1960 Olympics in Rome. The first winner of the event, when it was introduced to the Games in Los Angeles in 1932, had been another Brit – 38-year-old railway worker Tommy Green. Whitlock's younger brother Rex took part in the 50km walk at the 1948 Games in London and in Helsinki four years later, finishing fourth at that second event.

HAROLD WHITLOCK

ABOVE: The official poster of the Berlin 1936 Games, which depicts an athlete and the Brandenburg Gate

ABOVE RIGHT: Churchman cigarette card of Hector Harold Whitlock. Card no. 48 of a series of 50 cards titled "Kings of Speed"

BORN: December 16, 1903, in Hendon, London

DIED: December 27, 1985, aged 82, in Wicklewood, Norfolk

EVENT: 50km walk

GOLD (1): 50km walk (Berlin 1936)

TOTAL MEDALS: 🥇

BADMINTON

Badminton made its Olympics debut in Barcelona in 1992 and has been a mainstay since then, with men's and women's singles and doubles tournaments as well as mixed doubles which was introduced in Atlanta in 1996 – though it was first played at the 1972 Games in Munich as a demonstration sport. China has dominated, topping the badminton medals table with 47 – including 20 golds – ahead of Indonesia's 21 and South Korea's 20. China's triumphs include a clean sweep of all five gold medals in the sport at the London 2012 Games. Since that summer's Olympics each badminton competition has involved a group stage followed by knock-out rounds.

GAIL EMMS

Britain had never won an Olympic medal for badminton since its introduction to the Games in 1992 until Joanne Wright-Goode and Simon Archer claimed bronze in the mixed doubles in Sydney eight years later, beating Denmark's Rikke Olsen and Michael Søgaard in their medal play-off 15-4, 12-15, 17-14. Gail Emms and Nathan Robertson went a step better in Athens in 2004, surprising many by reaching the final after defeating Olsen and Jonas Rasmussen in the semi-finals before losing at the last to Chinese duo Zhang Jun and Gao Ling 15-1, 12-15, 15-12. Emms began playing badminton at the age of four, initially coached by her mother Janice who had played for the England women's football team in the 1970s. Emms and Donna Kellogg reached the second round of the women's doubles at Athens 2004 and the first four years later where this time Emms and Robertson could only make the quarter-finals in the mixed event. She retired after those Beijing Games and has since worked as a motivational speaker, TV commentator and coach with Badminton England. Her other medals include World Championships gold with Robertson in Madrid in 2006 as well as two Commonwealth Games golds, in Manchester in 2002 and Melbourne four years later.

BORN: July 23, 1977, in Hitchin, Hertfordshire

EVENT: Badminton - women's doubles, mixed doubles

SILVER (1): Athens 2004

TOTAL MEDALS:

NATHAN ROBERTSON

Nathan Robertson, alongside Gail Emms, achieved Britain's best badminton achievement at an Olympics, winning silver in Athens in 2004 – yet when asked for his career highlight he picked their World Championship triumph two years later, beating compatriots Anthony Clark and Donna Kellogg. Robertson was part of the British team for the 2009 World Badminton Championships in Hyderabad, India, but Badminton England pulled out before the opening round fearing a terror threat. Like Emms, he has spent time since retiring as a coach with Badminton England. Britain's only badminton medal since then, the country's third overall, was bronze for Marcus Ellis and Chris Langridge in the men's doubles at the 2016 Olympics in Rio. They had lost to the eventual champions, China's Fu Haifeng and Zhang Nan in the semi-final but clinched a medal in the play-off by defeating Chai Biao and Hong Wei – also from China – 21-18, 19-21, 21-10. Ellis and Langridge went on to claim gold together at the 2018 Commonwealth Games and the European Games the following year, before Smith and Lauren Smith reached the quarter-finals of the mixed doubles in the Tokyo 2020 Olympics.

LEFT: Gail Emms and Nathan Robertson of Great Britain celebrate winning the second set against Jun Zhang and Ling Gao of China in the mixed doubles badminton gold medal match on August 19, 2004 during the Athens 2004 Summer Olympic Games

BORN: May 30, 1977, in Nottingham

EVENT: Badminton - men's doubles, mixed doubles

SILVER (1): Athens 2004

TOTAL MEDALS:

BOXING

The United States has topped the boxing medals table since its introduction at the 1904 Olympics in St Louis, with 117 overall including 50 golds – well ahead of second-placed Cuba's 78, with Britain ranked third with 62 medals including 20 golds. The only Games where the sport was missing was in Stockholm in 1912, because the Swedish government banned boxing at the time. The 2024 Paris Olympics will have the men competing in seven different weight divisions and the women in six. Women's boxing was only added as an Olympic sport at London 2012 and until 2016 Olympic boxing was for amateur or state-funded competitors only.

NICOLA ADAMS

Nicola Adams made history as the first woman to win an Olympic boxing gold, at London 2012 on August 9 that year – and four years later she retained her title. The International Olympic Committee decided in 2009 to introduce women's boxing to the Games at three weights: flyweight (51kg), lightweight (60kg) and middleweight (75kg). Adams's flyweight final against China's world number one Ren Cancan came first, with the home favourite winning 16-7 on points in front of a 10,000-capacity crowd in London's ExCel arena. Adams, beaming as ever afterwards, avenged previous defeats to the same opponent in the 2010 and 2012 World Championship finals. Four years later in Rio, Adams again reached this final – this time defeating France's Sarah Ourahmoune by three rounds to nil, having already added world and European championship titles to her tally. She announced in 2017 she would turn professional, having first taken up boxing as a 12-year-old after her mother took her to a Leeds gym as "something to do". Adams became WBO flyweight world champion July 2019. She retired in November 2019, with a professional record of five wins and a draw.

BORN: October 26, 1982, in Leeds, West Yorkshire

EVENT: Boxing – flyweight

GOLD (2): Flyweight (London 2012), Flyweight (Rio 2016)

TOTAL MEDALS: 🥇🥇

No British boxer had won Olympic bantamweight gold since Henry Thomas at the London Games back in 1908 until Luke Campbell did so in the same city in 2012. Campbell – one of many gold medallists from Yorkshire that summer – beat Ireland's John Joe Nevin 14-11 in the 56kg final, having previously beaten Italy's Vittorio Parrinello, Detelin Dalakliev of Bulgaria and in the semi-finals Japan's Satoshi Shimizu. That was the second of three boxing golds for Team GB at that Olympics, coming in between Nicola Adams's flyweight triumph and Anthony Joshua's in the super heavyweight division. Campbell revealed after the final he almost gave up boxing four years earlier after a series of injury setbacks but was convinced to keep going by new coach Rob McCracken. Campbell turned professional the year after his Olympic glory and became WBC International lightweight champion in August 2015 and WBC Silver lightweight champion the following July. He announced his retirement at the age of 33 in July 2021, after 20 professional wins and four defeats.

LUKE CAMPBELL

BELOW: Luke Campbell celebrates defeating John Joe Nevin of Ireland to win the Men's Bantam (56kg) Boxing final bout on Day 15 of the London 2012 Olympic Games

BORN: September 27, 1987, in Kingston upon Hull, East Yorkshire

EVENT: Boxing – bantamweight

GOLD (1): Bantamweight (London 2012)

TOTAL MEDALS: 🥇

JAMES DEGALE

James DeGale was given the nickname "Chunky" as a boy and it has stuck ever since. But it looked like his opponent in the 2008 Olympics middleweight final in Beijing wanted to take a chunk out of him, with Cuba's Emilio Correa docked two points in the opening round for biting his shoulder. DeGale went on to win the bout and Olympic gold 16-14, having earlier in the tournament defeated 2004 Olympic welterweight champion Bakhtiyar Artayev, from Kazakhstan, and then Ireland's Darren Sutherland in the semi-finals – Sutherland went on to win bronze. DeGale paid tribute to Sutherland after his death from an apparent suicide in September 2019, aged 27, and go on to fight wearing shorts bearing the initials DS. DeGale turned professional in December 2008. When he beat the US's Andre Dirrell by unanimous decision in May 2015 to claim the IBF super-middleweight crown, DeGale

became Britain's first Olympic boxing gold medallist to win a professional world championship. He lost the title to another American, Caleb Truax, in December 2017 in London's Copper Box Arena – venue for his Olympics triumph – only to regain it in a rematch four months later in Las Vegas. DeGale retired in February 2019, after 25 professional wins, three defeats and a draw.

BORN: February 3, 1986, in Hammersmith, London

EVENT: Boxing – middleweight

GOLD (1): Middleweight (Beijing 2008)

TOTAL MEDALS:

RIGHT: Olympic Gold medalist boxer James DeGale poses during a portrait session at the Peacock Gym on December 22, 2008 in London

AUDLEY HARRISON

Audley Harrison won Olympic gold for Britain in the super heavyweight division, the unlimited weight category which had been known as heavyweight between 1904 and 1980. His triumph came in Sydney in 2000, where he comfortably defeated Kazakhstan's Mukhtarkhan Dildabekov 30-16 in the final – despite being troubled by a swollen knuckle. By that time Harrison had already become British super heavyweight champion in 1997 and added Commonwealth Games gold in Kuala Lumpur the following year. He celebrated his Olympic triumph by rapping to reporters in a post-match press conference.

He launched his professional career by knocking out US boxer Mike Middleton at London's Wembley Arena in May 2001, having signed a £1 million deal with the BBC who would broadcast his first 10 professional fights. Yet he also faced criticism for allegedly picking weak opponents – earning him the nickname "Fraudley Harrison" – yet did get a shot at the world title in 2010, only to be stopped in the third round by defending champion and fellow Brit David Haye. Harrison announced retirements and comebacks several times in the following years, before finally confirming the end of his career in March 2014 – with a professional record of 31 victories and seven defeats.

BORN: October 26, 1971, in Park Royal, London

EVENT: Boxing - super heavyweight

GOLD (1): Super heavyweight (Sydney 2000)

TOTAL MEDALS: 🥇

ANTHONY JOSHUA

Anthony Joshua brought Team GB's triumphant London 2012 performances to a fitting end on the Olympics' final day, just hours ahead of the closing ceremony when he beat Italy's Roberto Cammarelle – defending champion from Beijing 2008 in the super heavyweight final. The pair finished tied at 18-18 but Joshua was given gold on the count-back rule, with each judge asked who they felt deserved to win. The towering 6ft 6in Joshua had only taken up boxing five years earlier at the late starting age of 18, training at Finchley and District Amateur Boxing Club in north London. He turned down a £50,000 offer to turn professional in 2010, insisting he wanted to win medals, but after his Olympics success he made the move in 2013. He won the IBF heavyweight championship against the US's Charles Martin in April 2016 and unified the world belts in April 2017 at London's Wembley Stadium, knocking out Ukraine's Wladimir Klitschko in the 11th round of their WBA title fight. After a surprise defeat to another American boxer Andy Ruiz Jr in June 2019, he regained his titles in a rematch the following December – before another upset when beaten on points by Ukraine's Oleksandr Usyk at north London's Tottenham Hotspur Stadium in September 2021.

BORN: October 15, 1989, in Watford, Hertfordshire

EVENT: Boxing – super heavyweight

GOLD (1): Super heavyweight (London 2012)

TOTAL MEDALS: 🥇

BELOW: Anthony Joshua celebrates during the awards ceremony for the Super-Heavyweight boxing category of the 2012 London Olympic Games

Lauren Price kept the British boxing success story going at the delayed Tokyo 2020 Games held in 2021. She became the first Welsh boxer to win an Olympic title, claiming gold in the 75kg middleweight division with a 5-0 points victory over China's Li Qian. She told of being inspired by fellow Brit Nicola Adams's flyweight triumphs at London 2012 and Rio 2016. The 2020 Games was the first with five different women's boxing events, with featherweight at a maximum 57kg and welterweight at 69kg added to the roster. Price previously played football for Cardiff City, helping them win the Welsh Premier Women's Football League in 2012–13 and winning two caps for Wales before giving up the game in 2014 to prioritise boxing – going on to win middleweight bronze at that year's Commonwealth Games in Glasgow and then gold at the Gold Coast one in Australia in 2018. Britain's other boxing gold medallist at Tokyo 2020 was Galal Yafai, born in Birmingham to parents from Yemen. He beat the Philippines' Carlo Paalam 4-1 on points in the men's 52kg flyweight final, having knocked his opponent down in the opening round.

LAUREN PRICE

BORN: June 25, 1994, in Newport

EVENT: Boxing – middleweight

GOLD (1): Middleweight (Tokyo 2020)

TOTAL MEDALS: 🟡

Melbourne 1956 champion Dick McTaggart, unlike many of Britain's recent Olympic boxing medallists, steadfastly rejected any suggestions he turn professional – despite only earning £8 per week as a labourer. Dundee-born McTaggart, one of five boxing brothers, earned the right to fight in the lightweight division – for competitors of up to 60kg – in Melbourne after winning the 1956 ABA Championships in London. He was given the judges' decision in all four of his fights at that Games, ultimately beating West Germany's Harry Kurschat in the final. McTaggart also competed at the next two Olympics, where he was defeated both times by the eventual champion – Poland's Kazimierz Paździor in their 1960 Rome semi-final, again at lightweight, and by that same country's Jerzy Kulej in the light welterweight division round of 16 at Tokyo 1964. McTaggart retired in 1965 having won four more ABA Championships titles as well as Commonwealth Games gold in Cardiff in 1958 and silver in Perth four years later, with an overall record of 610 victories in 634 fights. He later coached Scotland's boxers for the 1990 Commonwealth Games in Auckland as well as accompanying the British team to two Olympics. He has said he "boxed for fun, for laughs" – describing the professional sport as "all work and wages, no fun".

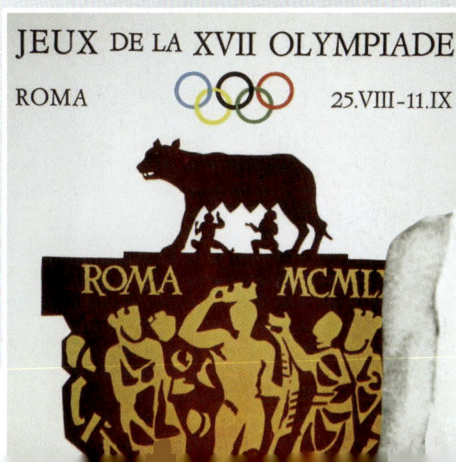

DICK McTAGGART

BORN: October 15, 1935, in Dundee

EVENT: Boxing – lightweight, light welterweight

GOLD (1): Lightweight (Melbourne 1956)

BRONZE (1): Lightweight (Rome 1960)

TOTAL MEDALS: 🟡 ⚪

BELOW: 1960 Rome Olympic Games poster

JEUX DE LA XVII OLYMPIADE
ROMA   25.VIII–11.IX
ROMA   MCMLX

CYCLING

Cycling has been an ever-present at every Olympics since the first modern-day Games in Athens in 1896, with a variety of speed races – as well as BMX freestyle events which were introduced at the delayed Tokyo 2020 Olympics in 2021. Britain has emerged this century among the most dominant forces in the sport, with the country's most decorated Olympians including cyclists Sir Jason Kenny, Sir Chris Hoy and Sir Bradley Wiggins. Road and track races are staged, though it was only in Los Angeles in 1984 that women's road events were introduced and women's track races four years later in Seoul.

ED CLANCY

Britain went 72 years without a cycling gold medal before Chris Boardman raced to glory in the 4000m individual pursuit at the 2000 Games in Sydney, finishing more than a lap ahead of German world champion Jens Lehmann. Since then Team GB's cyclists have dominated cycling at the Olympics, piling up record-breaking medal hauls. Ed Clancy has three golds and a bronze, with consecutive team pursuit triumphs at Beijing 2008, London 2012 and Rio 2016. In Beijing, his team pursuit side – which also featured Paul Manning, Geraint Thomas and Bradley Wiggins – broke the world record in qualifying heats with a time of 3:55.202 then topped that in the final, finishing ahead of silver medallists Denmark in 3:53.314. His team followed that up with consecutive world records of 3:52.499 and 3:51.659 at London 2012 and then 3:50.570 and 3:50.265 at Rio 2016. Clancy also won five team pursuit golds at the Track Cycling World Championships, before announcing his retirement in 2021 during the delayed Tokyo 2020 Olympics. Two years later he was announced as the new active travel commissioner for South Yorkshire, where he had been born and brought up in Barnsley.

BELOW: Ed Clancy, Steven Burke, Owain Doull and Bradley Wiggins of Team Great Britain prepares to compete in the Men's Team Pursuit Final for Gold on Day 7 of the Rio 2016 Olympic Games

BORN: March 12, 1985, in Barnsley, South Yorkshire

EVENT: Track cycling – omnium, team pursuit

GOLD (3): Team pursuit (Beijing 2008), Team pursuit (London 2012), Team pursuit (Rio 2016)

BRONZE (1): Omnium (London 2012)

TOTAL MEDALS: 🥇🥇🥇🥉

NICOLE COOKE

Britain's 200th medal at the Olympics was also the first ever in road cycling and the first medal for a British woman in any cycling event at the Games. Nicole Cooke raced through to overtake the four ahead of her in the final 350m of the 126km women's road race at Beijing 2008, in torrential rain she later likened to her native Wales. Cooke was given her first bike at six and is said to have insisted at the age of 11 she wanted to "win a golden medal", according to her parents. She had been one of the hopefuls at the 2004 Olympics in Athens but preparations had been disrupted by two crashes the previous year, one with a police outrider, and she could only finish fifth in the road race and 19th in the time trial. But her triumphant 2008 saw her become the first cyclist of either sex to win the road race World Championships and Olympic gold in the same year. Her other achievements include twice winning the Grande Boucle, the Women's Tour de France, in 2006 and 2007. After retiring aged 29 in 2013, she has spoken out against doping and sexism in the sport.

BORN: April 13, 1983, in Swansea

EVENT: Road cycling – road race, time trial

GOLD (1): Road race (Beijing 2008)

TOTAL MEDALS: 🥇

RIGHT: Cycling Gold medalist Nicole Cooke shows her medal during the Olympic and Paralympic Heroes Parade on October 16, 2008 at the Mansion House, London

CHRIS HOY

The hosts Great Britain – now branded as Team GB – won 65 medals at the London 2012 Olympics, their biggest tally since the 146 claimed in the same city back in 1908, though they would go on to take 67 at Rio 2016. Among the big winners at London 2012 was cyclist Chris Hoy, from the Scottish capital Edinburgh. His two golds in the team sprint and Keirin races made him the first British competitor to have won six Olympic titles, one more than rower Steve Redgrave. His first had come in Athens in 2004, in the 1km "kilo" time trial – the last time that event was part of the Olympics. Four years later he added another three golds in Beijing, the first Briton to win as many at a single Games for a century, and in 2012 he was Team GB's flag-carrier at the opening ceremony in London's Olympic Stadium before his team sprint triumph alongside Jason Kenny and Philip Hindes and his individual win in the Keirin. He retired in 2013, having said in the immediate aftermath of his London 2012 glory that there was only a "0.01 per cent chance" of targeting Rio 2016. He also vowed to down plenty of celebratory beers, ending four years of abstinence – telling reporters: "I'll definitely be making up for my lost units." He had been knighted in 2009, making him Sir Chris Hoy.

ABOVE RIGHT: Athens 2004 Olympic Games official poster

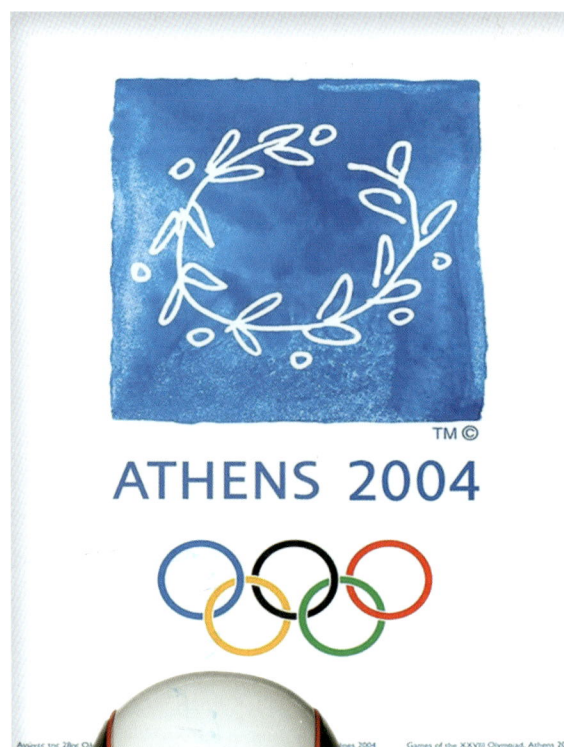

BORN: March 23, 1976, in Edinburgh

EVENT: Track cycling – 1km time trial, Keirin, sprint, team sprint

GOLD (6): 1km time trial (Athens 2004), Keirin, sprint, team sprint (Beijing 2008), Keirin, team sprint (London 2012)

SILVER (1): Team sprint (Sydney 2000)

TOTAL MEDALS: 🥇🥇🥇🥇🥇🥇🥈

Jason Kenny, then 20, was beaten by Great Britain team-mate Chris Hoy in the Beijing 2008 final of the cycling sprint – which since 2004 challenges the two cyclists to ride for 750m, though only really racing for the last 200m. The pair were both gold medallists on the same side in that summer's team sprint event. Kenny has since gone on to overtake Hoy as Britain's most successful Olympian, with more medals than anyone else – nine – as well as most golds, seven. He also has more Olympic medals of any cyclist. His latest came in the Keirin at Tokyo 2020, where he surged clear of Malaysia's Azizulhasni to successfully defend the title he won at Rio 2016 – just as he had repeated Olympic gold in the team sprint in 2008, 2012 and 2016 and the individual sprint in 2012 and 2016. That triumph justified his decision in 2017 to reverse his post-Rio 2016 retirement from competing. After his Tokyo 2020 success he was knighted in the 2022 New Year Honours List, while his fellow cyclist wife Laura Kenny – née Trott – was made a Dame. In February 2022 he revealed he really was retiring from the track, taking up a coaching post with British Cycling.

RIGHT: One of the posters used at the 2008 Beijing Olympics

BELOW: Kenny during the team sprint at the 2012 Olympic Games

JASON KENNY

BORN: March 23, 1988, in Bolton

EVENT: Track cycling – Keirin, sprint, team sprint

GOLD (7): Team sprint (Beijing 2008), Sprint, team sprint (London 2012), Keirin, sprint, team sprint (Rio 2016), Keirin (Tokyo 2020)

SILVER (2): Sprint (Beijing 2008), Team sprint (Tokyo 2020)

TOTAL MEDALS: 🟡🟡🟡🟡🟡🟡🟡⚪⚪

VICTORIA PENDLETON

Cycling's "Queen Victoria" bounced back from feeling "devastated" to miss out on a medal at the 2004 Olympics in Athens by claiming gold in the one event open to her in Beijing four years later. Victoria Pendleton beat long-time rival Anna Meares, from Australia, 2-0 in the final of the best-of-three-laps match sprint. Another battle between the pair ended in gold for Meares, silver for Pendleton, at London 2012 – after the British rider was controversially penalised by judges in the first round for edging out of the sprinting lane on the final bend. That was the last race of Pendleton's career but she had already added another Olympic gold that summer, becoming the first woman to win the Keirin as it was added to the Olympics for the first time. After retiring following London 2012, Pendleton later set her sights on becoming a horse racing jockey and met her target of competing in the 2016 Foxhunter Chase at the Cheltenham Festival, finishing fifth. She has also competed on the BBC's *Strictly Come Dancing* in 2012 and attempted a charity ascent of Everest in May 2018 but was forced to abandon it when suffering from a lack of oxygen. She has said: "After London 2012 I thought I'd really enjoy having a lot more time to myself – I've got a lovely veg patch at home and I do like a bit of gardening – but I felt I was missing out on what life has to offer."

RIGHT: Victoria Pendleton celebrates after victory in the Women's Sprint Final against Anna Meares of Australia in the track cycling event at the Laoshan Velodrome on Day 11 of the Beijing 2008 Olympic Games

BORN: September 24, 1980, in Stotfield, Bedfordshire

EVENT: Track cycling – Keirin, sprint, team sprint

GOLD (2): Sprint (Beijing 2008), Keirin (London 2012)

SILVER (1): Sprint (London 2012)

TOTAL MEDALS: 🥇🥇🥈

Versatile rider Geraint Thomas has achieved great success in both track and road cycling, alternating between the different disciplines throughout his career. He was part of the prolifically world-record-breaking team pursuit gold medallists in the velodromes at both the Beijing 2008 and London 2012 Olympics – in Beijing alongside Ed Clancy, Paul Manning and Bradley Wiggins and four years later with Clancy, Steven Burke and Peter Kennaugh. He switched to the road for the 2016 Games in Rio but crashed 10km from the finishing line of the 241.5km men's road race and came 11th, before finishing in ninth place in the time trial. Two years later he became Britain's third Tour de France winner – after Wiggins and Chris Froome – and the first from Wales and to be born in Britain, before he was voted BBC Sports Personality of the Year for 2018. Thomas, who joined his first cycling club at the age of ten, has also won three Cycling World Championship golds for team pursuit, in 2007, 2008 and 2012, as well as Commonwealth Games gold in the road race at Glasgow 2014 and time trial bronzes that same year and at Birmingham 2022.

BORN: May 25, 1986, in Cardiff

EVENT: Road cycling – road race, time trial; Track cycling – team pursuit

GOLD (2): Team pursuit (Beijing 2008)
Team pursuit (London 2012)

TOTAL MEDALS: ● ●

GERAINT THOMAS

LAURA TROTT

Laura Kenny, maiden name Trott, is the most successful Olympics cyclist of all time and the British woman with the most medals at the Games. She had been born a month premature and with a collapsed lung, before later being diagnosed with asthma, but took up cycling as a child alongside her mother who wanted to lose weight and Laura's elder sister Emma. Her major breakthrough came in the velodrome at London 2012, where she won team pursuit gold alongside Dani King and Joanna Rowsell in a world record time of 3:14.051 – and then another gold, riding solo two days later, in the omnium. She retained both titles in Rio four years later, then at the Covid-19 pandemic-delayed Tokyo 2020 event in 2021 she added a fifth gold in the Madison but had to settle for silver this time in the team pursuit, finishing six seconds behind the German team. No British woman before her had ever won gold medals at three Olympics in a row and she was chosen to carry the GB flag at the Tokyo 2020 closing ceremony. She and fellow cycling star Jason Kenny married in September 2016, not long after they had come home from Rio laden with yet more Olympic gold medals – Jason three that time to Laura's two.

ABOVE RIGHT: 2020 Tokyo Olympic Games poster design

BORN: April 24, 1992, in Harlow, Essex

EVENT: Cycling - Madison, omnium, team pursuit

GOLD (5): Omnium, team pursuit (London 2012), Omnium, team pursuit (Rio 2016), Madison (Tokyo 2020)

SILVER (1): Team pursuit (Tokyo 2020)

TOTAL MEDALS: 🥇🥇🥇🥇🥇🥈

radley Wiggins was already an accomplished and successful track cyclist, winning individual pursuit Olympic gold in Athens in 2004 before team pursuit and individual pursuit triumphs in Beijing four years later, when he added road cycling's ultimate honour in July 2012 – becoming Britain's first ever Tour de France champion. A mere week later he was sitting on a makeshift throne in the grounds of Hampton Court Palace after adding Olympic gold in the 27.3-mile time trial, finishing 42 seconds faster than Germany's silver medallist Tony Martin. His eight Olympic medals – the last of them team pursuit gold at Rio 2016 – are now only bettered by former team-mate Jason Kenny's nine. Wiggins, whose Australian father Gary had been a professional cyclist, is the first and so far only person to win the Tour de France and Olympic gold in the same year. He also rang the Olympic bell as part of London 2012's opening ceremony in the athletics stadium in Stratford, east London. Wiggins was made a Sir in 2013 though made light of the honour, saying he would only use the title for "comedy purposes". He retired from competitive cycling after the Rio 2016 Olympics though later competed in the following year's British Indoor Rowing Championships.

Rachel Whiteread LOndOn 2012

ABOVE: 2012 London Olympic Games poster

BRADLEY WIGGINS

BORN: April 28, 1980, in Ghent, Belgium

EVENT: Cycling – road time trial; track individual pursuit, Madison, team pursuit

GOLD (5): Track individual pursuit (Athens 2004), Track individual pursuit, team pursuit (Beijing 2008), Road time trial (London 2012), Track team pursuit (Rio 2016)

SILVER (1): Track team pursuit (Athens 2004)

BRONZE (2): Track team pursuit (Sydney 2000), Track Madison (Athens 2004)

TOTAL MEDALS: ⬤⬤⬤⬤⬤⬤ ⬤⬤

EQUESTRIAN

Equestrian events were first held at the Olympics in Paris in 1900 and have been a regular feature since 1912. Three disciplines are competed in – dressage, eventing and show jumping, in individual and team competitions open to both men and women. These and the equestrian element of the modern pentathlon are the only Olympic sports to feature animals, with the horses involved often becoming at least as popular with spectators as their riders. Ahead of the 2024 Olympics in Paris, Britain was fourth in the overall medal table with 40 including 13 golds – with Germany top, having won 56 medals, half of them gold.

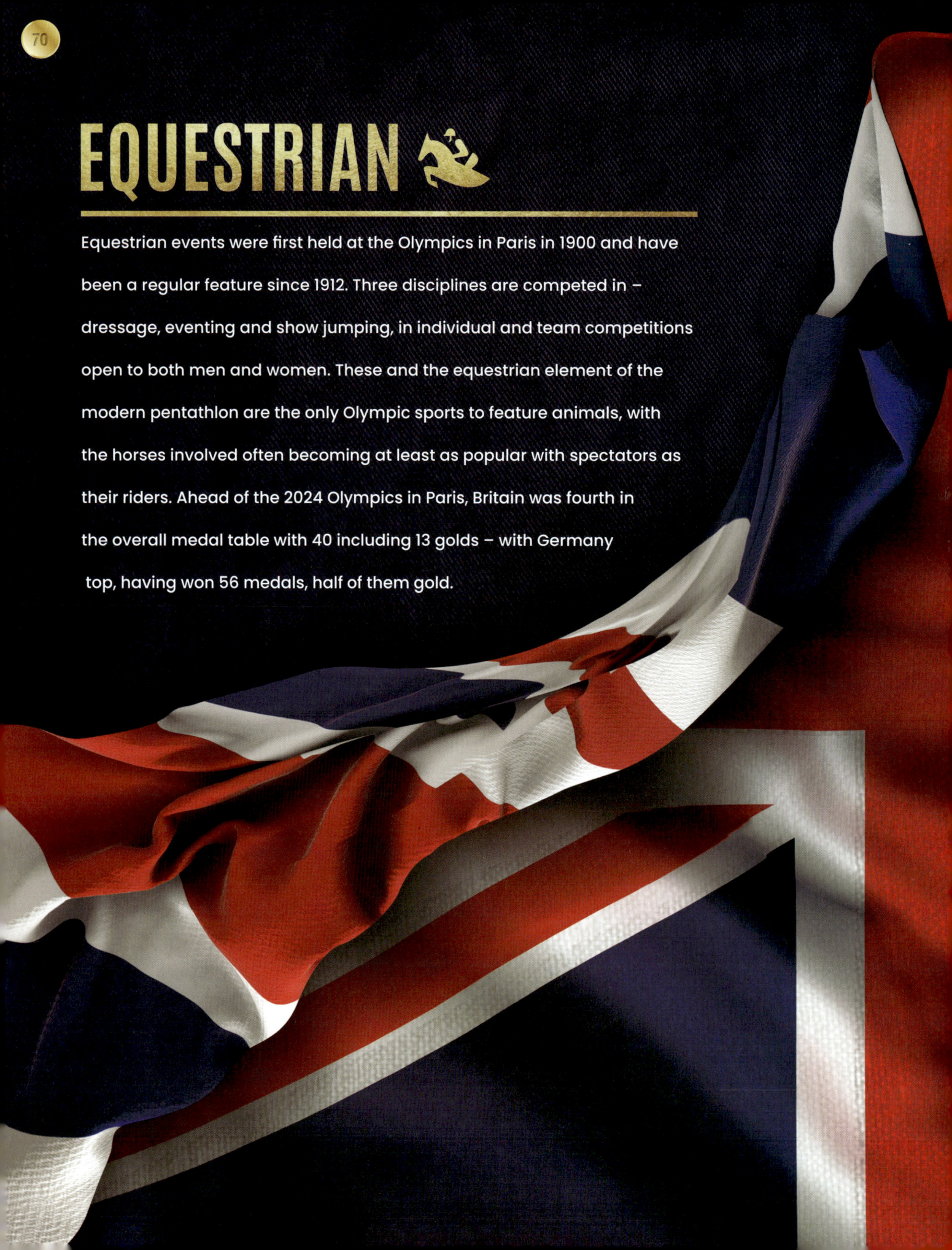

CHARLOTTE DUJARDIN

Charlotte Dujardin, who began riding horses aged two, shares with cyclist Laura Trott the record for most Olympics medals won by a British female competitor. Her three golds, a silver and two bronzes have come in the dressage – in which riders guide their horses through a series of pre-determined movements and are marked by judges for their performance. The individual dressage finals are set to music – and at London 2012, Dujardin and her beloved horse Valegro were accompanied by a patriotic soundtrack including "Land Of Hope And Glory", the theme to the movie *The Great Escape* and Big Ben's chimes. She not only won the individual dressage gold but four years later at the Rio Olympics she became the first British woman to retain an Olympic title. Dujardin's final winning score in the Rio individual dressage final was an Olympic record 93.857. Her fiancé Dean Golding responded to that triumph by wearing a T-shirt asking, "Can we get married now?" Dujardin retired Valegro after the Rio triumph, which also included team dressage silver to go with another gold in that event from London 2012, before taking individual and team dressage bronzes at Tokyo 2020 with new mount Gio.

BORN: July 13, 1985, in Enfield, London

EVENT: Equestrian – dressage

GOLD (3): Individual dressage, team dressage (London 2012), Individual dressage (Rio 2016)

SILVER (1): Team dressage (Rio 2016)

BRONZE (2): Individual dressage, team dressage (Tokyo 2020)

TOTAL MEDALS: ⬤⬤⬤⬤⬤⬤

BEN MAHER

Ben Maher was a key part of Britain's first show jumping Olympics gold for 60 years, suitably enough at London 2012 in the team jumping event. The country's last previous winners had been Wilfrid White, Douglas Stewart and Henry Llewellyn at the 1952 Helsinki Games, an event which made a national hero of Llewellyn's horse Foxhunter whose skeleton was later preserved and put on display after his death in 1959 by London's Royal Veterinary College. Maher, riding his horse Tripple X III, had team-mates Scott Brash on Hello Sanctos, Peter Charles on Vindicat W and Nick Skelton on Big Star. The British team and their Dutch rivals were level on scores after completing the scheduled set of rounds, where riders are judged depending on their progress across an obstacle course – but Maher and team-mates clinched gold in a tie-breaking "jump-off" – helped by

Charles' clear round on Vindicat W, who was sold the following month to rock star Bruce Springsteen for his daughter Jessica. Maher – from Enfield in north London, like fellow Olympic equestrian champion Charlotte Dujardin – added an individual jumping gold to his collection at Tokyo 2020, this time on his horse Explosion W. Maher completed the final jump-off round over a six-obstacle course in a time of 37.85 seconds, ahead of the 38.02 managed by Sweden's Peder Fredricson.

BELOW: Gold medalist Ben Maher rides Explosion W after the medal ceremony for the Jumping Individual Final on day twelve of the Tokyo 2020 Olympic Games

BORN: January 30, 1983, in Enfield, London

EVENT: Equestrian – individual jumping, team jumping

GOLD (2): Team jumping (London 2012)
Individual jumping (Tokyo 2020)

TOTAL MEDALS: 🥇🥇

RICHARD MEADE

Richard Meade excelled at eventing, a multi-discipline equestrian sport that combines dressage, cross-country jumping and show jumping. He helped Britain win team eventing gold at both the Mexico City Olympics in 1968 and in Munich four years later, the first time riding a horse named Cornishman V and the second time on Laurieston. Meade also won the individual eventing gold in Munich, making him the first British rider to clinch an Olympics individual title. Meade carried the British flag at the 1972 closing ceremony, but only after returning from a trip back to London to read a lesson at a memorial service for the victims of that summer's Munich massacre. The terror attack had left 17 people dead including 11 members of Israel's Olympics team. Meade went on to finish fourth, on a horse called Jacob Jones, in the individual eventing at the 1976 Olympics in Montreal. He later served as chairman of the British Horse Foundation and president of the British Equestrian Federation while training riders himself, before his death after treatment for cancer in January 2015, aged 76. His son James is godfather to the Prince and Princess of Wales' daughter Charlotte and James's wife Laura godmother to the royal couple's youngest son Louis.

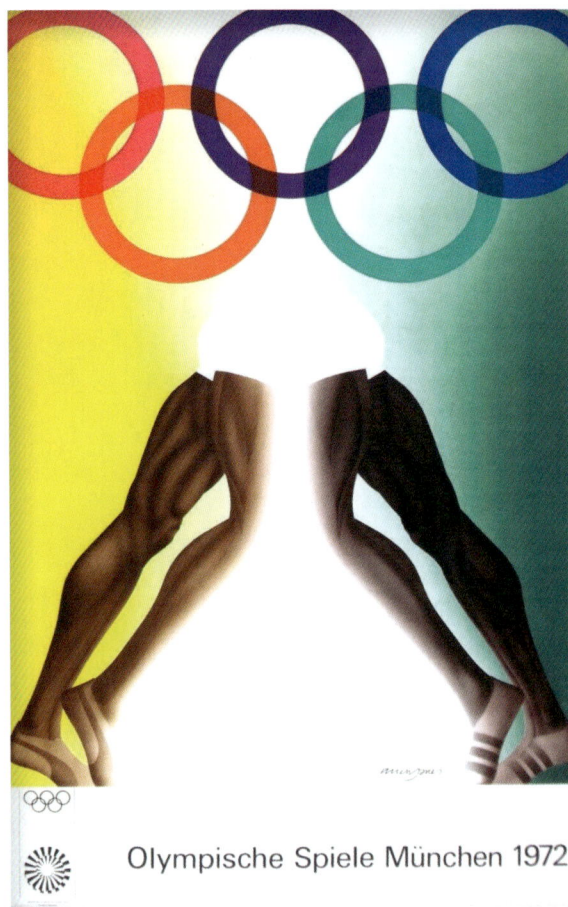

Olympische Spiele München 1972

ABOVE RIGHT: 1972 Munich Olympic Games poster

RIGHT: Richard Meade in 1974

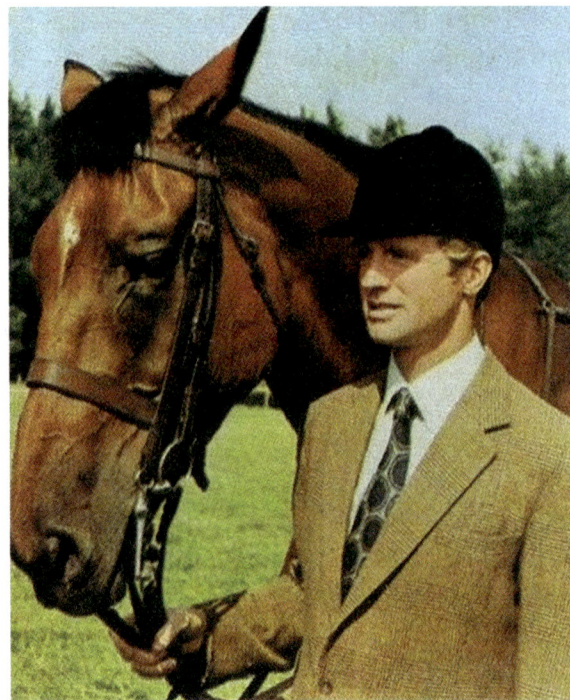

BORN: December 4, 1938, in Chepstow, Monmouthshire

DIED: January 8, 2015, aged 76, in West Littleton, Gloucestershire

EVENT: Equestrian – individual eventing, team eventing

GOLD (3): Team eventing (Mexico City 1968), Individual eventing, team eventing (Munich 1972)

TOTAL MEDALS: ● ● ●

Nick Shelton was not so much the comeback "kid" by London 2012 but then, at 54, he finally fulfilled his Olympic dream with gold – before adding another four years later in Rio. This was despite breaking his neck in a fall in September 2000 and retiring the following year – only to recover and reconsider. His first Olympics saw him finished joint seventh at the Seoul Games in 1988 and he came close to a medal at Athens 2004 when leading going into the final round only to fall short. That team jumping triumph at London 2012 came after a final jump-off in which Skelton, Scott Brash, Peter Charles and Ben Maher saw off their Dutch opponents – Skelton riding Big Star, the youngest horse in the competition and who also helped him to fifth in the individual jumping. The pair went on to glory in that individual event in Rio. Again, it took a jump-off to settle the final before Skelton and Big Star completed their run of the course in 42.82 seconds, ahead of Sweden's Peder Fredricson in 43.35 – Fredricson would later be similarly beaten by Maher at Tokyo 2020. At 58, Skelton became Britain's oldest Olympic champion since 61-year-old shooter Joshua Millner won 1000-yard rifle gold at the 1908 Games in London – though Millner was from Dublin and was competing for what was at the time Great Britain and Ireland.

BORN: December 30, 1957, in Bedworth, Warwickshire

EVENT: Equestrian – show jumping

GOLD (2): Team jumping (London 2012), Individual jumping (Rio 2016)

TOTAL MEDALS: ●●

BELOW: Nick Skelton riding Big Star competes in the 2nd Qualifier of Individual Jumping on Day 9 of the London 2012 Olympic Games

NICK SKELTON

GYMNASTICS

Olympic gymnastics has three disciplines: artistic, rhythmic and trampoline.

Artistic events see gymnasts judged on how they perform on a series of apparatus, while rhythmic – for female competitors only – involves graceful movements to music holding different implements and trampolinists are marked for their skills on those sprung surfaces. Gymnastics has played a part at every Olympics since Athens 1896, initially for men only until women's events were added in Amsterdam in 1928.

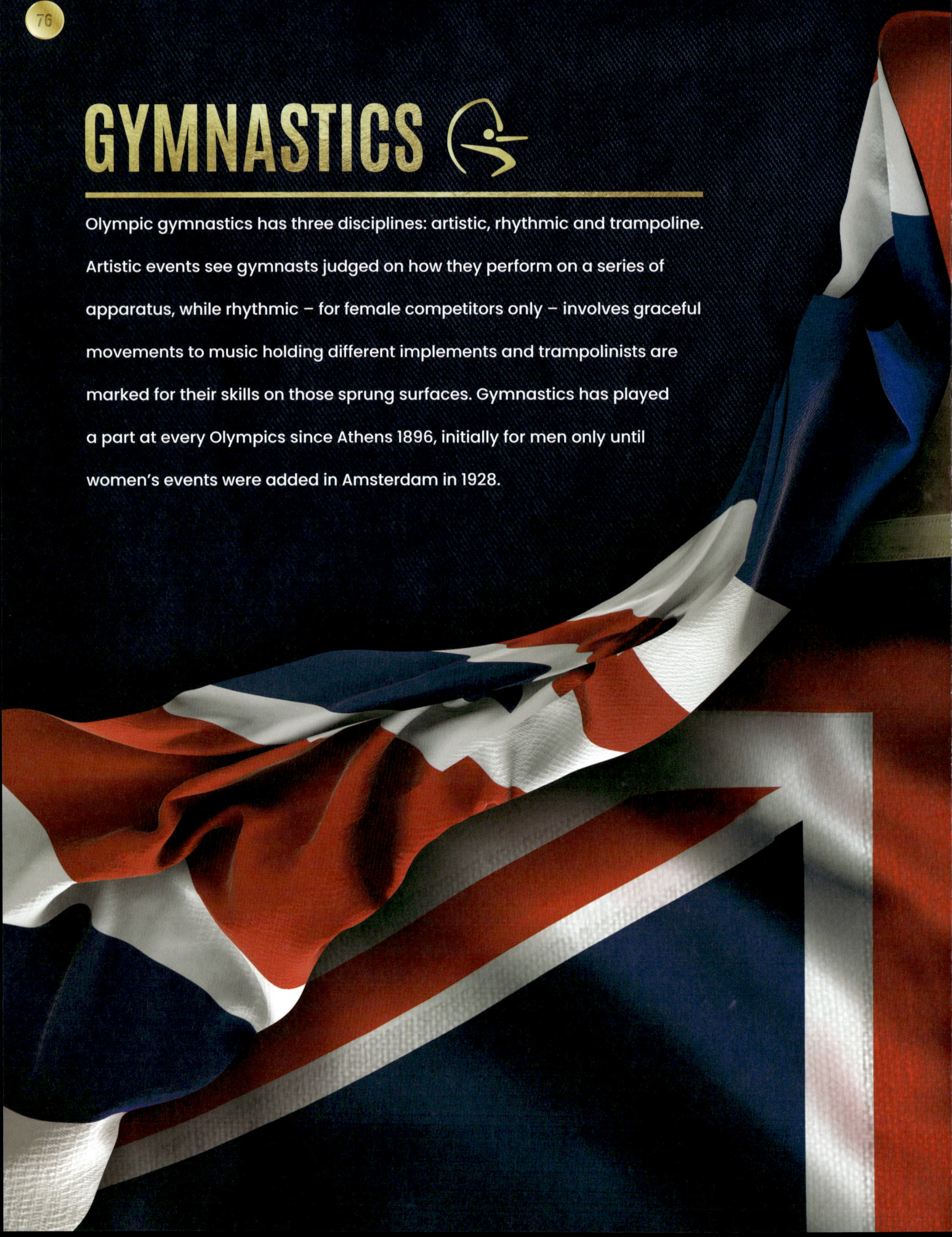

BRYONY PAGE

Bryony Page has described her personal philosophy as: "If you know you still enjoy it, just keep going and fight through those hard times." The competitor who began trampolining at the age of nine has certainly endured setbacks before becoming the first female British gymnast to win medals across two separate Olympics. Injury and illness forced her to miss the London 2012 Games, while she also suffered struggles with "the yips" – a nervous anxiety condition which can block sportspeople from carrying out certain actions. In the build-up to Rio 2016 she spent ten months out with a bone stress injury in her leg yet went on to win silver in the women's trampoline event – Britain's first ever trampolining Olympic medal. Her points score of 56.040 was only beaten by Canada's Rosannagh MacLennan with 56.465. Page took with her to Rio her "lucky" dinosaur lunchbox, having graduated in biology the previous year from Sheffield University having written a dissertation studying sounds dinosaurs made. Another two years of injury woes followed after Rio, this time afflicting Page's ankle, yet she added bronze in the same event at the Tokyo 2020 Games. Her other achievements include four Trampoline Gymnastics World Championships golds – two individual, two team.

ABOVE RIGHT: Bryony Page poses on the podium with her bronze medal after in the women's final of the Trampoline Gymnastics event during Tokyo 2020 Olympic Games

BORN: December 10, 1990, in Crewe, Cheshire

EVENT: Gymnastics – trampoline

SILVER (1): Individual trampoline (Rio 2016)

BRONZE (1): Individual trampoline (Tokyo 2020)

TOTAL MEDALS: ⚪🟡

LOUIS SMITH

One contestant on Britain's TV music talent show *The X Factor* in 2009 would have been a familiar face to many yet when he told the judging panel he was a gymnast, music mogul Simon Cowell asked: "Are you any good?" Louis Smith replied: "Not bad – I have got an Olympic bronze medal." He insisted his brief bid for pop stardom on that series was just for "fun" but his gymnastics achievements are seriously impressive. That pommel horse gold at the Beijing 2008 Olympic was the first medal for a British gymnast since Walter Tysall's all-around silver in London 100 years earlier and the country's first for any gymnastics since the women's team claimed bronze at Amsterdam 1928. Smith came agonisingly close to gold at London 2012, finishing tied on 16.066 points apiece with Hungary's Krisztián Berki only for his rival to have a higher execution score – based on the difficulty level of routines performed. Smith, who won BBC's *Strictly Come Dancing* series later that year, retired from gymnastics in 2014 but returned to again win silver at Rio 2016, this time only beaten by compatriot Max Whitlock with whom he had won team all-around bronze at London 2012. Smith became the first British gymnast to claim medals at three separate Olympics.

MAX WHITLOCK

Nineteen-year-old Max Whitlock served notice of his gymnastics abilities – especially on his favoured equipment, the pommel horse – with a pair of bronze medals at the London 2012 Olympics, and has gone on to become the world's most successful pommel horse performer and Britain's most decorated gymnast. He, Louis Smith, Sam Oldham, Daniel Purvis and Kristian Thomas won mean's team all-around that summer – in a event combining floor, pommel horse, rings, vault, parallel bars and horizontal bar routines, Britain's first men's gymnastics medal for 100 years. They had actually looked on course for silver, before a successful appeal by the Japanese competitors over scoring. Four years later, Whitlock became Britain's first gymnast ever to win Olympics individual gold, in the floor exercise – and added another just two hours later in the pommel horse, in which he'd won his other bronze at London 2012. He decided to try defending only one of these titles at the pandemic-delayed Tokyo 2020 Games in 2021, dropping the floor exercise but yet again triumphing in the pommel horse. He said afterwards: "People doubted me during this Olympic cycle and there were challenges and times when things didn't go to plan. But that just made it more rewarding in the end." He has also won three Artistic Gymnastics World Championships golds in the pommel horse.

BORN: January 13, 1993, in Hemel Hempstead, Hertfordshire

EVENT: Artistic gymnastics – floor exercise, pommel horse, team all-around

GOLD (3): Floor exercise, pommel horse (Rio 2016), Pommel horse (Tokyo 2020)

BRONZE (3): Pommel horse, team all-around (London 2012), Team all-around (Rio 2016)

TOTAL MEDALS:

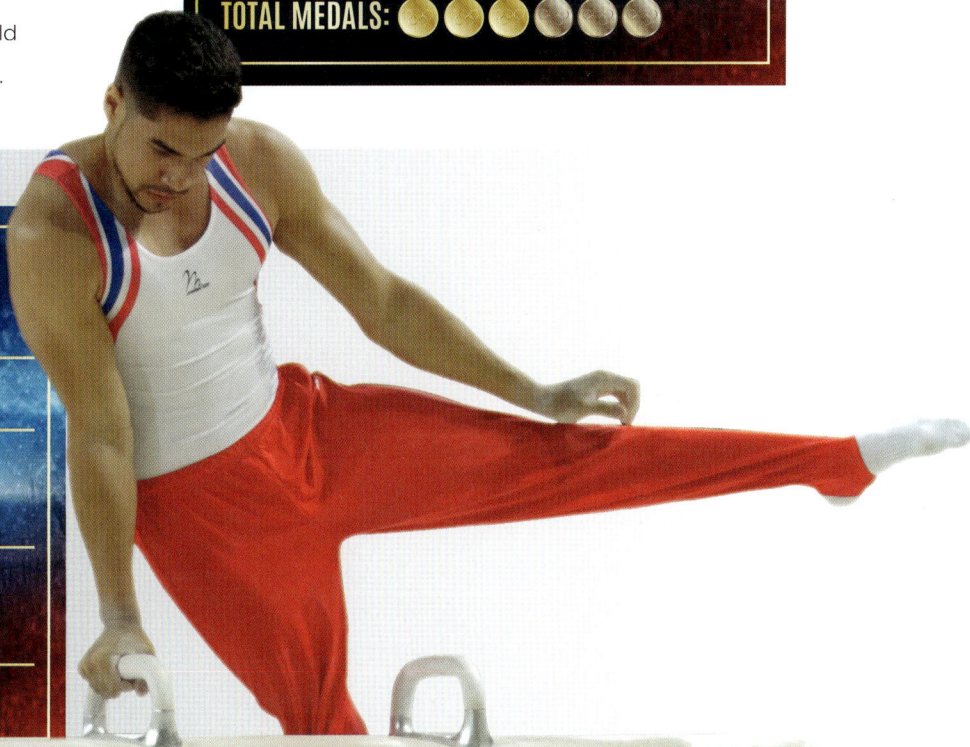

BORN: April 22, 1989, in Peterborough, Cambridgeshire

EVENT: Artistic gymnastics – pommel horse

SILVER (2): Pommel horse (London 2012), Pommel horse (Rio 2016)

BRONZE (2): Pommel horse (Beijing 2008), Team all-around (London 2012)

TOTAL MEDALS:

HOCKEY

Field hockey was first played at the Olympics in London in 1908 but did

not return until 20 years later in Amsterdam, though has been an

ever present since. The women's team event was only introduced,

however, at the 1980 Olympics in Moscow. Nine different countries have

won Olympics hockey gold, with India leading the way on eight triumphs –

followed by the Netherlands with six and Australia, Britain and Germany

on three apiece. The Netherlands has won the most hockey medals

overall, 18, with Australia and Britain on 13 each and India 12.

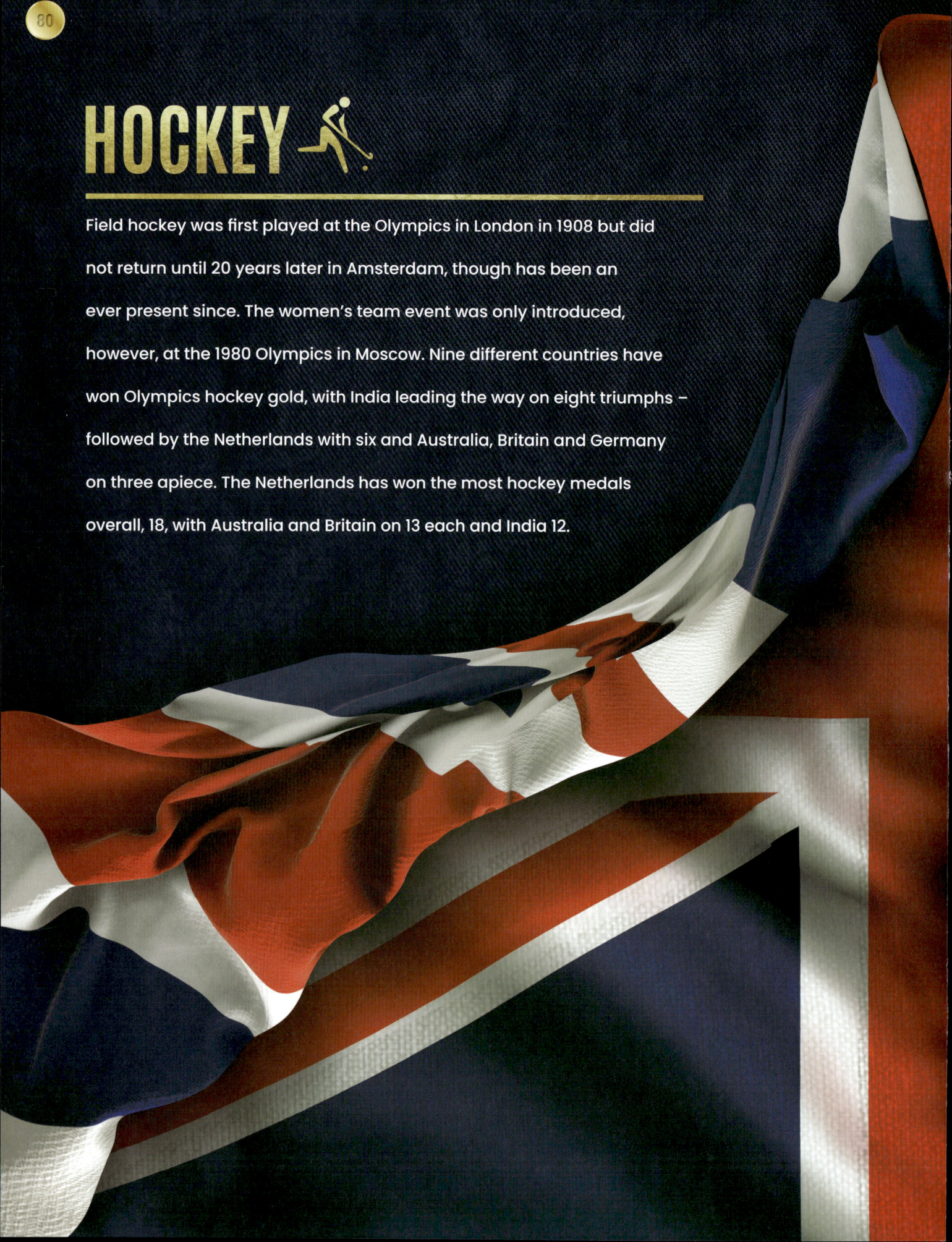

MADDIE HINCH

BORN: October 8, 1988, in West Chiltington, West Sussex

EVENT: Hockey

GOLD (1): Rio 2016

BRONZE (1): Tokyo 2020

TOTAL MEDALS: ⚫⚪

There were no half-inches to Maddie Hinch's heroics as she claimed a major hand in Britain's women's hockey gold at the 2016 Rio Olympics. After her side's final against the Netherlands ended in a 3-3 draw, Hinch saved not one, two nor three but all four of the Dutch penalties to claim only the country's fourth Olympics hockey gold and the first for Britain's women. Hinch had consulted a little black book containing notes on her opponents ahead of the shoot-out. She later took a break from hockey in 2018 but returned in time to help qualify for the Tokyo 2020 Olympics and then, after semi-finals defeat, she played masterfully in goal to help Britain claim consolation bronze by beating India 4-3 in the medal play-off. A teacher at primary school had highlighted her hockey potential after being impressed by her diving and catching when playing rounders and although Hinch was initially reluctant to go in goal, she became one of the world's top specialists – and played 97 times for England, 60 games for Great Britain, despite being disappointed to miss out on selection for London 2012 where Britain's women also won bronze. Hinch – nicknamed not only "The Wall" but also "Mad Dog" by team-mates – retired from internationals in March 2023 though continued playing for her club, HC Tilburg in Holland.

SEAN KERLY

Australia's men were many people's favourites to win their first Olympics gold medal in 1984 in Los Angeles, after two years' unbeaten, or else after disappointment there then four years later in Seoul. On both occasions they were defied by Great Britain – and winning goals each time by Sean Kerly. After Australia lost their semi-final 1-0 to Pakistan, and Britain theirs to West Germany by the same scoreline, the bronze medal play-off finished 3-2 to Britain – with Kerly scoring the winner. In Seoul in 1988 he hit a hat-trick against the same opponents, including the winner in another 3-2 victory – this time with just a minute and 22 seconds left on the clock in their semi-final. Kerly also scored in the 1988 final, along with two by Imran Sherwani, as Britain beat West Germany 3-1 to claim gold – having lost to the same opponents not only in Los Angeles but also 2-1 earlier in 1988 in the preliminary round. Kerly scored eight that summer, behind only the nine hit by Floris Jan Bovelander who won bronze with the Netherlands. Kerly, who won 99 caps for Great Britain and 93 for England, has told of wanting to play football as a striker as a child – only for his father to move the family back to birthplace Kent from Manchester, and he was sent to Chatham House Grammar School where pupils could not play football but were encouraged to take up hockey instead.

Maddie Hinch was not the only one to stand up to the pressure of penalty shoot-out which ultimately brought the first women's Olympic hockey gold for Britain in Rio in 2016. The goalkeeper saved all four of the Netherlands' efforts, but her team-mates still needed to score – and it was Helen Richardson-Walsh and Hollie Webb who found the net for a 2-0 victory, following a 3-3 draw in normal time. Richardson-Walsh had also scored in semi-final, helping the side – captained by her wife Kate – to a 3-0 victory over New Zealand. This was Helen Richardson-Walsh's fifth Olympics, having first featured as a 18-year-old at the 2000 Games in Sydney – Britain's youngest player that summer – and also been a bronze medallist at London 2012. Back then in London the Netherlands went on to gold, with Britain beaten 2-1 by Argentina in the semi-finals before defeating New Zealand 3-1 in the medal play-off in the London Olympic Park's Riverbank Arena. Helen Richardson married international team-mate Kate Walsh in 2013, both taking the surname Richardson-Walsh. Their Rio 2016 triumph made them the first same-sex married couple to win Olympic gold on the same team – and the first British married pair to triumph at an Olympics on the same side since sailors Cyril and Dorothy Wright at the 1920 Games in Antwerp.

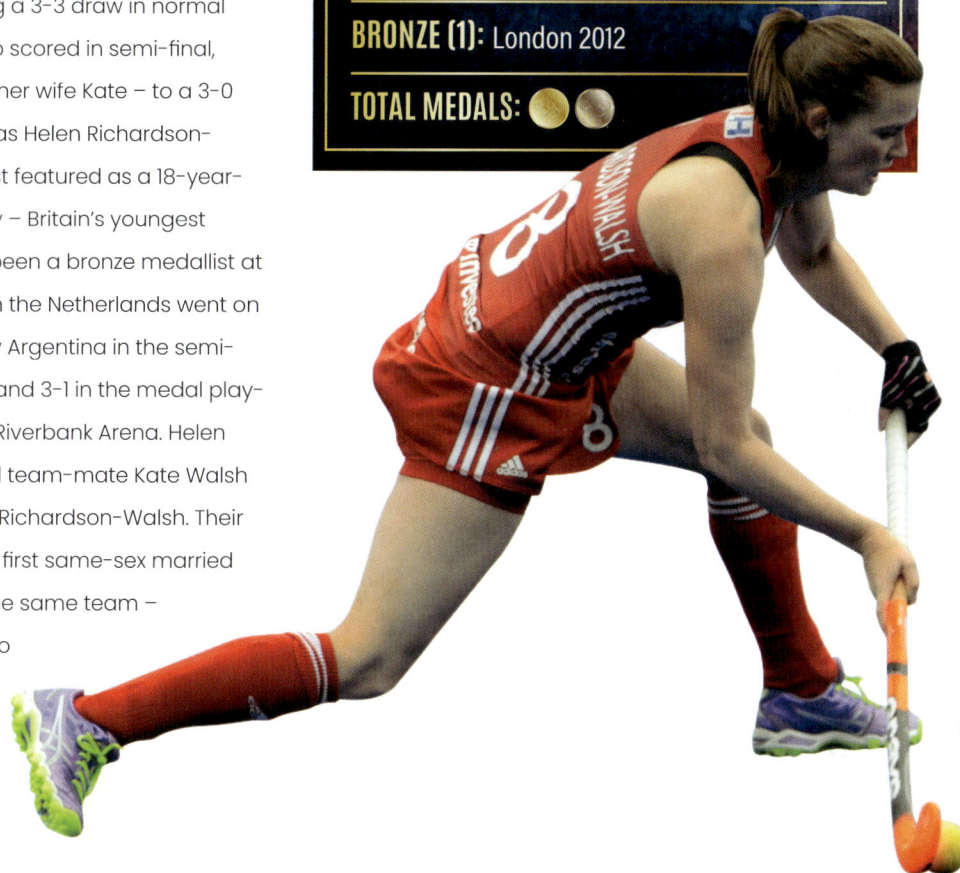

HELEN RICHARDSON-WALSH

BORN: September 23, 1981, in Hitchin, Hertfordshire

EVENT: Hockey

GOLD (1): Rio 2016

BRONZE (1): London 2012

TOTAL MEDALS: ●●

BORN: January 29, 1960, in Whitstable, Kent

EVENT: Hockey

GOLD (1): Seoul 1988

BRONZE (1): Los Angeles 1994

TOTAL MEDALS: ●●

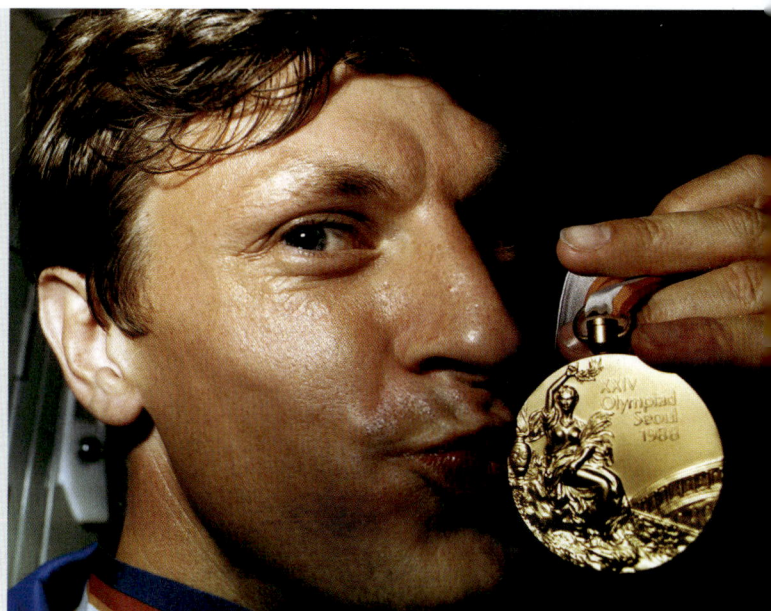

RIGHT: Sean Kerly kisses his 1988 Olympic gold medal at Heathrow

KATE RICHARDSON-WALSH

Kate Richardson-Walsh enjoyed the perfect farewell at Rio 2016 she retired from hockey with a record 375 caps for her country, Olympic gold as captain and the honour of carrying the Team GB flag at the Summer Olympics' closing ceremony. She led her side to eight wins out of eight in Brazil. She had made her Olympics debut in Sydney in 2000 – in the squad alongside future wife Helen Richardson – and also skippered the country to bronze at London 2012, though Helen stood in for her as captain for three matches that summer after Kate suffered a broken jaw when hit by a stick in the opening game against Japan. After five EuroHockey Nations Championships bronzes and a silver in 2013, she had led England to gold in London in 2015 – meaning she bowed out a year later as both European and Olympic champion. She said after the victory over the Netherlands: "To win an Olympic medal with your wife there next to you, taking a penalty in the pressure moments, is so special." She and Kate were later invited to a state banquet at Buckingham Palace in 2018 for the King and Queen of the Netherlands – and Kate has said she feared the special guests were horrified to see two of the hockey players who denied their nation Olympic gold were there.

BORN: May 9, 1980, in Withington, Manchester

EVENT: Hockey

GOLD (1): Rio 2016

BRONZE (1): London 2012

TOTAL MEDALS:

BELOW: Kate Richardson-Walsh in action for Great Britain v Japan

Before Sean Kerly and company won Olympic gold in Seoul in 1988, Britain's only two previous triumphs at the Games were back in 1908 in London and 12 years later in Antwerp. On both occasions one of the star players was the so-called "Prince of Centre-Forwards", Stanley Shoveller. The 1908 Olympics was the first to feature hockey and actually featured four different British sides in a six-team group – made up respectively of players from England finishing first, Ireland second, Scotland third and Wales fourth, ahead of Germany in fifth and France sixth. The English players beat France 10-1, Scotland 6-1 and Ireland in the final game 8-1, with Reggie Pridmore top-scoring with 10. Shoveller's second triumph in 1920 again saw Britain achieve three victories as they finished ahead of silver medallists Denmark, bronze medallists Belgium and France again last. Shoveller was the only Olympic champion to feature at both events – and scored 12 of Britain's 17 goals, to go with his seven at London 1907. In between the two Olympics, stockbroker Shoveller served with the Rifle Brigade during the First World War and was awarded the Military Cross, Britain's third-highest military decoration. He later served as vice-president of the Hockey Association and also as an England national team selector.

STANLEY SHOVELLER

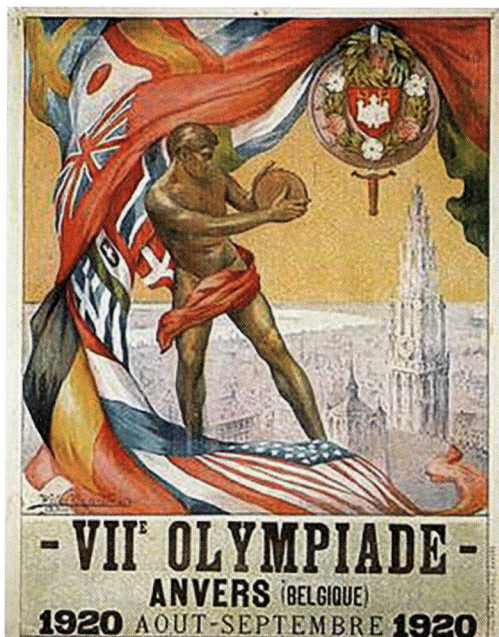

BORN: September 2, 1881, in Kingston-upon-Thames, Surrey

DIED: February 24, 1959, aged 77, in Broadstone, Dorset

EVENT: Hockey

GOLD (2): London 1908, Antwerp 1920

TOTAL MEDALS:

ABOVE: Poster of the 1920 Olympic Games

ABOVE: Winners of the 1908 Olympics Hockey Gold in London: N.I. Wood, L.C. Baillou, H.S. Freeman, A.F. Noble, E.W. Page, J.Y. Robinson, E. Green, R.G. Kidmore, S.H. Shoveller, G. Logan and P.M. Rees

MODERN PENTATHLON

The modern pentathlon, which first appeared at the Olympics in 1912, is based on the premise of a nineteenth-century soldier behind enemy lines – testing competitors' skills in riding an unfamiliar horse, fencing, swimming, shooting and running. The ancient Olympics had featured a pentathlon which included a foot race, wrestling, long jump, javelin and discus. As well as individual contests, a team event was included from 1952 in Helsinki until Barcelona in 1992, while the women's modern pentathlon was only added to the Olympic roster in Sydney in 2000. The event used to be stretched across four or five days, but this was reduced to just one at the Tokyo 2020 Games with plans to compress the semi-finals and finals into 90-minute periods at Paris 2024.

JOE CHOONG

The Tokyo 2020 Olympics might have been delayed by a year by the Covid-19 pandemic but it also finally brought a first men's modern pentathlon gold for Britain after 109 years of waiting, since the event's first appearance at the 1912 Games in Stockholm. Joe Choong triumphed in the five-discipline event which combines air pistol shooting, fencing, freestyle swimming, riding and cross-country running. That did come just two days after compatriot Kate French won the women's event, making this the first time one country had won both modern pentathlon contests at one Games. His overall score of 1,482 was not only five ahead of his closest challenger, Egypt's Ahmed El-Gendy, but also set a new Olympic record. Choong managed to sprint ahead of El-Gendy on their last bend of their climactic 800m race to confirm gold – and later told of being inspired by watching French's earlier triumph while feeling under pressure to "get one for the boys". Choong, whose parents were both doctors, followed up his Olympic glory by winning World Modern Pentathlon Championships golds in Alexandria in Greece the following year and again back home in England in Bath in 2023.

BORN: May 23, 1995, in Orpington, Kent

EVENT: Modern pentathlon

GOLD (1): Tokyo 2020

TOTAL MEDALS: 🥇

STEPH COOK

After being competed only among men since the 1912 Olympics, the modern pentathlon was first run as a women's event at Sydney in 2000 – where the inaugural champion proved to be Britain's Steph Cook. Although born and brought in Scotland, she became a true Oxbridge competitor – taking up rowing while studying at Cambridge University's Peterhouse College before switching to modern pentathlon when she finishing her clinical medicine course at Oxford University's Lincoln College. Her Oxford modern pentathlon team-mates would find themselves on the medal podium for the event at Sydney 2000 – the US's Emily deRiel winning silver, Kate Allenby of Britain bronze. Yet it was Cook who was at the top, brandishing gold, after putting her career as a doctor on hold. She triumphed on the final day of that summer's Games despite having been outscored by deRiel in the first four events. Strong runner Cook made up 49 seconds to win the climactic 3000m run, overtaking DeRiel in the final 300m and finishing with an overall score of 5,318 – ahead of second-place 5,310 and Allenby's 5,273. Cook followed that up with world and European championship successes the following year before retiring. Allenby would finish eighth in the same event at the Athens 2004 Olympics then directed the fencing discipline of the modern pentathlon at London 2012.

Just as compatriot Joe Choong in her aftermath, Kate French won modern pentathlon gold for Britain at Tokyo 2020 and with an Olympic record score. She finished with a total of 1,385 points – comfortably clear of the 1,370 racked up by Lithuania's Laura Asadauskaitė, who had won gold at London 2012. The 2020 event culminated in four back-to-back 800m "laser runs" – with three rounds of pistol shooting in between – which began with French placed fifth, the position she finished in at Rio 2016. Yet here she raced through the field to cross the line in first, then collapsed on the track in relief and celebration at clinching gold – Britain's first in the modern pentathlon since Steph Cook in Sydney in 2000. French had earlier performed comfortably on her horse Clintino in the show jumping part of the event – in stark contrast to Germany's Annika Schleu whose tearful tantrum on horse Saint Boy after it shied away then collided with an obstacle saw her plummet from 1st to 31st in the rankings. French's other honours include one world and six European championship titles. Britain did win another modern pentathlon Olympic gold, back in 1976 in Montreal, in the men's team event which was discontinued after Barcelona 1992.

KATE FRENCH

BORN: February 11, 1991, in Gravesend, Kent

EVENT: Modern pentathlon

GOLD (1): Tokyo 2020

TOTAL MEDALS: 🥇

RIGHT: Steph Cook won the gold medal for Modern Pentathlon at the Sydney Olympics in 2000

BORN: February 7, 1972, in Irvine, West Ayrshire

EVENT: Modern pentathlon

GOLD (1): Sydney 2000

TOTAL MEDALS: 🥇

ROWING

Bad weather forced planned rowing events at the first modern-day Games in Athens in 1896 to be called off, but it has been an Olympic sport since belatedly making its debut in Paris four years later. Men and women now have seven events apiece – with women only first taking part in Olympic rowing in Montreal in 1976 – ranging from individual races to those involving duos as well as teams of four and eight across a 2000km course. Since 1936 in Berlin, races have involved six competing boats – the only exception being Helsinki in 1952, when four or five took part in each.

JACK BERESFORD

Before Steve Redgrave, there was Jack Beresford. Long before the future Sir Steve rowed his way to six Olympic medals in five Games, the highest standards were set by Beresford and his five in four – including golds in the single sculls at Paris 1924, coxless fours at Los Angeles 1932 and double sculls in Berlin four years later. His Olympic career actually began in Antwerp in 1920, when he finished second in the single sculls – just a second behind the US's Jack Kelly who finished the two-oars-per-person race in seven minutes and 35 seconds. Both men were too exhausted afterwards to even shake hands. Beresford went one better along the Seine in the same event four years later, beating the US's William Gilmore into second having finished behind him in the semi-finals. His coxless fours team-mates winning gold in Los Angeles were John Badcock, Hugh Edwards and Rowland George, finishing in 6:58.2, well clear of Germany's 7:03.0. At the Berlin Games in 1936, Beresford not only added a third gold – this time in the double sculls alongside Dick Southwood – but he also carried the British flag at the opening ceremony and became the first rower to compete at five Olympics. His father Julius Beresford had won rowing silver as part of Britain's coxed four at the 1912 Olympics in Stockholm.

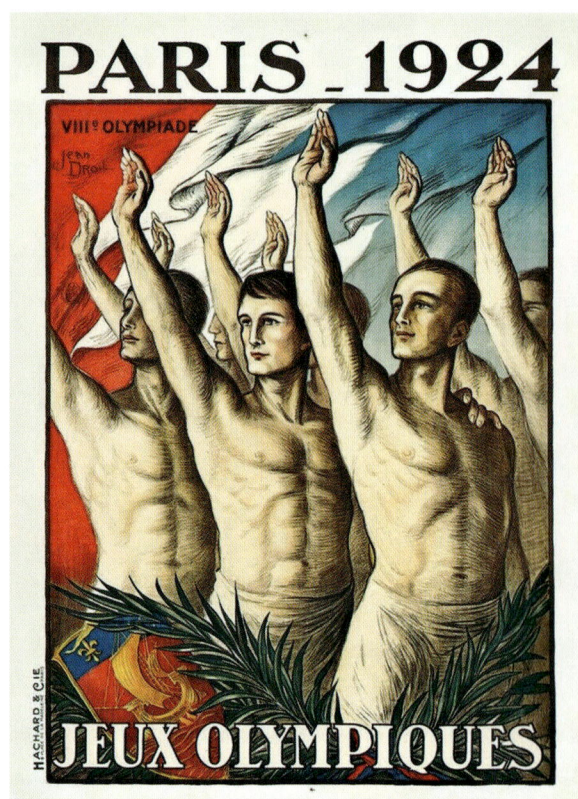

ABOVE: An official poster of the 1924 Paris Olympic Games

BELOW: Jack Beresford at the 1920 Antwerp Olympic Games

BORN: January 1, 1899, in Chiswick, London

DIED: December 3, 1977, aged 78, in Shiplake, Oxfordshire

EVENT: Rowing - coxless fours, double sculls, eights, single sculls

GOLD (3): Single sculls (Paris 1924), Coxless fours (Los Angeles 1932), Double sculls (Berlin 1936)

SILVER (2): Single sculls (Antwerp 1920), Eights (Amsterdam 1928)

TOTAL MEDALS:

KATHERINE GRAINGER

Always the bridesmaid, never the bride? Not so for Katherine Grainger, at London 2012, where she made it fourth time lucky by finally winning gold after silver at the three previous Olympics. She and Anna Watkins triumphed in the double sculls at Dorney Lake in Buckinghamshire, finishing in 6:55.82 minutes – ahead of silver medallists Kim Crow and Brooke Pratley from Australia. Grainger looked at the sky and raised her arms in the air as the glory sunk in, after her hat-trick of previous near misses. She even added another silver medal in Rio four years later, making her Britain's most decorated female Summer Olympian, before being voted in as the new chair of governing body UK Sport in April 2017. Grainger's silver medals included twice in the quadruple sculls – in 2000 with Gillian Lindsey and sisters Guin and Miriam Batten at Sydney 2000 and with Debbie Flood, Frances Houghton and Annabel Vernon in 2008 – as well as in the coxless pair with Cath Bishop at Athens 2004 and the double sculls with Vicky Thornley at Rio 2016. Grainger was made a Dame in 2017. Watkins, who set a new Olympic record with Grainger at London 2012 with 6:44.33 in their semi-final heat, previously won double sculls bronze at Beijing 2008 with Elise Laverick.

BELOW: One of the posters from the 2000 Sydney Olympic Games

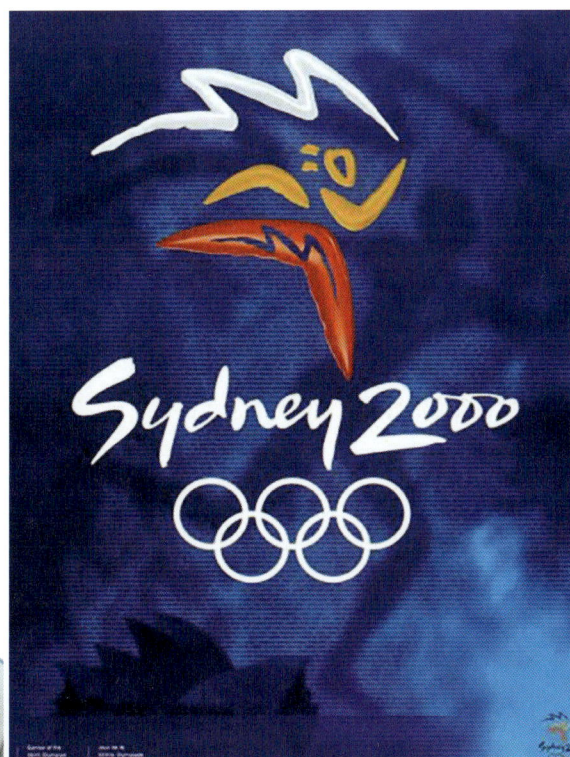

BORN: November 12, 1975, in Glasgow

EVENT: Rowing – coxless pair, double sculls, quadruple sculls

GOLD (1): Double sculls (London 2012)

SILVER (4): Quadruple sculls (Sydney 2000, Beijing 2008), Coxless pair (Athens 2004), Double sculls (Beijing 2008)

TOTAL MEDALS: ●●●●●

HELEN GLOVER

Great Britain, now rebranded as Team GB, won 65 medals including 29 golds at the home Olympics of London 2012 – making this the country's most successful since the same city staged the Games back in 1908. Yet after the opening ceremony on Friday, 27 July it was a nervous wait until the following Wednesday for the first of those golds, finally won by Helen Glover and Heather Stanning on Dorney Lake in the women's coxless pair – also Britain's first female Olympic rowing gold ever. The duo had set a new Olympic record of 6:57.29 in their semi-final before completing the final in 7:27.13, ahead of Australia's Kate Hornsey and Sarah Tait in 7:29.86. Glover, who had also excelled in hockey and cross-country running as a youngster, first worked as a teacher before giving this up in 2010 to concentrate on rowing. She and Stanning first teamed up in April that year and almost won their 2011 World Rowing Championships only to lose by 0.1 seconds on the line. They were inspired by this narrow miss towards Olympic gold at London 2012 – and successfully retained their title at Rio 2016, this time in 7:18.29 minutes, more than a second ahead of New Zealand's Genevieve Behrent and Rebecca Scown. Glover later became the first mother to row at an Olympics for Britain, finishing fourth with Polly Swann in the coxless pair at Tokyo 2020. She and naturalist, explorer and TV presenter Steve Backshall wed in 2016.

ABOVE RIGHT: Women's coxless pair gold medalists at the 2012 Summer Olympics; Heather Stanning and Helen Glover (R)

BORN: June 17, 1986, in Truro, Cornwall

EVENT: Rowing – coxless pair

GOLD (2): Coxless pair (London 2012, Rio 2016)

TOTAL MEDALS: 🥇🥇

MATTHEW PINSENT

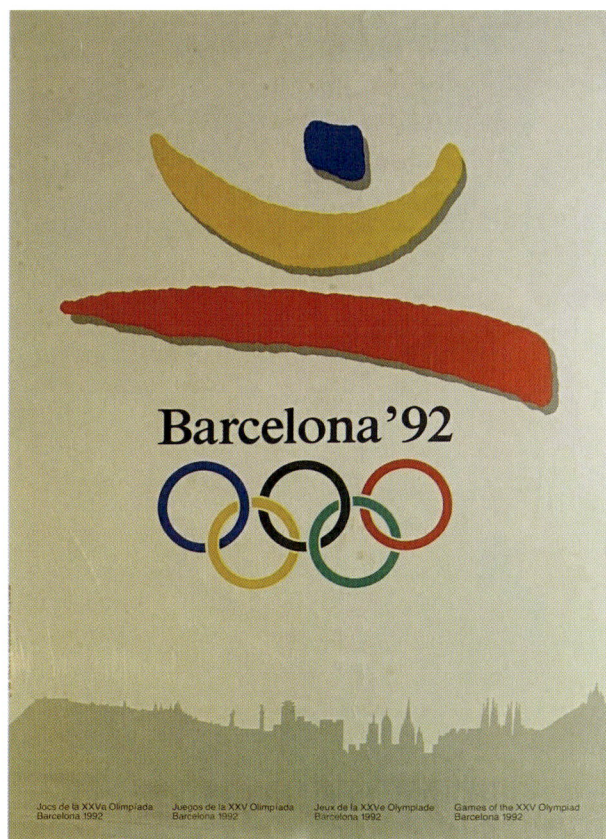

icar's son Matthew Pinsent was an initially reluctant schoolboy rower, only choosing the sport over rugby because his friends did so first – yet he went from only good enough for the second team at Eton to becoming a four-time Olympic gold medallist and another sporting knight of the realm. Pinsent's immense physique and stamina – with lung capacity capable of taking in 8.5 litres of air – quickly impressed coaches at Oxford University where he helped beat Cambridge in the 1990 and 1991 Boat Races. British Rowing's German technical consultant Jürgen Gröbler teamed him up with Steve Redgrave, eight years older, in 1990 – and their first world title the following year began a nine-year unbeaten run including Olympic golds in the double sculls at Barcelona 1992 and Atlanta 1996, Britain's only gold of that Games. For the 2000 Olympics in Sydney the pair joined forces with James Cracknell and Tim Foster in the coxless four, again winning gold in Pinsent and Redgrave's 100th and final race together. Four years later in Athens, Pinsent won his fourth gold, again in the coxless four, this time alongside Cracknell, Ed Coode and Steve Williams – clinching victory over Canada by just eight-hundredths of a second. Pinsent retired two months later and was knighted in the following New Year's Honours list.

BORN: October 10, 1970, in Holt, Norfolk

EVENT: Rowing - coxless pair, coxless four

GOLD (4): Coxless pair (Barcelona 1992, Atlanta 1996), Coxless four (Sydney 2000, Athens 2004)

TOTAL MEDALS: ●●●●

Jocs de la XXVa Olimpíada Barcelona 1992   Juegos de la XXV Olimpiada Barcelona 1992   Jeux de la XXVe Olympiade Barcelona 1992   Games of the XXV Olympiad Barcelona 1992

ABOVE: Barcelona 1992 Olympic Games - one of the official posters

HEATHER STANNING

eather Stanning was tipped for Olympic gold in her school yearbook, having risen to the heights of head girl at independent Gordonstoun School in Moray, Scotland – the alma mater of King Charles III. She took up rowing in 2006 and within six years had fulfilled that promise with Team GB's first gold of London 2012, alongside Helen Glover in the women's coxless pair, a title they would successfully defend in Rio four years later. Stanning had been given special dispensation from her role in the British Army to take part in the 2012 Games – having graduated from Sandhurst and joined the Royal Artillery in 2008. Both her parents Timothy and Mary served in the Royal Navy. Stanning herself was posted to Helmand Province in Afghanistan for a tour of

duty in 2013, before resuming her partnership with Glover – saying it was "brilliant to be back racing with Helen". Glover has described them as "great friends on and offer the water". Their renewed partnership brought not only that second Olympic gold at Rio 2016 but also two World Rowing Championships golds and two silvers. Stanning returned to military service after announcing her rowing retirement following the 2016 Games.

BORN: January 26, 1985, in Yeovil, Somerset

EVENT: Rowing – coxless pair

GOLD (2): Coxless pair (London 2012, Rio 2016)

TOTAL MEDALS: 🥇🥇

RIGHT: Heather Stanning (L) and Helen Glover compete in the women's pair final A to win the gold medal in the rowing event on Day 5 of the London 2012 Olympic Games at Eton Dorney

An exhausted Steve Redgrave told TV crews after clinching his fourth Olympic gold in Atlanta 1996: "If anyone sees me going anywhere near a boat again, they have my permission to shoot me." Yet four years later he was on top of the winners' podium for a then-British record fifth time, this time in Sydney. Redgrave had overcome health setbacks such as being diagnosed with ulcerative colitis in 1992 and diabetes five years later. That coxless pairs victory in Atlanta, alongside Matthew Pinsent who would go on to end his career with four Olympic titles of his own, was Great Britain's solitary gold at the Atlanta Games. Redgrave was knighted in 2001 for services to rowing and was one of seven Olympic legends chosen to carry the torch inside London's Olympic Stadium in Stratford at the opening ceremony in 2012. His first Olympic gold, in Los Angeles in 1984, came in a boat with Martin Cross, Adrian Ellison, Andy Holmes and Richard Budgett, before he and Holmes teamed up for gold four years later, Pinsent accompanied him to glory in 1992 and 1996 and those two plus James Cracknell and Ed Coode triumphed in 2000. That last victory saw the British team lead from the start yet were closely pursued by their Italian rivals, with Redgrave and Co ultimately finishing in a time of 5:56.24 – marginally ahead of Italy's 5:56.62.

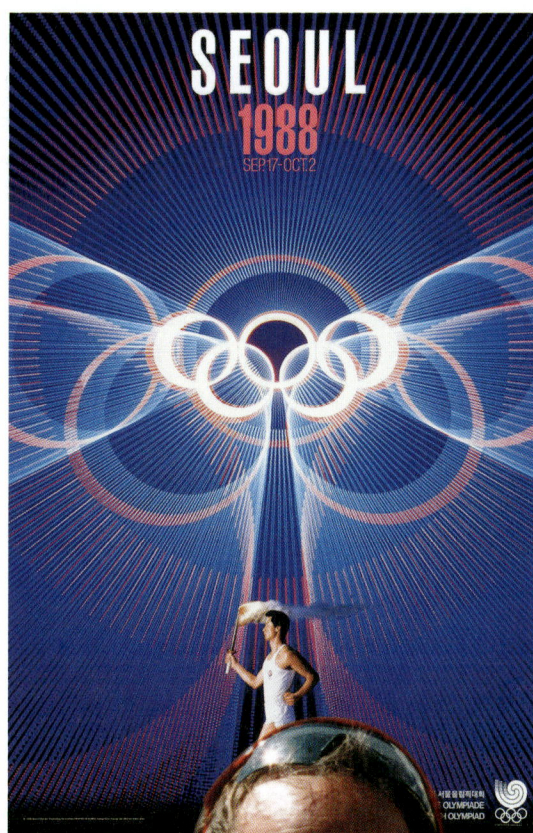

ABOVE RIGHT: One of the official posters of the 1988 Seoul Summer Olympics

BORN: March 23, 1962, in Marlow, Buckinghamshire

EVENT: Rowing – coxed four, coxed pair, coxless pair

GOLD (5): Coxed four (Los Angeles 1984), Coxless pair (Seoul 1988, Barcelona 1992), Coxless four (Sydney 2000)

BRONZE (1): Coxed pair (Seoul 1988)

TOTAL MEDALS:

STEVE REDGRAVE

SAILING

Competitors taking part in Olympic sailing events are awarded points correlating to their finishing place in each of various race – one for first, two for second and so on – and the person with the fewest points at the end is declared the champion. Like rowing, it fell victim to bad weather at the 1896 Games in Athens but has been a part of every Summer Games since other than the 1904 Olympics in St Louis. The sizes, styles and names of different boats used in Olympic categories have varied widely over the years – men and women now have four different events each, while there are also two mixed events. Britain tops the overall medal table with 64 including 31 golds, ahead of the US's 61, 19 of which were gold.

BEN AINSLIE

Ben Ainslie, the Olympics' most successful sailor, has said he pursued the sport as a youngster to distract from being bullied at a new school. Yet his own aggressive tactics on the water have played a significant part in his success. He had to settle for silver at his first Olympics, in Atlanta in 1996, behind long-time rival and future friend Robert Scheidt from Brazil when both were disqualified for a false start in the final race – but the positions were reversed four years later in Sydney, when two protests from the Brazilian about Ainslie's approach in that last race were rejected. Ainslie competed in those two Games in the Laser class, for 4.24m, 59kg boats, but he switched to Finn for the following Olympics – involving larger 4.5m, 126kg dinghies. He prepared with a rigorous weight-training regime and consuming 5,000 calories each day, putting on 15kg – and triumphed in Athens despite being disqualified in the second race. Four years later in Beijing he achieved his aim of not only winning gold but marking it with victory in the final race. Ainslie carried the British flag at the opening ceremony of the London 2012 Olympics, where he would equal the four-gold sailing tally of Denmark's Paul Elvstrøm but with that added silver from making his Olympics debut as a 19-year-old in Atlanta. Ainslie was knighted in 2013.

BORN: February 5, 1977, in Macclesfield, Cheshire

EVENT: Sailing – Finn, Laser

GOLD (4): Laser (Sydney 2000), Finn (Athens 2004, Beijing 2008, London 2012)

SILVER (1): Laser (Atlanta 1996)

TOTAL MEDALS: 🥇🥇🥇🥇🥈

BELOW LEFT: Ben Ainslie of Great Britain celebrates overall victory after competing in the Men's Finn Sailing Medal Race on Day 9 of the London 2012 Olympic Games at the Weymouth & Portland Venue at Weymouth Harbour on August 5, 2012

BELOW: One of the official posters from the 1996 Atlanta Games

NICK DEMPSEY

BORN: August 13, 1980, in Norwich, Norfolk

EVENT: Sailing – windsurfing: Mistral, RS:X

SILVER (2): RS:X (London 2012, Rio 2016)

BRONZE (1): Mistral (Athens 2004)

TOTAL MEDALS: ⬤⬤⬤

Nick Dempsey is the only windsurfer to win three Olympic medals – stretching across 12 years, from his bronze in the Mistral event at Athens 2004 to twin RS:X silvers at London 2012 and Rio 2016. Brazil's Ricardo Santos was leading the field going into the 11th and final race in the Athens 2004 event, but fell to fourth in the overall rankings – with Dempsey overtaking him by a point to claim bronze, thanks to winning three of the last five races. He himself finished fourth in Athens four years later, when the Mistral boat was first replaced by the 2.86m, 15.5kg RS:X board with a 9.5sq m sail. In the London 2012 event held at the Weymouth and Portland National Sailing Academy in Dorset, Dempsey won two of his 11 races and finished with silver behind Dutch windsurfer Dorian van Rijsselberghe who won six – and it was the same top two four years later in Rio. Dempsey turned 36 on the eve of the final Rio 2016 race, knowing he was guaranteed silver – going on to sign off by crossing the line in fourth. Dempsey, windsurfing world champion in 2009 and 2013, was married for four years to yachtswoman Sarah Ayton – one of the so-called "Three Blondes In A Boat" who won Yngling gold for Britain at Beijing 2008.

HANNAH MILLS

Hannah Mills and Saskia Clark suffered relative disappointment at the London 2012 Olympics, "only" winning silver in the women's 470 class for 4.7m-long two-handed dinghies – despite going into the 11th and final race at Weymouth and Portland National Sailing Academy in Dorset on equal points for gold. Yet they only finished ninth in that race and second overall behind New Zealand's Jo Aleh and Polly Powrie. But they triumphed four years later in the same event in Rio, and Mills added a second gold at the delayed Tokyo 2020 Games – this time alongside Eilidh McIntyre. Mills was also one of Britain's flagbearers at the opening ceremony in Tokyo along with rower Mohamed Sbihi, who had won coxless four gold at Rio 2016. Welsh-born Mills had first tried sailing as a child during a family holiday in Cornwall. Clark was initially expected to pair up with Sarah Ayton at London 2012 but Mills stepped in after Ayton's decision to retire. Ayton had previously won two Olympic sailing golds of her own, in the Yngling class of three-person keelboats at both Athens 2004 with Shirley Robertson and Sarah Webb and Beijing 2008 with Webb and Pippa Wilson, the latter trio nicknamed "Three Blondes in a Boat". This category was discontinued after the 2008 Games.

BORN: February 29, 1988, in Cardiff

EVENT: Sailing – women's 470

GOLD (2): Women's 470 (Rio 2016, Tokyo 2020)

SILVER (1): Women's 470 (London 2012)

TOTAL MEDALS: ⬤⬤⬤

RODNEY PATTISSON

Three years after Britain's Julie Andrews won the Best Actress Oscar for playing Mary Poppins, a boat named after perhaps that movie musical's best-known song was used to clinch sailing gold for Britain at the 1968 Olympics in Mexico City. That was the first of two golds and a silver for sailor Rodney Pattisson in the Flying Dutchman category, for dinghies with a crew of two – one of the sailors attached with a rope and trapeze. Royal Navy submarine sub-lieutenant Pattisson's 1968 triumph alongside London lawyer Iain Macdonald-Smith was on a boat called *Supercalifragilisticexpialidocious*, although race officials shortened this to Superdocious. They finished first in six of their seven races, though were disqualified from the first, before coming in second in the last. Pattisson retained his title in Munich four years later, this time alongside Christopher Davies, before again winning the opening race at Montreal 1976 with Julian Brooke Houghton but ultimately having to settle for silver. Pattisson was given the honour of carrying the British flag at that summer's opening ceremony. He was denied a shot at another medal when the Royal Yachting Association boycotted the 1980 Games in Moscow. Britain's only subsequent medal in the Flying Dutchman was bronze for Jonathan Richards and Peter Allam in Los Angeles in 1984, before the category was discontinued after Barcelona 1992.

ABOVE: Rodney Pattisson and Christopher Davies in 1972

BORN: August 5, 1943, in Campbeltown, Argyll and Bute

EVENT: Rowing – Flying Dutchman

GOLD (2): Flying Dutchman (Mexico City 1968, Munich 1972)

SILVER (1): Flying Dutchman (Montreal 1976)

TOTAL MEDALS: 🥇🥇🥈

IAIN PERCY

The friendship between Iain Percy and Andrew Simpson, which began when they were seven, was such that – after winning gold in the Finn sailing class at the 2000 Olympics in Sydney, where Simpson was his understudy – Percy switched to the Star category for the Athens Games four years later. That was meant to give Simpson – nicknamed "Bart" after the TV cartoon character – his shot in the Finn class, only for Ben Ainslie to take the British qualifying place instead. Yet Percy and Simpson teamed up in the two-man Star boat event – in which Percy finished sixth with Steve Mitchell at Athens 2004 – and won gold together at the 2008 Beijing Games, then silver in London four years later. They had been second going into the final Beijing 2008 race but were encouraged by windy and rainy conditions that day and did what they needed to do, finishing fifth to clinch gold ahead of Brazil's silver medallists Robert Scheidt and Bruno Prada. Percy later said of the weather: "We are Brits – we live for that stuff." Simpson tragically died aged just 36 in December 2013, when crewing a catamaran which capsized in San Francisco Bay during training for the America's Cup.

Giles Scott admitted he was in "a pretty dark place" after missing out on selection for the London 2012 Olympics to Ben Ainslie – but what better way to lighten the mood than by then winning gold at not only the Rio 2016 but also the Tokyo 2020 Games? After spending most of the London 2012 regatta drinking, Scott has since admitted that disappointment gave him "the desire and the drive" to make sure Rio 2016 glory was his. He has now triumphed at both subsequent Games in the Finn, the heaviest Olympic boat category for single-handed sailors – and was so comfortable in Rio that he knew he had gold with a day to spare. Old rival Ainslie hailed him for winning "in serious style". Despite being born in Cambridgeshire, Scott's introduction to sailing was on dinghies on the Ottawa River after his family moved to Canada when he was one – though they returned to Britain five years later and was encouraged by his parents to take up junior competitive sailing. His Tokyo triumph meant Finn gold for Britain at six successive Olympics, going back to Iain Percy in Sydney in 2000 and taking in Ainslie's three back-to-back victories in between.

GILES SCOTT

BORN: June 23, 1987, in Huntingdon, Cambridgeshire

EVENT: Sailing – Finn

GOLD (2): Finn (Rio 2016), Tokyo 2020)

TOTAL MEDALS: 🥇🥇

LEFT: Iain Percy, during the kitting out of the British Olympic Team for the 2004 Olympic Games in Athens

BORN: March 21, 1976, in Southampton

EVENT: Sailing – Finn, Star

GOLD (2): Finn (Sydney 2000), Star (Beijing 2008)

SILVER (1): Star (London 2012)

TOTAL MEDALS: 🥇🥇🥈

TAEKWONDO

Taekwondo is a relative newcomer to the Olympics, only making its competitive debut at the Sydney Games in 2000 – having previously been a demonstration sport at Seoul 1988 and Barcelona 1992. Martial arts fighters in the men's event fight three three-minute rounds, while women have three two-minute rounds per match. Points are awarded for striking four different parts of an opponent's body – either with kicks of the feet or with the knuckles of the index and middle fingers. Competitors can also win by knocking their rival down for ten seconds. There are four events each for men and women – flyweight, featherweight, middleweight and heavyweight events.

JADE JONES

Nineteen-year-old Jade Jones won Britain's first taekwondo Olympics gold medal at the London 2012 Games – then the country's second four years later in Rio. Jones, who was encouraged to take up the sport aged eight by her grandfather Martin Foulkes, earned the nickname "The Headhunter" for her fighting style which targets her opponent's head, winning more points than delivering kicks to the body. Supporters in her Welsh home town of Flint raised £1,600 to help send her to qualifiers for the 2010 Summer Youth Olympics in Singapore where she won gold – two years before her first Summer Olympics triumph in London, beating China's Hou Yuzhuo 6-4 in the final. In Rio in 2016 she came up against Spain's Eva Calvo in the gold medal match, winning 16-7. Yet she was devastated to go out in the first round at the Tokyo 2020 Games, losing to Kimia Alizadeh who was part of the Refugee Olympic Team – the second time, after Rio 2016, for such a group to take part. Jones – who has told of pre-fight preparations which involve tucking into pasta and jelly – had been hoping to become the first person to win three Olympic golds for taekwondo.

ABOVE: Jade Jones proudly receives her gold medal during the 2016 Rio Olympics 57kg Taekwondo ceremony

BORN: March 21, 1993, in Bodelwyddan, Denbighshire

EVENT: Taekwondo – 57kg

GOLD (2): 57kg (London 2012, Rio 2016)

TOTAL MEDALS: ⬤ ⬤

Controversy surrounded Lutalo Muhammad's selection as Britain's male representative in the taekwondo at the London 2012 Olympics, ahead of the then-world number one Aaron Cook. Muhammad, nicknamed the "Walthamstow Warrior" for his east London upbringing, told of receiving hate mail following the decision in his favour. But he went on to win bronze in the 80kg division, beating Armenia's Arman Yeremyan 9-3 in a medal play-off. Muhammad went one better in Rio four years later, winning silver – though was only just denied the gold. He had been leading Cheick Sallah Cissé from the Ivory Coast 6-4 in the final only for his opponent to deliver a spinning hook kick in the very last second which was enough to inflict on Muhammad an 8-4 defeat. Muhammad wept in the arms of his father Wayne Mohammed, also his coach, and later called the agonising loss "the lowest moment of my life". Cook also competed in Rio, having switched allegiance to Moldova after gaining citizenship there – he finished 11th at the 2016 Games. After missing out on selection for Tokyo 2020, Muhammad indicated in 2022 his taekwondo career was over – and insisted he was now "at peace" with his Rio 2016 silver instead of gold.

BORN: June 3, 1991, in Walthamstow, London

EVENT: Taekwondo – 80kg

SILVER (1): 80kg (Rio 2016)

BRONZE (1): 80kg (London 2012)

TOTAL MEDALS: ⚪⚪

LUTALO MUHAMMAD

TENNIS

After being played at every Summer Olympics between 1896 and 1924, tennis was dropped as a medal event until 1988 in Seoul – though it did feature as a demonstration sport in Mexico City in 1968 and Los Angeles 16 years later. Mixed doubles was only restored to the Olympic roster at London 2012. The playing surface used varies between Olympics – predominantly hard courts have been used, though London 2012 was on grass and the Paris events are on clay as they were in Barcelona in 1992. Great Britain has won the most tennis medals at the Olympics – 43, including 17 golds – although the United States has the most golds, 21 of its 39 overall.

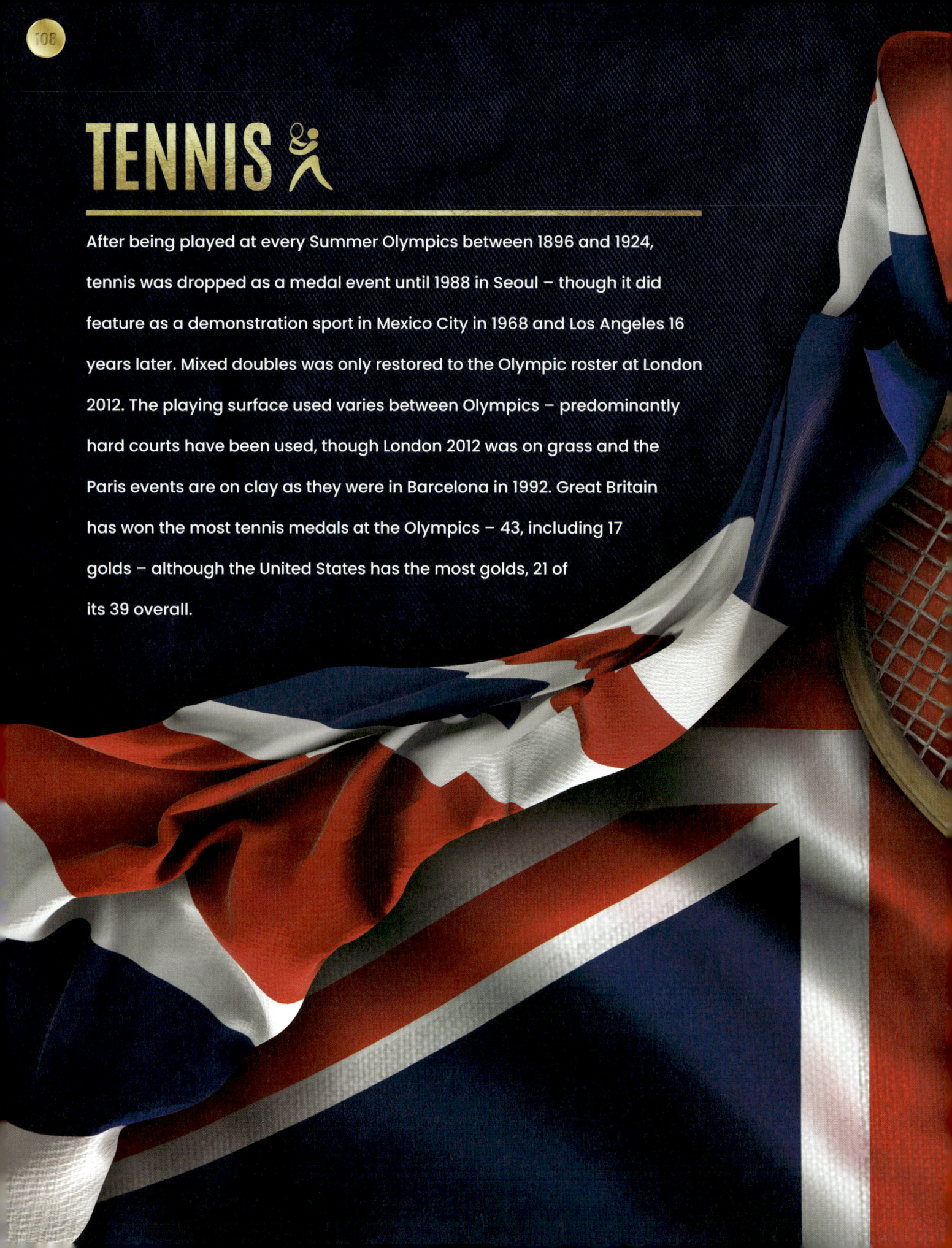

JOHN BOLAND

Irish-born, English-educated John Boland became a double Olympic champion in tennis at the first modern-day Games in Athens in 1896 – twice defeating in a final one of the men who convinced him to take part. Boland, a student at Christ Church college Oxford, was told about the forthcoming Games by a Greek friend Thrasyvoalos Manaos speaking at the Oxford Union. Then, on an Easter holiday trip to Athens, Boland was persuaded to sign up for the tennis tournament by Manaos and Dionysios Kasdaglis. Three victories put Boland through to the men's singles final, where he beat that same Kasdaglis 6-2, 6-2 – despite having considered forfeiting the match as a gesture of goodwill to the man who had encouraged him to enter in the first place. Boland teamed up with the man he defeated in the opening round, Germany's Fritz Traun, and the pair won the final 5-7, 6-3, 6-3 against Kasdaglis and Demetrios Petrokokkinos. Boland protested when Britain's Union Jack flag was raised, prompting officials to add the Irish flag. Boland served in the House of Commons as Irish Parliamentary Party MP for South Kerry between 1900 and 1918 and later received a papal knighthood. The proud Irish patriot died on St Patrick's Day in 1958.

BORN: September 16, 1870, in Dublin, Ireland

DIED: March 17, 1958, aged 87, in Westminster, London

EVENT: Tennis – men's singles, men's doubles

GOLD (2): Men's singles, men's doubles (Athens 1896)

TOTAL MEDALS: ⬤ ⬤

ABOVE: Boland (right) at the 1896 Olympics tennis men's doubles final

CHARLOTTE COOPER

Women's tennis was added to the Olympics at the second modern-day Games, held in Paris in 1900, where Britain's Charlotte Cooper became not only the first female tennis champion but the first woman to win any individual Olympics event. She beat France's Hélène Prévost in the women's singles final 6-1, 6-4 – then added another triumph in the mixed doubles, alongside Reginald Doherty, as they defeated Prévost and Great Britain and Ireland's Harold Mahony 6-2, 6-4. Cooper had already won three of her five Wimbledon singles titles by then. She reached eight consecutive Wimbledon singles finals between 1895 and 1904 – a record only surpassed by Martina Navratilova in 1990 – and remains the oldest woman to win the championship, aged 37 in 1908. Cooper, who went deaf at the age of 26, married lawyer Alfred Sterry the January after her Olympic triumphs. He later became president of the Lawn Tennis Association and their children both became involved in the sport – son Rex served as vice-chairman of the All England Club based at Wimbledon while daughter Gwen competed eight times in the annual tournament and played for Britain's Wightman Cup team. The only Brit to win women's singles gold at the Olympics since Cooper was Edith Hannam at Stockholm in 1912, in an indoor tournament which was held separately from an outdoor event.

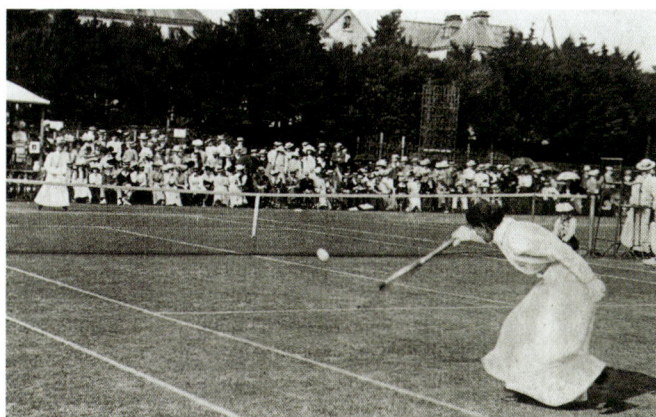

ABOVE: Charlotte Cooper Sterry vs Blanche Bingley Hillyard

BORN: September 22, 1870, in Ealing, London

DIED: October 10, 1966, aged 96, in Helensburgh, Argyll and Bute

EVENT: Tennis – women's singles, mixed doubles

GOLD (2): Women's singles, mixed doubles (Paris 1900)

TOTAL MEDALS: 🥇🥇

REGINALD DOHERTY

A century before American siblings Venus and Serena Williams won doubles gold at the Sydney Olympics, British brothers Reginald and Laurence Doherty had done similarly at the 1900 Games in Athens. The siblings comfortably defeated the US's Basil Spalding de Garmendia and France's Maxime Décugis 6-1, 6-1, 6-0 in the men's doubles final – a gold to go with the eight Wimbledon doubles titles they would win on eight occasions between 1897 and 1905. Laurie also won the men's singles that summer beating Great Britain and Ireland's Harold Mahony 6-4, 6-2, 6-3 in the final, after Reginald withdrew from the brothers' scheduled semi-final against each other. Reginald was rewarded with a second gold of his own, however, teaming up with women's singles champion Charlotte Cooper to win the mixed doubles tournament. He claimed a third Olympic gold eight years later in London, this time in the men's doubles alongside fellow Brit George Hillyard – winning 9-7, 7-5, 9-7 in the final against compatriots Josiah Ritchie and James Parke, having saved seven match points along the way. Reginald, the older brother by four years, won four Wimbledon singles titles while Laurence captured five as well as one US Open. Both brothers suffered from health problems even in their youth and Reginald died aged just 38, Laurence 43.

BORN: October 14, 1872, in Wimbledon, London

DIED: December 29, 1910, aged 38, in Kensington, London

EVENT: Tennis - men's singles, men's doubles, mixed doubles

GOLD (3): Men's doubles, mixed doubles (Paris 1900), Men's doubles (London 1908)

BRONZE (1): Men's singles (Paris 1900)

TOTAL MEDALS: ● ● ● ●

BELOW LEFT: One of the official posters of the 1900 Paris Summer Olympics

BELOW: Reginald Doherty (left) with his brother Laurence

ANDY MURRAY

Andy Murray finally ended British tennis fans' 76-year wait for a men's singles champion at Wimbledon in 2012 – but not in the All-England Club's annual tournament that July, where he lost his final against Switzerland's Roger Federer in four sets, but the following month when he won Olympic gold at the same venue. It was the same opponent too, and this time Murray comfortably saw off Federer 6-2, 6-1, 6-4. The following year he did win the actual Wimbledon title, beating Serbia's Novak Djokovic in the final – ending the hoodoo which appeared to exist since Fred Perry's last British male's singles triumph there in 1936 – and was champion again in 2016, against Canada's Milos Raonic. Murray had hoped for two golds at London 2012, but had to settle for silver alongside Laura Robson in the mixed doubles – defeated in three sets by Belarus's Victoria Azarenka and Max Mirnyi. But he successfully retained his Olympic title at the 2016 Rio Games, this time with a 7-5, 4-6, 6-2, 7-5 victory over Juan Martín del Potro of Argentina. Murray, who survived as an eight-year-old the Dunblane shooting massacre at his primary school in Scotland when a gunman killed 16 pupils and a teacher, was coached as a youngster by his mother Judy. He has also won the US Open in 2012 and would surely have claimed more Grand Slams had his time at or near the top in tennis not coincided with the careers of other all-time greats Federer, Djokovic and Rafael Nadal.

ABOVE RIGHT: Murray carrying the flag on behalf of athletes from Great Britain during the parade of nations at the 2016 Summer Olympics opening ceremony

BORN: May 15, 1987, in Glasgow

EVENT: Tennis - men's singles, men's doubles, mixed doubles

GOLD (2): Men's singles (London 2012, Rio 2016)

SILVER (1): Mixed doubles (London 2012)

TOTAL MEDALS: 🥇🥇🥈

TRIATHLON

The triathlon was introduced for men and for women at the 2000 Olympics in Sydney. It involves a 1500m swim in open water followed by 40km cycling and a 10,000-metre run. Britain tops the overall medals table with three golds, three silvers and two bronzes – and is the only country to win medals in all three of the men and women's individual events and the mixed relay which was first held at the Tokyo 2020 Games and involves four team members – two men and two women – each completing a 300m swim, an 8km cycle and a 2km run.

ALISTAIR BROWNLEE

The Brownlee brothers Alistair and Jonathan have five Olympic triathlon medals between them, including three golds – two of them won by elder sibling Alistair in the individual event at both London 2012 and Rio 2016, making him the only man to achieve such a double. Their father Keith was a keen runner and mother Cathy a swimmer, but they were introduced to the triathlon as youngsters by their uncle Simon Hearnshaw – and became familiar sights pounding the streets of their native Leeds in dogged daily training in the early hours, Alistair even doing so the day after his gruelling London 2012 victory. He was the best British finisher in the triathlon at the 2008 Beijing Olympics but only finished 12th overall. Yet he dominated the field four years later, completing the course in London's Hyde Park in a time of one hour, 46 minutes and 25 seconds – surging clear in the concluding 10km run ahead of Spain's Javier Gómez and with Jonathan in third. Alistair recorded an even better time of 1:45.01 at Rio 2016, in an event whose 1.5km-long swim was along Brazil's renowned Copacabana beach. Alistair told after his London 2012 success how an 89-year-old pensioner wrote to the brothers enclosing a £10 note for each one.

ABOVE RIGHT: Alistair Brownlee during the London 2012 Olympic & Paralympic Games Victory Parade, 10th September

BORN: April 23, 1988, in Dewsbury, West Yorkshire

EVENT: Triathlon - individual

GOLD (2): Individual triathlon (London 2012, Rio 2016)

TOTAL MEDALS: 🥇🥇

JONATHAN BROWNLEE

If Jonathan Brownlee ever felt overshadowed by his elder brother Alistair, winning bronze to his gold at London 2012 and silver to his gold at Rio 2016, then at last at the delayed Tokyo 2020 he could finally claim an Olympic title of his own. He was part of the four-person British team to triumph in the mixed relay triathlon, alongside Jess Learmonth, Georgia Taylor-Brown and Alex Yee – finishing in one hour, 23, minutes and 41 seconds, 14 seconds ahead of the US silver medallists. Yee also won silver in the men's individual triathlon that summer. That third-place finish for Jonathan, or Jonny, at London 2012 came after he was given a 15-second penalty for his transition between the swimming and cycling legs – a decision later criticised by Alistair who said it cost his brother silver, though he did finish 20 seconds behind Spain's Javier Gómez. Jonathan was taken to hospital after collapsing at the Hyde Park finishing line but was later given the all-clear. He suffered again from heat and exhaustion in the final moments when leading a 2016 World Triathlon Series race in Cozumel, Mexico – prompting Alistair to abandon his own chances of winning to help his brother over the line, Jonathan in second and the elder sibling third, while Rio 2016 bronze medallist Henri Schoeman from South Africa finished first.

No female triathlete has ever done better for Britain at the Olympics than Georgia Taylor-Brown's silver in the women's individual event at Tokyo 2020 – which she then followed up with gold in the mixed relay event, alongside Jonathan Brownlee, Jess Learmonth and Alex Yee. Tokyo 2020 was the first time a mixed relay triathlon was staged at an Olympics – with each of the four competitors on teams challenged to complete a combination of a 300m swim, a 6.8km cycle and a 2km run. Like the Brownlee brothers Taylor-Brown has been based for her training in Leeds, despite being born across the Pennines in Manchester. Her individual event in Tokyo saw her finish the course in one hour, 56 minutes and 50 seconds – 74 seconds behind Bermuda's first Olympic gold medallist Flora Duffy. Taylor-Brown's strong performance in the final run, again second only to Duffy, helped make up for losing 20 seconds when suffering a puncture late on in the cycling section. Taylor-Brown's other titles include golds at the 2020 World Triathlon Championships and the 2022 Commonwealth Games in Birmingham. Her Tokyo 2020 team-mate Learmonth, another Leeds triathlete, finished ninth in the women's individual triathlon that summer.

GEORGIA TAYLOR-BROWN

BORN: March 15, 1994, in Manchester

EVENT: Triathlon – individual, mixed relay

GOLD (1): Mixed relay triathlon (Tokyo 2020)

SILVER (1): Individual triathlon (Tokyo 2020)

TOTAL MEDALS: 🥇🥈

BORN: April 30, 1990, in Leeds, West Yorkshire

EVENT: Triathlon – individual, mixed relay

GOLD (1): Mixed relay triathlon (Tokyo 2020)

SILVER (1): Individual triathlon (Rio 2016)

BRONZE (1): Individual triathlon (London 2012)

TOTAL MEDALS: 🥇🥈🥉

WEIGHTLIFTING

One-hand lift and two-hand lift were the weightlifting contests at the 1896 Olympics in Athens, while the sport returned eight years later in St Louis with two-hand lift and all-around dumbbell categories. It was then absent again until 1920 in Antwerp, which introduced different weight categories to pit competitors of equivalent sizes against each other. One-handed lifts have not been used since the 1924 Olympics in Paris. Women's weightlifting was only introduced to the Games in 2000 in Sydney though has been a part of every Olympics since. Britain's one and only weightlifting triumph, back in 1896, also happened to be the country's first ever Olympic gold in any sport.

EMILY CAMPBELL

Emily Campbell only made her international debut weightlifting for Great Britain in 2018 but within three years she not only became European champion in the 87kg division in Moscow on April 21 but also, three months later in Tokyo, the country's first ever female Olympic weightlifting medallist. Her silver, again in the 87kg class, was also Britain's first at all in weightlifting since David Mercer won bronze in the 90kg at the 1984 Games in Los Angeles. Campbell was outside the medals in fourth, at Tokyo 2020, after the snatch round – which involves lifting a bar above the head in one movement. But in her follow-up clean and jerk – a two-part lift – managed 161kg, giving Campbell an overall score of 283kg, one ahead of the US's bronze medallist Sarah Robles. China's Li Wenwen was the clear winner, setting an Olympic record of 320kg overall. Campbell's performance set new British and Commonwealth bests. Campbell went on to retain her European title in both 2022 and 2023, while also winning 2022 Commonwealth Games gold in Birmingham and World Weightlifting Championships silver that same year. Campbell had taken up weightlifting as a youngster to help improve her performance in athletics – only to decide to concentrate on it as her main focus instead.

BORN: May 6, 1994, in Nottingham

EVENT: Weightlifting – 87kg

SILVER (1): 87kg (Tokyo 2020)

TOTAL MEDALS: ⚪

Launceston Elliot took part in the 100m, wrestling and rope climbing at the first modern-day Games in Athens in 1896, but it was in the weightlifting that he became Britain's first Olympic champion. He had to settle for silver first in the two-hand lift event – although he and Viggo Jensen both managed 111.5kg, Greek supervisor Prince George awarded the victory to Elliot's Danish rival for doing so "with better style". The one-hand lift contest was held almost immediately afterwards and Elliot triumphed by raising a 71kg barbell, while the injured Jensen could only do 57kg. Vicar's son Elliot was born in British colonial India before the family moved to Essex in England when he was 13. The well-built young man started training in weightlifting, becoming British champion aged 20 before heading to that first

Olympics. Four years after his Athens success Elliot was disappointed to find no weightlifting on the roster at the 1900 Paris Olympics, so instead took part in the discus competition – finishing 11th. He later travelled widely as a music-hall strongman showing off his strength – such as riding a bicycle while carrying two people perched on a bar across his shoulders. He also worked as a farmer in England before moving to Australia in 1923, where he died with cancer of the spine seven years later.

LAUNCESTON ELLIOT

ABOVE: Elliot on a postcard from 1910

ABOVE: Cover of the official report of the 1896 Athens Summer Olympics

BORN: June 9, 1874, in Hubli, India

DIED: August 8, 1930, in Melbourne, Australia

EVENT: Athletics – 100m; rope climbing; weightlifting – one-hand lift, two-hand lift; wrestling

GOLD (1): One-hand lift (Athens 1896)

SILVER (1): Two-hand lift (Athens 1896)

TOTAL MEDALS:

MISCELLANEOUS OLYMPIC EVENTS

Summer Olympics typically feature 28 mandatory sports with up to another six added for each addition. The likes of athletics, aquatics and cycling attract plenty of attention – and have featured much success for British competitors. But stars have also been made in many other events, whether sports which have a high worldwide profile such as football and golf or others which may slip beneath the mainstream public radar away from their appearances in the Games every four years. Some such as fencing date back to the very first modern-day Olympics, in Athens in 1896 – while the most recent new addition was skateboarding, at the delayed Tokyo 2020 Games in 2021.

SKY BROWN

t was in the park event that Sky Brown became Britain's youngest-ever Olympic medallist, aged 13 years and 28 days, at the Tokyo 2020 Olympics. She won bronze, behind Japanese pair Sakura Yosozumi, 19, taking gold and 12-year-old Kokona Hiraki silver – after the competitors were judged on their skills and tricks during 45-second runs inside a large bowl. Despite falling in her first two rounds, she scored 56.47 in her last attempt, to Yosozumi's 60.09 and Hiraki's 59.04. Brown herself was born in Japan to British father Stuart and Japanese mother Mieko and lives for half the year in the United States, but announced in 2019 she would compete for Great Britain. Self-tutored with the help of skateboarding videos on YouTube, she turned professional at the age of ten. She took part in the pandemic-delayed Tokyo Games in 2021 despite having suffered a severe fall from a halfpipe ramp in California in May 2020, fracturing her skull and breaking her left wrist and hand. But she recovered in time to become Britain's youngest ever competitor at a Summer Olympics, breaking the record previously set by 200m breaststroke swimmer Margery Hinton who was 13 years and 43 days old when she took part in the 1928 Olympics in Amsterdam.

RIGHT: Sky Brown competes during the Women's Skateboarding Park Preliminary Heat on day twelve of the Tokyo 2020 Olympic Games

BORN: July 7, 2008, in Miyazaki, Japan

EVENT: Skateboarding – park

BRONZE (1): Tokyo 2020

TOTAL MEDALS:

It was third time lucky for Liam Heath after twice giving up kayaking before taking it up again and going on to become Britain's most success canoeist at the Olympics. After being introduced to the sport as a ten-year-old, he gave it up while at Loughborough University to concentrate on his studies – then after resuming after graduation in 2006, he quit again in disillusionment at not being picked by GB Canoeing. But he was convinced to return in 2009 after the International Olympic Committee added 200m sprint canoe events at the 2012 Olympics in London. He teamed up with Jonathan Schofield and the pair won bronze in the London 2012 K-200m race held at Dorney Lake, known during the Games as Eton Dorney, in Buckinghamshire. The pair went one better in same race in Rio four years later, taking silver behind Spain's Saúl Craviotto and Cristian Toro, while Heath won individual gold in the K-1 200m race – following that up with bronze in the same event at the Tokyo 2020 Olympics. Heath retired in April 2022. His medal haul puts him ahead of Tim Brabants, who won a gold and two bronzes – among them a bronze in the K-1 1000m at the 2000 Sydney Games, Britain's first ever Olympics medal for canoeing.

LIAM HEATH

BORN: August 17, 1984, in Guildford, Surrey

EVENT: Canoeing – K-1 200m, K-2 200m

GOLD (1): K-1 200m (Rio 2016)

SILVER (1): K-2 200m (Rio 2016)

BRONZE (2): K-2 200m (London 2012), K-1 200m (Tokyo 2020)

TOTAL MEDALS:

Judo was first opened to women at the Olympics only at the 1992 Games in Barcelona, where Nicola Fairbrother became Britain's first medal-winning judoka. She took home silver after losing the 56kg division final to Spain's Miriam Blasco, in what could be called a later love match – the two competitors married each other in 2016. Winning bronze in the 66kg judo category that summer was Kate Howey, who eight years later in Sydney claimed silver in the 70kg division – only beaten by Cuba's Sibelis Veranes. Howey nevertheless became the first and still only British woman to win two Olympics judo medals, across four Games which are a joint record with London 2012 78kg bronze medal-winning judoka Karina Bryant. Howey carried Britain's flag at the Athens 2004 opening ceremony. Also at London 2012, Gemma Gibbons won silver in that same 78kg category – having been not only tipped for a medal but also coached by Howey. Gibbons pointed to the sky in tears on winning silver, in honour of her mother Jeanette who had died aged 49 of leukaemia two years earlier. Britain's other judo medals at the Olympics include 73kg silver for Neil Adams at Moscow 1980 and another for him at 81kg in Los Angeles four years later, as well as silver for Hackney sweet shop owner Dave Starbrook in the 100kg category at Munich 1972.

KATE HOWEY

BORN: May 31, 1973, in Andover, Hampshire

EVENT: Judo - 66kg, 70kg, 72kg

SILVER (1): 70kg (Sydney 2000)

BRONZE (1): 66kg (Barcelona 1992)

TOTAL MEDALS:

JUSTIN ROSE

North America dominated the Olympic medals for golf when it featured at the 1900 Games in Paris and in St Louis four years later – though the men's event in 1900 did see silver for Britain's Walter Rutherford and bronze for compatriot David Robertson. When golf finally returned to Olympics at the 2016 Games in Rio, it was a South African-born Brit who claimed gold in the men's event. Justin Rose first came to global attention when finishing fourth at the 1998 Open Championship as a 17-year-old amateur. He eventually won his first major 15 years later, triumphing at the 2013 US Open, before adding Olympic gold in 2016 as he finished

two strokes ahead of Sweden's Henrik Stensson on a course specially built for that summer's event at Rio's Marapendi Natural Reserve. Their duel came down to the final, 18th hole at climax of their fourth round – only for Stenson to finish with a one-over-par bogey while Rose putted for a one-under-par birdie. Rose, who had moved to Britain as a five-year-old with his family, had hit a hole-in-one on the opening day's play – the first golfer to do so at an Olympics – and would later proudly wear his gold medal around his neck at PGA tour event The Barclays. At Tokyo 2020, Britain's Paul Casey and Rory McIlroy were among six golfers beaten in a play-off for bronze by Chinese Taipei's Pan Cheng-tsung.

RIGHT: Justin Rose celebrates winning the men's golf at the Rio 2016 Olympic Games

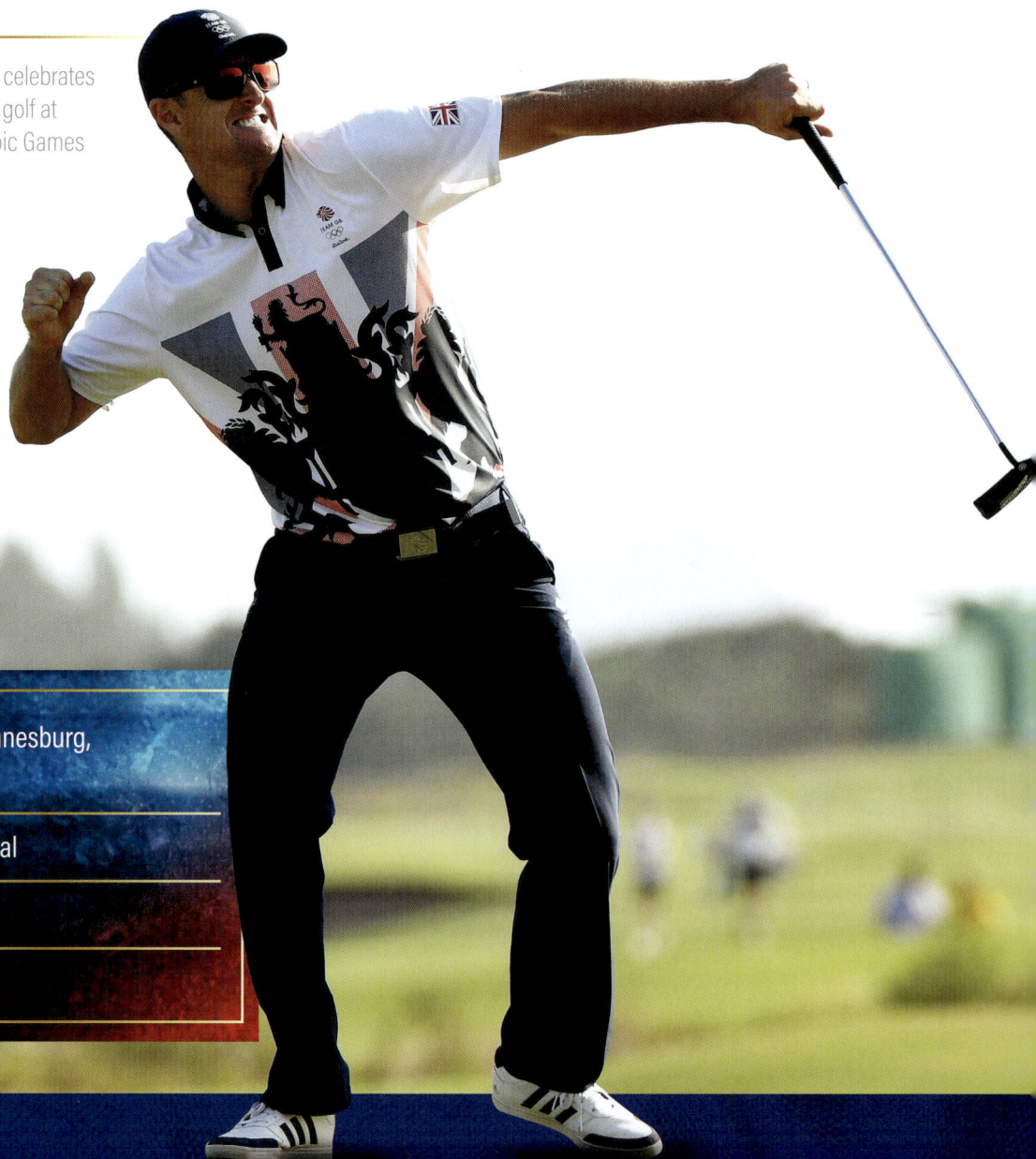

BORN: July 30, 1980, in Johannesburg, South Africa

EVENT: Golf – men's individual

GOLD (1): Rio 2016

TOTAL MEDALS: 🥇

GILLIAN SHEEN

Going in the 2024 Paris Games, Britain had eight silver medals for fencing at the Olympics but only one gold – won by dental surgeon Gillian Sheen at the 1956 event in Melbourne. Sheen only just got through to the women's individual foil final, defeating Hungary's Lídia Sákovicsné Dömölky in a tie-breaking "barrage" to qualify in fourth from their semi-final pool of six. Sheen lost her opening bout in the final round, to Romania's Olga Orban but won the next six against her other opponents to force a rematch with Orban for gold – and this time Sheen triumphed by four touches to two. She previously reached the second round at the 1952 Helsinki Olympics. Sheen followed up her Olympic title in 1956 with Commonwealth Games gold in Cardiff in 1958, four years after silver in Vancouver. She could only reach the quarter-finals when attempting to defend her Olympic crown at the 1960 Games in Rome. Sheen married orthodontist Bob Donaldson in 1962 and moved to his United States homeland where she set up a dental practice together. She was made an MBE in 2019, two years before her death in New York aged 92.

BELOW: 1956 Melbourne Olympics advertising poster

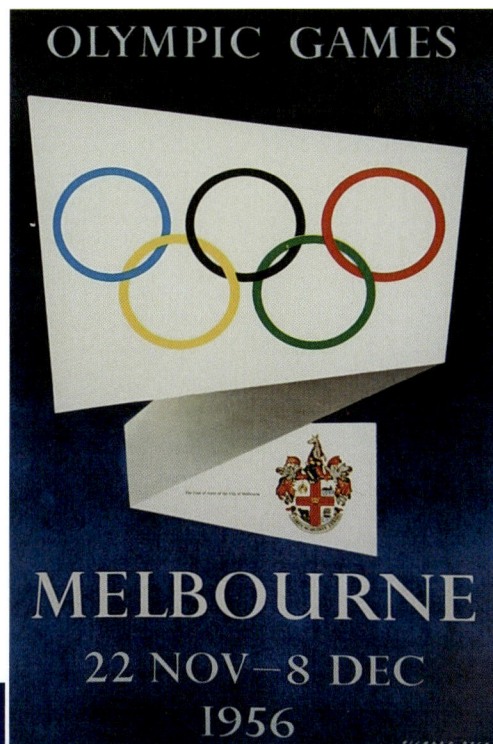

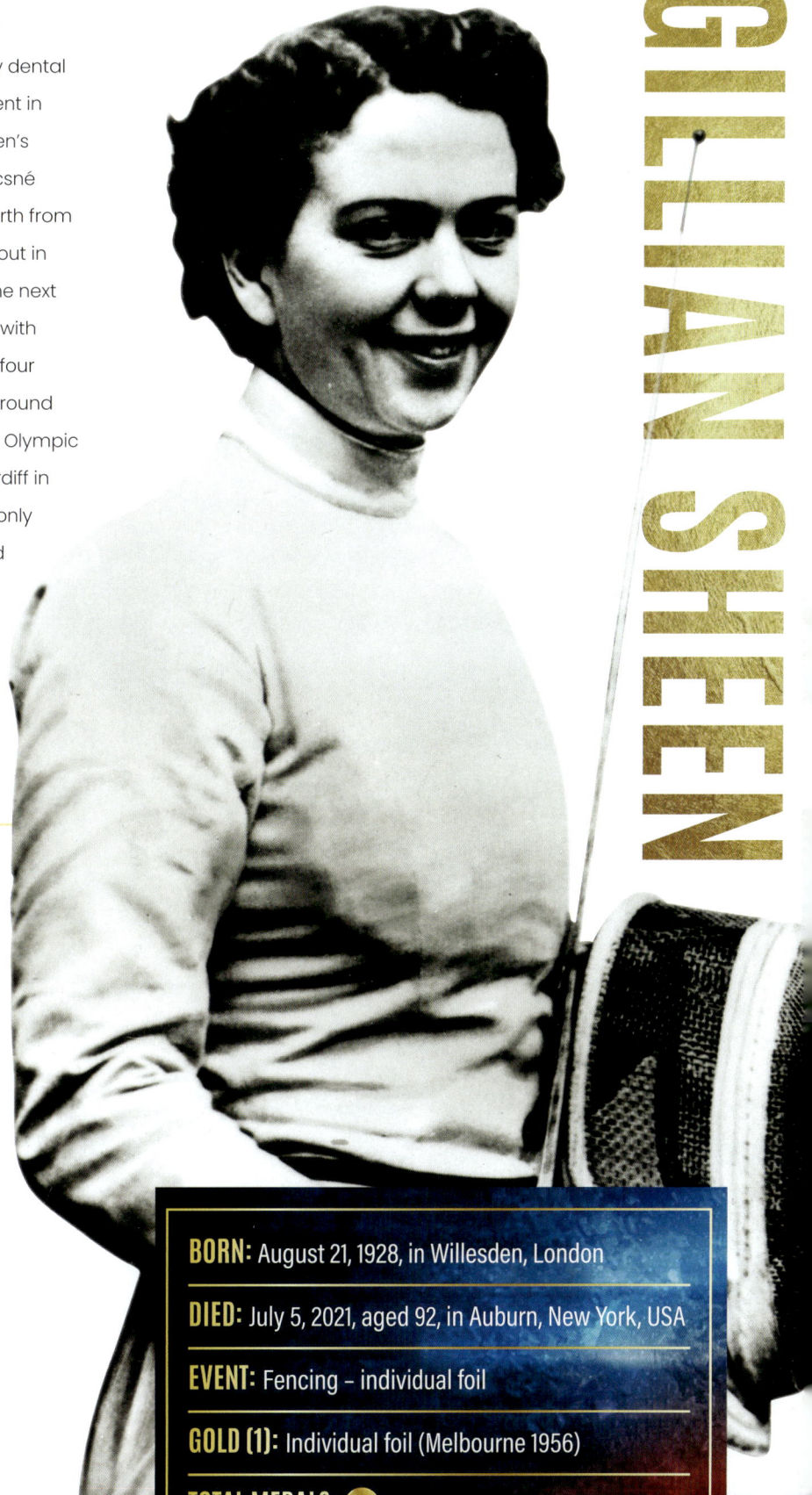

OLYMPIC GAMES

MELBOURNE
22 NOV – 8 DEC
1956

BORN: August 21, 1928, in Willesden, London

DIED: July 5, 2021, aged 92, in Auburn, New York, USA

EVENT: Fencing – individual foil

GOLD (1): Individual foil (Melbourne 1956)

TOTAL MEDALS: 🥇

PETER WILSON

Peter Wilson impressed youngsters discussing the London 2012 Olympics on a Tube carriage by plucking from his pocket and showing them the gold medal he had just won. The double trap event was introduced at the 1996 Olympics in Atlanta, challenging shooters to aim from each of five stations at 11cm-diameter targets launched into the air by three machines – with 150 to go for in the preliminary round and another 50 for the six shooters reaching the final. Wilson won his London 2012 gold at the Royal Artillery Barracks in Woolwich, with an overall score of 188 – two ahead of Sweden's Håkan Dahlby. In the run-up to the Games, he had set a new double trap world record score of 198 in March that year, at a World Cup event in Tucson, Arizona. At 25, Wilson was the youngest taking part in the London 2012 event – yet he retired from the sport just two years later. Wilson had originally taken up shooting after his hopes of playing squash and cricket were scuppered by a snowboarding accident which left him with nerve damage to his shoulder. Britain's only other Olympic gold medallist in the double trap was Richard Faulds in Sydney in 2000. Previously, Malcolm Cooper not only won 50m rifle 3 positions gold at Los Angeles 1984 but retained his title four years later in Seoul. Cooper died of cancer, aged 53, in 2001.

ABOVE: Peter Wilson, the London 2012 Gold Medallist in the Shooting Double Trap event shows off his Gold medal won the day before, to the crowd waiting outside the BBC Olympic Studio in the London Olympic Park

BORN: September 15, 1986, in Dorchester, Dorset

EVENT: Shooting – double trap

GOLD (1): Double trap (London 2012)

TOTAL MEDALS: 🥇

Britain's last two Olympic gold medals for football saw the men's team captained both times by England international star Vivian Woodward, back in London in 1908 and again in Stockholm four years later – each time with Denmark beaten in the final. Britain did actually claim gold in the first Olympics tournament in Paris 1900, when the Upton Park team from east London represented the UK, Paris champions Club Français took silver for France and bronze went to a mixed side mostly made up of Belgians but with one extra player each from Britain and the Netherlands. Woodward, a forward who played for Tottenham Hotspur at the time, scored the second in the 1908 final in London's White City Stadium, a 2-0 home win with former Nottingham Forest centre-half Frederick Chapman getting the opener. Woodward, by now playing club football for Chelsea, added another two goals at the 1912 tournament. Britain's top scorer in Sweden – including a strike in the 4-2 final victory over Denmark was 11-goal Harold Walden who later became a music hall comic performer. Woodward also scored 29 goals in 23 full internationals for England, as well as 40 in 24 appearances for England Amateurs. A thigh injury he suffered while serving on the Western Front in 1916 denied him a return to football after the First World War. Britain stopped sending men's teams to Olympic Games after 1960, other than a mixed English and Welsh squad which reached the London 2012 quarter-finals.

F. & J. SMITH'S CIGARETTES

CHELSEA.

V. J. WOODWARD.

VIVIAN WOODWARD

BORN: June 3, 1879, in Kennington, Surrey

DIED: January 31, 1954, aged 74, in Ealing, London

EVENT: Football

GOLD (2): London 1908, Stockholm 1912

TOTAL MEDALS: 🥇🥇

OLYMPIC LEGENDS FROM THE REST OF THE WORLD

Going into the 2024 Olympics in Paris, Great Britain was third overall for medals since the first modern-day Games in Athens in 1896, with 916 medals including 284 golds – behind the United States on 2,629 and the former USSR on 1,010. Six countries have provided competitors at all 29 Summer Olympics before Paris 2024: Australia, France, Great Britain, Greece, Italy and Switzerland. Only Britain has won at least one gold at every Summer Olympics. Yet many of the most impressive, successful and fondly recalled Olympic performers have come from other nations all across the world.

KENENISA BEKELE

E thiopia's Haile Gebrselassie won Olympic gold in the 10,000m at both the 1996 Olympics in Atlanta and the follow-up four years later in Sydney – a double that was then emulated by his compatriot Kenenisa Bekele in Athens in 2004, where Gebrselassie finished fifth, and at Beijing 2008 where the former champion this time came in sixth. Another Ethiopian, Sileshi Sihine, took silver behind Bekele in both Athens and Beijing – in Athens the pair waited for Gebrselassie to cross the finishing line before sharing a lap of honour with him. Both Bekele's victories came in Olympic record times – 27:05.10 in 2004, 27:01.17 in 2008. He also won 5,000m silver in 2004 then gold four years later, as well as five World Athletics Championships golds between 2003 and 2009. These included his victory in the 10,000m final in Helsinki in 2005 just months after Bekele's fiancée Alem Techale died of a heart attack, aged only 18, while doing a training run with him. Bekele held the 10,000m world record of 26:15.53 for 15 years until it was bettered by Uganda's Joshua Cheptegei, running 26:11.00 in October 2020 a year before he won 10,000m silver and 5,000m gold at the delayed Tokyo 2020 Games. Cheptegei had previously beaten Bekele's 5,000m world record of 12:37.35, taking it down to 12:35.36.

SIMONE BILES

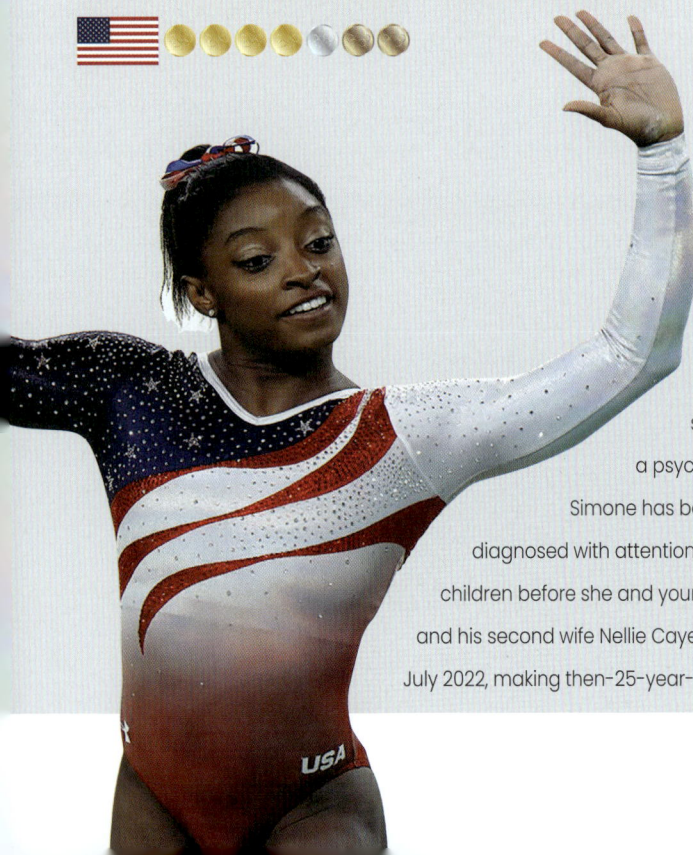

S imone Biles was one of the standout – while somersaulting – sensations of the Rio 2016 Summer Olympics, which ended with her becoming the first female gymnast given the honour of carrying the US flag at the Closing Ceremony. By that point she had become the first woman to win four artistic gymnastics golds at a single Summer Games since Romania's Ecaterina Szabo in Los Angeles in 1984 and only the fifth in history. Biles's first was in the all-around team event, where she was the only US gymnast to perform in all events in the final. She followed this triumph with individual golds in the all-around, vault and floor exercise finals and bronze in the vault. She reached all individual finals at Tokyo 2020 but pulled out of the team competition amid mental health struggles – only returning for the beam final, where she won bronze with a scaled-back routine of less complexity than her usual spectacular performances. Biles later explained she had been suffering "the twisties", a psychological state depriving her of the usual air awareness while carrying out twists. Simone has been praised for speaking publicly about mental health as well as how she has been diagnosed with attention deficit hyperactivity disorder. Biles and her three siblings spent time in foster care as children before she and younger sister Adria were formally adopted in 2003 by her maternal grandfather Ron Biles and his second wife Nellie Cayetano Biles. US president Joe Biden awarded her the Presidential Medal of Freedom in July 2022, making then-25-year-old Biles the youngest person to receive the country's highest civilian honour.

FANNY BLANKERS-KOEN

"The Flying Housewife" Francina "Fanny" Blankers-Koen was the unexpected star of the 1948 Olympics in London – having been written off by many as too old at 30 and as a mother-of-two. Yet she surged to 100m gold in 11.9 seconds before adding three more triumphs – in the 80m hurdles, in an Olympic record 11.2 seconds, the 200m and as the anchor in the 4 x 100m relay when she recovered from third place on the final leg to finish first. Blankers-Koen's 80m hurdles victory was declared after a photo finish alongside Great Britain's Maureen Gardner, though she initially thought she had lost because a band inside Wembley Stadium began playing the UK national anthem. It transpired this was merely because the British royal family had arrived at that precise moment. Blankers-Koen previously competed at the 1936 Olympics in Berlin as an 18-year-old, finishing fifth in both the high jump and the 4 x 100m relay – while also getting the autograph of the USA's four-time gold medallist Jesse Owens, something she would treasure and from someone she would go on to emulate. The International Association of Athletics Federations honoured her in 1999 as the "Female Athlete of the Century", five years before her death aged 85 in January 2004 after suffering with Alzheimer's disease.

USAIN BOLT

Usain Bolt really did electrify athletics like the lightning bolt he would mimic in his celebratory poses on the track – of which there have been many. In 2008 in Beijing he became the first man since Carl Lewis in Los Angeles in 1984 to win both 100m and 200m Olympic gold, but the manner of his victories proved just as captivating. In the Bird's Nest Stadium he set new world records in both events. He finished in 9.69 seconds in the 100m despite a slow start, with his left foot trainer unlaced and while easing up to begin celebrating with 15m still to go, and ran the 200m in 19.30. He also helped Jamaica win 4 x 100m gold though this title was rescinded nine years later after team-mate Nesta Carter was found guilty of taking a banned substance. In 2009 Bolt set a new 100m best of 9.58 at the World Athletics Championship in Berlin – a world record which still stands, as does his 19.19 in the 200m at that same tournament. Bolt, who often joked about living on a diet of McDonald's chicken nuggets, retained his individual titles at London 2012 and Beijing 2016 as well as adding 4 x 100m golds both times. Bolt's London 2012 winning times were 9.63 seconds in the 100m and 19.32 in the 200m, which he followed up in Rio by running 9.81 and 19.78.

NADIA COMĂNECI

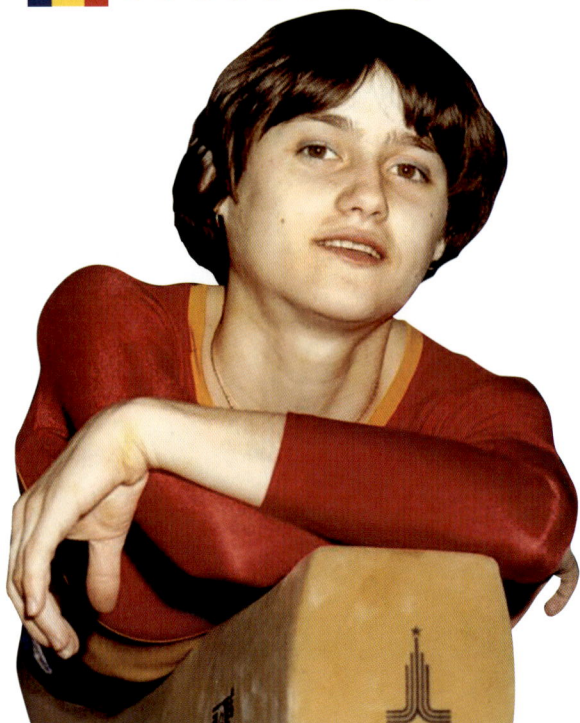

No gymnast had ever been awarded a perfect score of 10 out of 10 by judges at an Olympic Games, until Romania's Nadia Comăneci managed it not just once in Montreal in 1976 but seven times. The Romanian 14-year-old won three golds that summer, in the all-round, uneven bars and balance beam individual events – before adding another two in Moscow four years later, in the balance beam and floor exercise disciplines. The USSR's Nellie Kim, who won silver to Comăneci's gold in the 1976 all-around final, was given two 10.0 scores that summer – in the uneven bars and the balance beam. Four of Comăneci's top scores came for her athletic, graceful and speedy performances on the uneven bars, three on the balance beam. Such a performance was so unexpected, the electronic scoreboards were not programmed to display a perfect 10 – instead first showing her mark from the judges as 1.00. She remains the youngest Olympic all-around champion, with the rules now stipulating competitors must turn 16 in the same calendar year as their Games. Comăneci defected from Communist Romania to the United States in November 1989 and became a US citizen 12 years later. In 1996 she married Bart Conner, a former gymnast who won team and parallel bars gold medals for the US at the 1984 Los Angeles Olympics.

BIRGIT FISCHER

Birgit Fischer is the most successful Olympics kayaker, winning eight golds and 12 medals overall across seven Games representing first East Germany and then Germany following reunification. Her first Olympic title came aged 18, her latest at the age of 42 in Athens in 2004 – having twice come out of retirement, vowing to quit after both the 1988 and 2000 Games but later changing her mind. Her former husband Jörg Schmidt won silver for East Germany at the 1988 Seoul Olympics, in the men's C-1 1000m race in a summer which saw his wife capture not only a silver of her own but also two golds. Her niece Fanny Fischer won gold in the women's K-4 500m race at the 2008 Olympics in Beijing, an event Birgit won in Atlanta in 1996 and in Athens four years before Fanny's success. Birgit also won 38 ICF Canoe Sprint World Championships medals, including 28 golds, while her brother Frank won nine – four of his being gold. Her triumph in the K-2 500m final at Sydney 2000, alongside Katrin Wagner, made her the first woman to win at least two medals at four different Olympics – having already won gold with Wagner, Manuela Mucke and Anett Schuck in the K-4 500m that summer.

ALADÁR GEREVICH

Aladár Gerevich has been labelled "the greatest Olympic swordsman ever" and few could disagree, simply looking at his record of seven Olympic golds stretching across an amazing 28-year reign from the 1932 Games in Los Angeles to the 1960 event in Rome. He would surely have won even more had the Second World War not meant there were no Olympics in 1940 nor 1944. All his golds came in the sabre team event, except for his individual triumph at the 1948 Olympics in London where he won all seven of his contests – two more than Italy's Vincenzo Pinton. Hungarian teams won gold in eight of the first ten team sabre Olympic events up to 1960, where Gerevich bowed out with his last victory at the age of 50, but their most recent since then was in Seoul in 1988. Hungary took bronze in the men's team sabre at Tokyo 2020, behind gold medallists South Korea and silver-winning Italy, while the women's event that summer was won by a Russian Olympic Committee team, followed by France in second and South Korea third. Gerevich's wife Erna Bogen won fencing bronze at the 1932 Olympics in Los Angeles, in the women's individual foil – 20 years after her father won team sabre silver for Austria at the 1912 Games in Stockholm. Aládar and Erna's son Pál Gerevich went on to win bronze in the team sabre at Munich 1972 and Moscow 1980.

FLORENCE GRIFFITH JOYNER

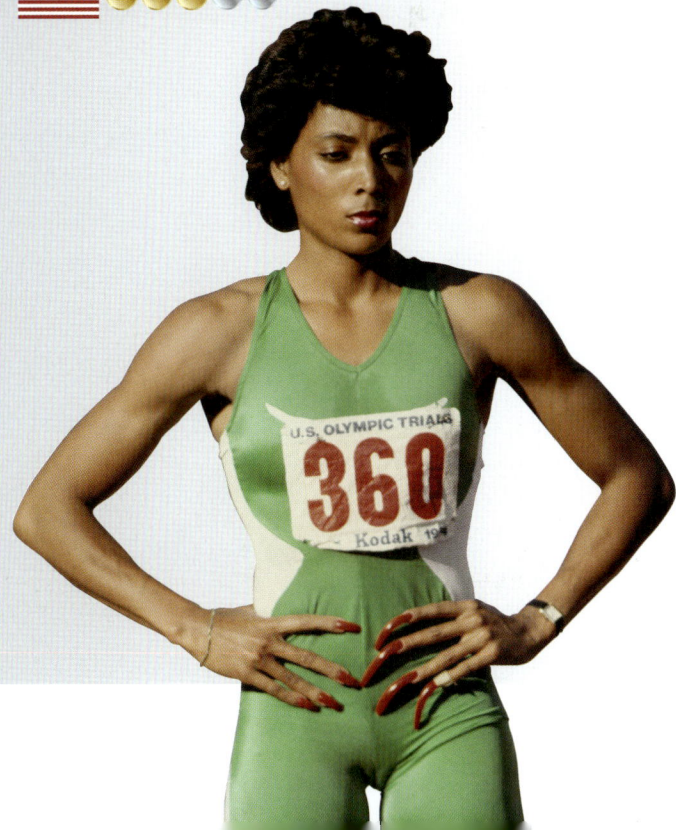

Florence Griffith Joyner became a sensation at the 1988 Olympics in Seoul, attracting attention for her colourful running suits, her long painted fingernails – and of course her blistering times as she sprinted to three golds, setting new Olympic and world records as she went. Competing as Florence Griffith, she had won 200m silver at the 1984 Games in Los Angeles but devoted herself to a new training regime ahead of the Seoul Olympics – and set a 100m world record of 10.49 at the US qualifying trials. Griffith Joyner, a former bank teller, ran the 1988 100m final in 10.54 seconds, ahead of US team-mate Evelyn Ashford. Meanwhile, in the 200m the semi-final run by the athlete dubbed "Flo-Jo" was a world record 21.56 before she bested that in the final – clinching gold in just 21.34 seconds. She added another gold in the 4 x 100m but abruptly retired the following February aged just 30. She died in her sleep in September 1998 at the age of 38, having suffered an epileptic seizure. Her widower Al Joyner, who she married in 1987, had previously won triple jump gold for the US at the 1984 Olympics and was her coach ahead of the Seoul Games. Griffith Joyner's 100m and 200m world records both still stand.

JACKIE JOYNER-KERSEE

Few sporting all-rounders can compare with the feats achieved by Jackie Joyner-Kersee – named after former US first lady Jacqueline Kennedy. She only just missed out on heptathlon gold at the 1984 Olympics in Los Angeles, falling short by just 0.06 in the final 800m event, but went one better not only in Seoul four years later but again in Barcelona in 1992 – making her the first heptathlete to win Olympic gold twice in a row. In Seoul she also won the USA's first ever gold in the women's high jump, leaping an Olympic record 7.40m, while her 7,291 points in that summer's heptathlon remains a world record. That heptathlon triumph involved running the 100m hurdles in 12.69 seconds, the 200m in 22.56 and the 800m in 2:06.51, covering 1.86m in the high jump and 7.27m in the long jump, and throwing 15.80m in the shot put and 45.66m in the javelin. Despite suffering from a right hamstring injury she added bronze in the long jump at the 1996 Olympics in Atlanta before enjoying a brief professional basketball career later that year, playing for the Richmond Rage. Her brother was 1984 Olympic triple jump gold medallist Al Joyner and her husband Bob Kersee was also her coach, though said she could only use his surname when she broke a world record – which she first did in July 1986 when breaking the 7,000-point mark in the heptathlon event at the Goodwill Games in Moscow.

SAWAO KATŌ

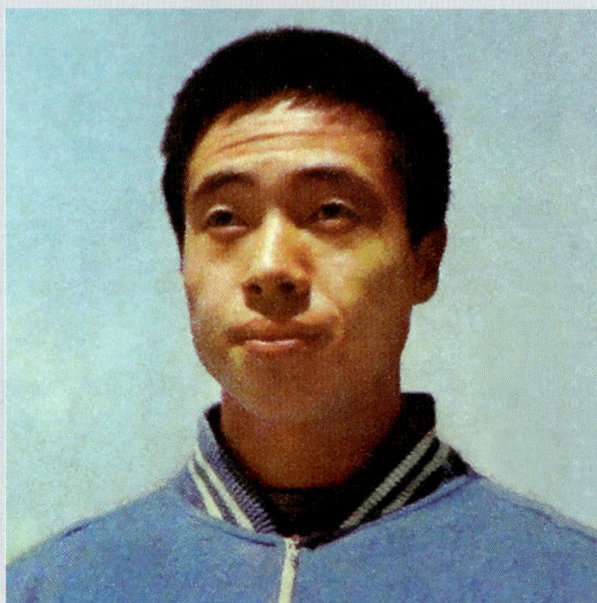

No male gymnast has won more Olympic golds than Japan's Sawao Katō, who clinched eight across the Mexico City 1968, Munich 1972 and Montreal 1976 Games – while only three men have more gymnastics medals overall: Russia's Nikolai Andrianov on 15, his compatriot Boris Shakhlin two further back and Japan's Takashi Ono also with 13. Kato, standing at just 1.63m but with superb composure, became in 1976 the first man to successfully defend the parallel bars title. Katō's brother Takeshi, four years older, won team gold alongside him in Mexico City as well as bronze in the floor exercise. The younger brother's team gold in Montreal four years later was a painful ordeal for Japanese colleague Shun Fujimoto, who broke his leg at the knee during his floor exercise routine but went ahead with the side horse exercise and dislocated his knee further in the dismount – but did enough to help Japan win gold with an overall score of 576.85, ahead of the USSR's 576.45. Katō later served as head judge for the gymnastics at the 2004 Olympics in Athens.

LARISA LATYNINA

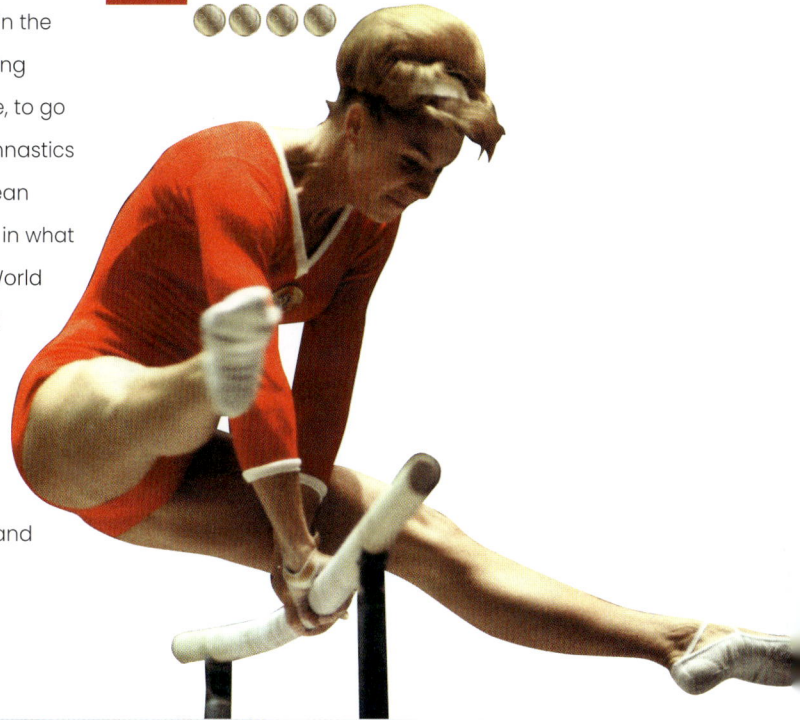

Only US swimmer Michael Phelps, with 23, has more Olympic gold medals than Larisa Latynina's nine – while her 18 medals overall put her ahead of all other gymnasts. She made her Games debut as a 21-year-old in Melbourne in 1956, where she clinched her first four golds – in the all-around, floor exercise, team and vault finals. She was still winning multiple medals in Tokyo eight years later, two golds and a bronze, to go with not only her Olympic medals but also 14 from the Artistic Gymnastics World Championships (nine gold) and another 14 from the European Women's Gymnastic Championships (seven gold). Latynina, born in what is now Ukraine, lost both parents in the aftermath of the Second World War. She took up gymnastics as an 11-year-old, impressing school teachers with her skills doing exercises with balls and hoops. Latynina later said: "I repeat my old routine hundreds, sometimes thousands of times. Monotonous? Not at all." After retiring as a competitor she became coach of the USSR's Olympics team, helping guide them to golds at the Mexico City 1968, Munich 1972 and Montreal 1976 Olympics.

CARL LEWIS

Carl Lewis is one of only six people to have won Olympic gold in the same event four times in a row – yet his long jump feats from 1984 in Los Angeles to Atlanta 12 years later are only part of his phenomenal story. He won 10 Olympics medals in all, nine of them gold – including one which was upgraded from silver when Canada's Ben Johnson was infamously disqualified after the 100m final at Seoul 1988 upon failing a drugs test. Lewis's four golds in Los Angeles in 1984 matched the tally of compatriot Jesse Owens at the Munich Olympics in 1936, and in the same four events – the 100m, 200m, 4 x 100m and long jump. Lewis was so confident that his first attempt in that summer's long jump final, measuring 8.54m, would be enough to win gold that after a foul in his next try he chose not to make any more – saving himself for the 200m and 4 x 100m races to come. Only swimmer Michael Phelps has more Olympic gold medals than the nine won by Lewis as well as Finnish runner Paavo Nurmi, Soviet gymnast Larisa Latynina and US swimmer Mark Spitz. Lewis has part-credited his late-career success to becoming a vegan in 1990.

PAAVO NURMI

The "Flying Finn" Paavo Nurmi ruled the world when it came to middle- and long-distance running through the 1920s, winning nine Olympic golds and three silvers at Antwerp 1920, Paris 1924 and Amsterdam 1928 – while still feeling annoyed his country failed to enter him for the 10,000m in Paris, an event he remained unbeaten in elsewhere. One protest by Nurmi did work out – he was upset to discover in Paris there was only 30 minutes between the men's 1500m and 5,000m events, but he and Finland's officials managed to get the gap widened to two hours. But he was denied his hope of running the marathon at the 1932 Olympics in Los Angeles after having his amateur status questioned. Nurmi, who would often run clutching a stopwatch in his hands, later ran into the host stadium carrying the Olympic torch when his homeland hosted the 1952 Summer Games in the country's capital Helsinki. Nurmi, who set 22 world records during his running career, later worked an athletics coach and successful businessman before dying aged 76 in October 1973, prompting Finland to grant him a state funeral where six of his country's other gold medallists were pallbearers. Nurmi was the running hero of Hollywood actor Dustin Hoffman's character in the 1976 movie *Marathon Man*.

LEFT: Poster for the 1928 Summer Olympics in Amsterdam

JESSE OWENS

Germany's Nazi dictator Adolf Hitler declared the 1936 Olympics in Berlin open, hoping it would promote "Aryan supremacy". But to his chagrin it was the USA's black athlete Jesse Owens who was the star of the Games, winning four gold track and field medals – in the 100m, 200m, 4 x 100m and long jump. Owens, son of a sharecropper, won the 200m in a world record time of 20.7 seconds – while the relay team's finish of 39.80 seconds was another global best. He became friends with his German rival for the long jump title, Luz Long – whose silver medal-winning leap of 7.87m was bested by Owens' 8.06m – and remained in touch with Long's family after the German's death during the Second World War's Battle of St Pietro in Italy in June 1943. Owens had been born with the first names James Cleveland but a schoolmistress misheard his initials J.C. and her mistaken version stuck. Despite his triumphs in Berlin, Owens was stripped of his amateur status by US officials after returning to America to discuss commercial sportswear deals rather than go on a post-Games tour of Sweden with team-mates. He suffered racial discrimination, struggled to find work and often had to take menial jobs, while also taking part in stunt races for cash – including against motorbikes, cars and horses. Owens died of lung cancer in March 1980, aged 66.

LÁSZLÓ PAPP

Lászó Papp was the first boxer to win gold at three consecutive Olympics, first in the middleweight category at London 1948 before moving into the light middleweight events at the two Summer Games which followed – triumphing in all 13 of his matches and only dropping one round, in the 1956 final he nevertheless went on to win against future world light heavyweight champion José Torres. Papp's first Olympic victory in London was against the home favourite, Great Britain's John Wright. Papp's dominance was despite his height being a mere 1.65m yet he went through his entire career undefeated – winning 27 times and drawing twice. As well as being a triple Olympic gold medallist, he also won the European Amateur Championships as a middleweight in 1949 and as a light middleweight two years later. The Hungarian government allowed him to fight professionally, the first boxer from a Communist country given such permission, yet they did still bar him an exit visa in 1964 which prevented him from taking on the USA's Joey Giardello for the world middleweight title. Papp died aged 77 in October 2003, two years after being inducted into the International Boxing Hall of Fame.

MICHAEL PHELPS

Swimming phenomenon Michael Phelps stands alone as the most-decorated Olympian of modern times. In Beijing in 2008 he became the first athlete to win eight gold medals at a single Summer Olympics, going one better than fellow US swimmer Mark Spitz's seven in Munich in 1972. Seven of the eight set records and Phelps suggested he was the ultimate "morning person" by winning them all before Beijing lunchtime. Yet this was no breakthrough surprise – and nor was it enough for Phelps, who kept on winning and now owns an all-time Olympic record of 28 medals, including 23 golds (also more than anyone else). Four years before Beijing he won eight medals, six of them gold, at Athens 2004. He only missed the chance to equal Spitz's gold record back then when giving up his place in the 4 x 100m medley relay team to Ian Crocker – Phelps had beaten him by just 0.04 seconds in the 100m butterfly. Phelps – blessed with 1.93m in height, 2.01m in arm span and size 14 feet – began swimming as a seven-year-old and was soon setting national age group records. He followed Beijing with four golds and two silvers at London 2012 then another five golds and a silver in Rio four years later, where he was also chosen as his country's flag-bearer for the Opening Ceremony athletes' parade. Phelps – who began his Olympic career as a 15-year-old at Athens 2000, the youngest member of the US swimming team for 68 years – has made a point of regularly freshening up which events to target and train for between Games. He did announce his retirement after London 2012 but announced a return in April 2014. His aims included reclaiming the 4 x 100m freestyle title the US won in Beijing before finishing second in London – which of course Phelps, by now 31, helped them achieve in Rio, in an Olympic record time of 3:27.95.

DAVID RUDISHA

Kenya's David Rudisha ran the 800m final in London 2012's Olympic Stadium as if it were a sprint, leading from the start and finishing in 1:40.91 minutes – ahead of silver medallist Nijel Amos of Botswana crossing the line in 1:41.73. Rudisha retained his title four years later in Rio, this time in 1:43.88 though only surging clear off the chasing field after the final turn. His London 2012 performance remains an 800m world record, with the next two best times being recorded by him too. Rudisha had initially favoured the 400m before being convinced by Irish coach Colm O'Connell to focus on the 800m instead. London 2012's organising committee chair Sebastian Coe – himself a double Olympic gold medallist, in the 1500m at Moscow 1980 and Los Angeles 1984 – described Rudisha's display in the English capital as his favourite of that summer's Games, calling it "the most extraordinary piece of running I have probably ever seen". Rudisha himself labelled the race "nice and easy". No one since has yet matched his feat of running the 800m in under one minute and 41 seconds. His father Daniel Rudisha was a member of Kenya's 4 x 400m silver medal-winning team at the 1968 Olympics in Mexico City.

MARK SPITZ

The swimming legend dubbed "Mark the Shark" twice headed off to a Summer Olympics promising to return home with six golds. Spitz, born in California, spent his childhood swimming daily in the sea off Waikiki beach after his family moved to Hawaii when he was two and then with a club in Sacramento when they returned to California four years later. He was already setting age-group records by the time he was ten. Spitz came back from the Mexico City Olympics in 1968, aged 18, with "only" two golds – in the 4 x 100m and 4 x 200m freestyle relays, as well as 100m butterfly silver and 100m freestyle bronze. But he bettered his own repeat prediction four years later in Munich, where he became the first person to complete a haul of seven golds from one Summer Games. His record stood until fellow US swimmer Michael Phelps took eight in Beijing 36 years later. Spitz's seven 1972 triumphs also set records, including four individual races in the 100m and 200m freestyle and 100m and 200m butterfly. Spitz left the Games early, after completing his events, amid concerns for his safety – being Jewish – after the "Munich Massacre" which saw 11 Israeli athletes taken hostage and murdered by terrorists. He retired after Munich and went into the property business but did attempt a comeback 20 years later. Then 41, he failed to make it through US qualification trials for the 1992 Olympics in Barcelona.

TEÓFILO STEVENSON

Two men have gone on to emulate Hungary's László Papp in winning boxing gold medals at three Olympics in a row – and both came from Cuba. Teófilo Stevenson completed his hat-trick of heavyweight titles in Moscow in 1980, following on from triumphs in the same division at Munich 1972 and Montreal 1976. Stevenson, at 196cm, was a whole foot taller than Papp. He set his Olympic career off to the perfect start by knocking down Poland's Ludwik Denderys inside the opening 30 seconds of their first-round fight in Munich and went on to be given gold after his scheduled opponent in the final, Romania's Ion Alexe, had to miss out through injury. Stevenson turned down lucrative offers to go professional – despite the prospect of taking on Muhammad Ali – and remained amateur for his follow-up Olympic victories in 1976, beating Mircea Şimon of Romania in the final, and in 1980 where the USSR's Pyotr Zayev was seen off for gold. He was denied the chance to go for further medals at Los Angeles in 1984 and Seoul four years later as the Cuban government boycotted both Games. Stevenson retired in 1988 and died from a heart attack, aged 60, in the Cuban capital Havana in June 2012. The third boxer to win golds at three successive Olympics was fellow Cuban heavyweight Félix Savón, at Barcelona 1992, Atlanta 1996 and Sydney 2000.

EMIL ZÁTOPEK

Emil Zátopek made a sudden decision to run his first marathon on July 27 1952. He ended it winning Olympic gold, at the 1952 Helsinki Games – having already that summer successfully defended his 10,000m title from London 1948 and added 5,000m gold for good measure. Zátopek – dubbed the "Czech locomotive", and familiar for his ungainly running style and grimacing discomfort during races – was carried around the field by the Jamaican 4 x 400m relay team in Helsinki after completing his unprecedented hat-trick of long-distance golds at a single Olympics. He had been born on the very same day as his future wife Dana Zátopková, who herself won javelin gold at that 1952 Olympics – around the same time as Emil's 5,000m triumph – and then silver in the same event in Rome eight years later. Zátopek attempted to retain his marathon crown at Melbourne 1956 but finished sixth, hampered by a groin injury. Zátopek, a former lieutenant-colonel in the Czech army, was expelled from the country's Communist Party in 1968 after co-signing a pro-freedom letter and sent to work in a uranium mine, but was allowed to return to the capital Prague and reunite with his family in 1977. Prague's National Theatre hosted his funeral following his death at the age of 78 in November 2000 after suffering a stroke.

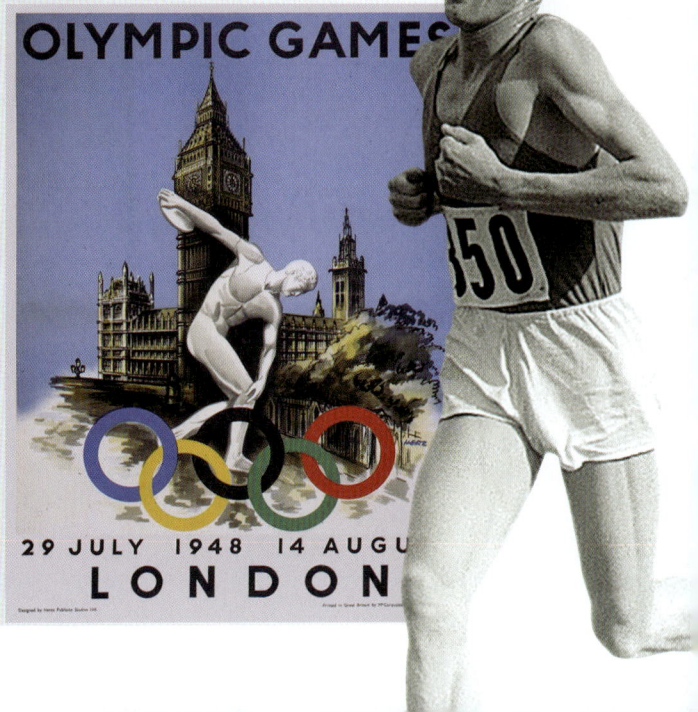

FAR RIGHT: A poster promoting the 1948 London Olympics

OLYMPIC GAMES

29 JULY 1948 14 AUGU

LONDON